MARK AND LIVY

MARK
AND LIVY

*The Love Story of Mark Twain
and the Woman Who Almost
Tamed Him*

RESA WILLIS

TV BOOKS
NEW YORK

Library of Congress Cataloging-in-Publication Data
Willis, Resa.
Mark and Livy : the love story of Mark Twain and the woman who almost tamed him / by Resa Willis.
p. cm.
Originally published: Atheneum Publishers, 1992.
Includes bibliographical references and index.
ISBN 1-57500-096-2 (pbk.)
1. Clemens, Olivia Langdon, 1845-1904—Marriage. 2. Authors, American—19th century—Biography. 3. Authors' spouses—United States—Biography. 4. Married people—United States—Biography. I. Title.
PS1332.W55 2000
818'.409—dc21
[B]
99-055505

TV Books, L.L.C.
1916 Broadway, Ninth Floor
New York, NY 10019
www.tvbooks.com

Manufactured in Canada.

This book is dedicated to
Mary Rose Sweeney and Gordon O. Taylor
because "A teacher affects eternity. . . ."

CONTENTS

CONTENTS

ACKNOWLEDGMENTS

Mark Twain felt that biographies were only "the clothes and buttons" of a person. I may have sat by myself researching, taking notes, and writing, but many helped me to stay in that chair and to keep looking for the connecting "threads." My gratitude to these people has only increased since this book was first published.

At the Mark Twain Project at the University of California at Berkeley, the director, Robert Hirst, and Sunny Gottberg helped me cull through a great deal of material and gave me access to unpublished information. On the other coast, Diana Royce of the Stowe-Day Foundation in Hartford, Connecticut, let me see unpublished letters and diaries from the Langdon family. Beverly Zell helped me select photographs of the Clemenses.

Giselda J. Lozada and Jonathan Miller at Louisiana State University Library in Baton Rouge gave me access to the Grace King Collection. Frank Lorenz of Hamilton College in Clinton, New York, allowed me to use the Susy Clemens-Louise Brownell Saunders unpublished letters.

Michelle Cotton and the Chemung County Historical Society guided me to information about the Langdons and their connec-

ACKNOWLEDGMENTS

tions with Elmira, New York. Mary Heller gave me access to the Park Church Archives in Elmira.

Livy came alive for me in the places where she and Clemens lived. The Executive Director, John Vincent Boyer, and Curator Marianne Curling of the Mark Twain Memorial in Hartford, Connecticut, have answered countless questions for me over the years and let me wander through that remarkable house. Herbert Wisbey, Jr. of Elmira College, the former director of Mark Twain Studies, gave me access to the files of Quarry Farm and the archives of the college and let me stay at the summer place that gave Livy so much pleasure. The present Director of Quarry Farm, Gretchen Sharlow, has continued that generosity toward me. Henry Sweets, the Curator of the Mark Twain Boyhood Home in Hannibal, remains a dear friend and colleague.

Closer to home, the librarians at my school, Drury University, are always available to help me track down yet another item or turn their heads at overdue books.

Lee Goerner first edited and published *Mark and Livy*. I am sorry that he isn't here to see the continued interest in her story. My special thanks goes to Peter Kaufman, my present publisher, who cared passionately about having the book republished. Thanks also goes to my agent Elaine Markson.

Finally, recognition for my cheerleaders, the friends and family who are always much more certain of my talent than I am—my friends Katherine Kurk Reichardt, Krystal Compas, my niece Theresa, and my husband, Michael. Then there are the people who make me look good—Jacqueline Lyn Brummel, J. D. Dunning, Jennifer Nelson, and Marline Ritter.

INTRODUCTION

This biography of Olivia Langdon Clemens, the woman married to America's most famous and favorite writer, Mark Twain, began when I discovered that among the numerous volumes about him there was no definitive biography of her. The story of their incomparable thirty-seven year romance needed to be told. And so it was published in 1992 by Atheneum. Since that time I have received many letters and questions from those who read the book. Often these fans of Livy and Clemens would ask: Will the book be out in paperback? Is a film going to be made of it? Well, I can now answer in the affirmative. I continue to be gratified by the interest in this quiet, dignified, but very influential woman in American letters just as I think Mark Twain would be.

Livy was not only Samuel Clemen's wife and the mother of his children, she was Mark Twain's editor. She read and proposed changes to nearly everything he wrote. She attended many of his lectures and made constant suggestions regarding material to include in his platform speeches. He relied on her judgment as to what his readers would and wouldn't accept.

Twain once remarked, "Mrs. Clemens has kept a lot of things from getting into print that might have given me a reputation I wouldn't care to have, and that I wouldn't have known any better than to have published." He readily recognized the civilizing effect she had on him, for he admitted that his wife not only edited his work but also edited him.

Americans love biographies, for in reading about others we hope to learn about ourselves. Olivia Langdon Clemens was no different. Her favorite type of reading concerned the lives of others. Her letters and journals are full of references to them. From Hartford, June 7, 1885:

> I am reading with great interest "George Eliot's Life" by her husband J.W. Cross. It is most delightful—you live with her in a most real way— The only thing in the book that annoys me is her constant mention of her ill health. How can a woman that was so great as she, be so interested and absorbed in how she feels, how her headache is, that she always mentions the fact in journal and her letters. It seems as if the remarks should have been left out in the editing. The only thing that would seem to excuse their being left in, is that they show how much a person may accomplish with great physical inability and much mental depression. At any rate the "life" carries you in giving strong impressions of all her moods & struggles in a most marvelous way.

This journal selection tells us so much about Livy. Here is a woman who was considered rather frail by her family and husband yet she dislikes the idea of Eliot capitalizing on her illness. More importantly, we see Livy in this passage as an editor— someone not only reading words but thinking about them—what works and what doesn't for the reader.

The Livy I discovered and Livy Mark Twain described weren't always the same woman. His word about her had been the only source for years. Mark Twain says in his autobiography, "When I was young I could remember anything, whether is had hap-

INTRODUCTION

pened or not; but my faculties are decaying now and soon I shall be so I cannot remember anything but the things that never happened." He probably didn't purposefully lie about the incidents in their life together. He may have unconsciously chosen, as we all do, to sometime remember things as they never happened in order to make a good story.

Mark Twain created many memorable characters; after all, he created Mark Twain from Samuel Clemens. Livy was another of those creations. The image he jokingly liked to project to friends and relatives was Livy the shrew. He wrote Mrs. Fairbanks, "When things don't go right she breaks the furniture & knocks everything endways. You ought to see her charge around. When I hear her warwhoop I know it is time to climb out on the roof." Anyone who knew the gentle Livy would have been amused by his outlandish characterization.

As his editor, the question has been: Did she stifle his creativity? Of course not. It was all a game to him. He created a Livy to reform his life and a Livy to edit his work. He wanted and needed to be tamed.

Mark Twain was his own man, but he trusted Livy's judgment. He once remarked to her sister Sue Crane, "Whenever I have failed to follow the advice of Livy to change this or that sentence or eliminate a page, I have always come to regret it, because in the end my better taste in thoughts and their expression rises up and says: You should have done as she said; she was right." If he felt strongly about something that he didn't want changed, he didn't change it. Of his autobiography, he told her, "You are not to edit it—it is to appear as it is written, with the whole tale told as truly as I can tell it." At her urging, he worked on his autobiography during her last illness and continued it after her death.

Livy died on June 5, 1904, but their love story was not over. Mark Twain's devotion to his wife shows in the difficulty he had in living and writing during the six years he survived her. He adored her; he would be happy his readers enjoyed reading about her and that curiosity about her has not waned since the first publication of this book. While this biographer has gone on to work on other subjects, interest in Livy and her life with Mark Twain continue to bring me back to her.

For both Mark and Livy, I hope this new edition of their love story once again does what Livy wanted in a good biography—make the subject "live in a most real way."

MARK AND LIVY

CHAPTER 1

"I feel so frightfully banished."

A death reflects the pattern of a life. It is one more daily incident, even if it is the last one. And so it was also for Olivia Langdon Clemens. Her death mirrored her life and her relationship with her husband, Samuel Clemens. As in all the events of her life, it was characterized by what she allowed her husband to see, what he wanted to see, and what really happened. As Mark Twain's greatest literary creation, the Livy he envisioned and the Livy that really existed lived together in an accepted tension in one very human woman.

Olivia Clemens spent the final day of her fifty-eight years, Sunday, June 5, 1904, at the Villa di Quarto, three miles from Florence, Italy. The villa had been her home since November 9, 1903 when her husband, her daughters—Clara, aged twenty-nine and Jean, aged twenty-three—moved her there from Riverdale, New York with the hope that her health would improve in a warmer, drier climate.

Clemens described Livy in her final illness as "being smitten helpless by nervous prostration complicated with an affection of the heart of several years' standing."

It was the "affection of the heart," the complications from hyperthyroidism, that ended her life. Livy had suffered intermittently all of her life from the elusive nervous disorders that struck the upper-class nineteenth-century woman. It was called by a number of names: nervous prostration, neurasthenia, hysteria. Diaries, letters, journals of this time record women and their invalidism. The disease was elusive, for it tended to strike only the upper class. Poor women simply could not afford to be delicate and frail. Illness was one way of not dealing with a world that did not know what to do with an intelligent woman who was not allowed to achieve on her own, let alone compete with men. Whether real or imagined, the symptoms were painful enough to the women who suffered from this malaise. The wealthy could literally afford to be idle; being sick just legitimized it—Olivia Clemens included.

Mysteriously paralyzed as a young woman, Livy spent two years on her back in a darkened room. She was eventually "cured" enough to marry Clemens, bear four children, and run an elaborate household as well as serve as literary editor for her husband. But she remained frail in the mind of her husband, despite his own words that "For from that day that she was eighteen until she was fifty-six she was always able to walk a quarter of a mile without stopping to rest; and more than once I saw her walk a quarter of a mile without serious fatigue."

A Countess Massiglia owned the villa that the Clemens family hoped would restore Livy as wife and mother to them. Clemens's private secretary Isabel Lyon remembered this countess as a pretentious American: "The Countess is none other than a vicious woman of whom I knew a little in Philadelphia about 15 years ago." Then her name was Mrs. Barney Campan. She was later divorced by her husband when she was found "tampering with the affections of her mother's boarder." Miss Lyon's dislike for the woman is obvious: "Count Massiglia is far away serving his country as Consul, in Persia or Siam, and he is likely to stay there too; and it seems to me that for the sake of peace or freedom, he has left this Villa in the hands of the Countess. . . . Here she remains, a menace to the peace of the Clemens household, with her painted hair, her great coarse voice, her slitlike vicious eyes, her dirty clothes, and her terrible manners."

MARK AND LIVY

The stormy atmosphere between the countess and Clemens proved worse than the damp and chill of Riverdale. The battle between them began the moment the Clemens family reached Florence. The countess forced the family to stay in a hotel because she would not allow anyone in the villa until the Clemens family occupied it. So an old friend and neighbor, Mrs. Janet Ross, could not prepare the villa as had been planned for their arrival. Mrs. Ross had found the Clemenses a Florentine villa twelve years before, and the fond memories of their stay at Villa Viviani had led the Clemens family to want to return to Italy.

His nerves no doubt frayed from Livy's ill health, Clemens saw the countess as determined to make him and his family as miserable as possible. Her actions seemed to confirm his beliefs. The lease stated a sick person could not be placed in the very room that had been chosen as the best one for Livy. He accused the countess of removing furnishings that were to go with the villa, smearing her dogs with kerosene so that they would rub against his daughters and visitors, cutting the telephone wires, shutting off the water, and locking the gates so Livy's doctors could not attend her. As Isabel Lyon stated, "Her viciousness seems to grow, as she realizes that she cannot make a tool of Mr. Clemens, nor use the lovely Clemens daughters as tools of another kind to give a place in society." The situation was aggravated by the fact that the countess and her mother lived nearby in a house on the villa's grounds. Clemens would seek restitution from this "excitable, malicious, malignant, vengeful, unforgiving, selfish, stingy, avaricious, coarse, vulgar, profane, obscene" woman through a series of lawsuits that were to drag on after Livy's death.

Clemens described the three-storied villa as "built for fuss & show . . . not for a home." It was a "huge confusion of rooms and halls and corridors and cells and wasted spaces." Miss Lyon felt the more than sixty rooms had been "tortured into hideousness by the atrocious taste of the present owner."

Even if the villa was not the best location for a frail woman, in the spring of 1904 Livy was able to enjoy some of the beauty of the Italian countryside. Her bedroom and private parlor were at the southern end of the house. This location allowed the sun to pour "its light in through the thirty-three glass doors or windows which pierce the side of the house." From mid-May when she had the strength, for she could rarely stand for more than five minutes at a time, and when it was not raining as it did a great deal that spring, she could sit in her wheelchair on the veranda. She could see Dante's city of Florence on the plain below, often shrouded in a mist. The hills were dotted with other villas and the domes of distant churches. Snowcapped mountains peaked beyond. Olive trees that provided the aromatic wood for the fireplaces in the villa draped their branches over the high iron fence that surrounded the villa and the high stone walls on either side of the road. Sheep and donkeys traversed this narrow road that meandered down into Florence. Clemens described the scenery as a "persistent inspiration . . . when the afternoon arrives there will be a new picture every hour till dark, and each of them divine— or progressing from divine to diviner and divinest."

Katy Leary, the Clemenses' faithful servant for twenty-four years, remembered the bounty of roses that grew in the garden. Even in December a person could "cut the roses by the bushel." Blossoms from the orange trees and the roses filled the house in the evening with smells while nightingales, owls, and church bells filled the nights with sound. Don Raffaello Stiattisi, a neighboring priest who became a friend of the family and who housed Miss Lyon and her mother when the countess had them evicted from a cottage on the villa grounds, had the bell ringing stopped when he learned it disturbed Livy. Although he could not silence the owls, he informed the family that they regularly nested at the villa. Despite the priest's reassurances about the hooting, Livy told Katy, "I know that's a sign of death."

Clemens was optimistic about his wife's recovery. On Livy's last day, Sunday, June 5, 1904, he and Jean had gone out looking for another villa. As a young wife in Hartford, Connecticut, Livy had written her husband, "I believe there is nothing that sooner ruins the happiness of a family than a worrying woman." After thirty-four years of marriage, Clemens was still sensitive to his wife's worries. He had written in January that Livy worried about the problems with the countess and about her mounting medical expenses so much that she often couldn't sleep. Both Clemens and the countess wanted to be rid of each other; now he felt that Livy was well enough to be moved.

Livy had seemed better to him and "the girls," as she had always called her daughters. After twenty months of watching her waste away, Clemens reported his wife "ceases to be a pallid, shrunken shadow, & looks bright & young & pretty. She remains what she always was, the most wonderful creature of fortitude, patience, endurance, and recuperative power that ever was." His constant fear was always of her "retrogression"; that "pathetic something in the eye which betrays the secret of a waning hope would return."

The heart problems, the rheumatism, an attack of tonsilitis in January had all taken their toll. Clemens wanted to believe his wife was getting better, would recover as she had done in the past, that she would live, but Livy had given up. The choking sessions left her "white, haggard, exhausted, & quivering with fright." She was terrified and told her husband that she didn't want to die. Fear of strangulation forced her to sit up in bed both day and night, getting very little sleep. She often had to have oxygen to make her breathing easier or an injection of brandy to relax her tense body. She frightened her husband by asking, "You don't think I am going to die, do you? Oh, I don't want to die." Yet she conceded to Katy that she knew she was dying.

A week before her death she asked Katy to dress her when she died in a certain lavender satin gown trimmed with lace. The dress was a particular favorite by Madame Fogarty of New York. Mrs. Fogarty had made most of Livy's dresses including her wedding dress and trousseau when she was a young bride. Despite Katy's Irish insistence not to speak of such things, Livy said, "I don't think I can live much longer." Although very weak and seldom strong enough to speak, Livy whispered that she missed America and desired to see her sister, Sue Crane, again before she died. Katy admitted later, "I'm sure Mrs. Clemens knew she was going to die, but she didn't let the family know how she felt."

Her fear of exciting the family and worrying them to excess and their mutual fears for Livy had been the basis of their family life. During her most serious illnesses, Livy's doctors limited Clemens to restricted visits at his wife's bedside for fear that in his anxiety and dependence on her he would overexcite her and bring on the one thing the doctors hoped to minimize by keeping him from her—a worsened condition.

In these last, lingering months of illness in Riverdale and now in Villa di Quarto, Clemens was permitted to see his wife only once a day to tell her good night. He was only to see her for five minutes, but Katy recounted, "He broke the rules pretty often and he'd slip in sometimes during the day, just for a glimpse of her. She'd put her arms around his neck the first thing, and he'd hold her soft, and give her one of them [sic] tender kisses. . . . It was a love that was more than earthly love—it was heavenly."

During much of their earthly married life, the Clemenses were often separated by the necessity of Clemens's lecture tours to earn money or his absence due to various other publishing or business ventures. In 1885 Livy had written her husband while he was away from home, "My wish now is that we might live yet together twenty or thirty-five years and never be one night seperated [sic]." She did not get her wish, but often had to communicate with her husband throughout their marriage in writing.

Clemens had first won Livy's heart through love letters. Now in the end of their life together, they again had to express their love on paper. Clemens's room was next to hers so they could hear each other's every move. He occupied his time by dictating, at Livy's suggestion, his autobiography to Isabel Lyon. When her health permitted, Livy still acted as her husband's editor by listening to portions of his autobiography during his brief visits. "Mrs. Clemens is an exacting critic," Clemens wrote Howells, "but I have not talked a sentence yet that she has wanted altered."

Livy felt their separation as keenly as her husband did. On a note folded in half and addressed to "S. L. Clemens Esq.," she expressed her love and loneliness:

Youth my own precious Darling:

I feel so frightfully banished. Couldn't you write in my bou-
doir? then I could hear you clear your throat & it would be such
a joy to feel you so near.

I miss you sadly sadly. Your note in the morning gave me
support for the day, the one at night peace for the night. With
the deepest love of my heart your Livy.

The last afternoon Clemens spent with his wife he thought her
health to be much better. When he and Jean returned from looking
for another villa, Clara, who usually sat with her mother in the
afternoons, greeted them with the news that she thought her
mother was much more animated than she had been in a long
time. The three of them then repeated, *"Unberufen,"* the German
word the Clemens family used for good luck, so as not to jinx
Clara's observation and all their hopes.

Clemens described his wife in her illness as "the most wonderful
creature of fortitude, patience, endurance, and recuperative power
that ever was." In the last few hours of her life Livy presented a
bright face to her husband, although she had been ill all afternoon
and the nurse had felt it necessary to give her oxygen.

Clemens was confident he had found the perfect villa for them.
In his grief a few days following Livy's death he described to his
old friend Joseph Twichell how she had wanted to hear all the
details. Clemens wrote, "She wanted a *home*—a home of her own;
that she was tired & wanted rest, & could not rest & be in comfort
& peace while she was homeless." Clemens had spent much of
his life blaming himself for often uncontrollable incidents that took
place in his life. He condemned himself for their firstborn son
Langdon's death at nineteen months of diphtheria and of their
favorite daughter Susy's death at twenty-four of spinal meningitis.
Now he added his wife's homelessness and death to his list of
self-recriminations. After her death, in an attempt to expiate his
self-induced guilt that he had made his wife homeless, he wrote
her brother Charles Langdon to assure him that he had not spared
any expense or consideration in caring for her.

At Livy's insistence about hearing of the new villa, Clemens remained in her room from 7:30 until 8:00 that evening although he was acutely aware that he was breaking the rules. "She was bright and cheerful—a rare thing these last weeks—and she *would* talk, although it was a forbidden privilege, because she was so easily exhausted. She was full of interest in the calls which Jean and I had been making, and asked all about the people, and was like her old self. And smiled!" He feared he would tire her. But she said no that he must come back and see her at his appointed time of 9:30 to say good night. Her interest, her smile, "It lifted me up and made me believe the impossible—that she would walk again, be our comrade again!"

As he left her room, they threw kisses to each other. He gloried in her expression, "her face all bright with that new-found smile—I not dreaming that I was looking upon that dear face for the last time in life." He left her room happy at the prospect of a future with his wife. In his "deep contentment," he did something he had rarely done since Susy's death eight years earlier, "whose death made a wound in her mother's heart which never healed"; he sat down at the piano to play and sing the Negro spirituals that Susy and Livy had so loved.

When Katy returned from church that evening, she went to attend Livy, as was her practice. Livy admitted to her, "Oh, I have been awful sick all the afternoon, Katy." She heard her husband playing "Swing Low, Sweet Chariot," "My Lord He Calls Me," and "Go Chain the Lion Down" on the piano. Her last words were, "He is singing a good-night carol to me."

The end came not by strangulation as she had feared but by heart failure. She died sitting up in bed. Katy recalled, "I was fanning her and then—she fell right over on my shoulder. She died right then in my arms. She drew a little short breath . . . just once, and was gone! She died so peaceful and a smile was on her face." The oxygen pipe to her mouth was no longer needed.

In writing the sad news to his friend Howells, Clemens placed himself in Livy's room at her death. "Last night at 9.20 I entered Mrs. Clemens's room to say the usual good-night—& she was dead! tho' no one knew it." Livy's obituary in the Elmira *Telegram* perpetuated the story that she died in his arms. Clemens placed himself with her at her death because he wished he had been. In reality, he had finished playing the piano, pausing only in surprise to find Jean listening to him. "She asked me to go on, only the astonishment remained, and it was a pleasant one and inspiring." When he finished, he went to his room. He pondered how he might tell Livy that Jean had enjoyed his playing and singing but decided not to for fear it would remind her of Susy. As Clemens was thinking of saying good night to his wife, Isabel Lyon came to him. Lyon recorded in her diary, " 'Is it an alarm?' he said— but I didn't know, they only told me to run and get him."

What Clemens found when he entered Livy's room, he set down in words a few hours later:

> Livy was sitting up in bed, with her head bent forward—she had not been able to lie down for seven months—and Katy was on one side of the bed and the nurse on the other, supporting her; Clara and Jean were standing near the foot of the bed, looking dazed. I went around and bent over and looked into Livy's face, and I think I spoke to her, I do not know; but she did not speak to me, and that seemed strange, I could not understand it. I kept looking at her and wondering—and never dreaming of what had happened! Then Clara said, "But is it *true*? Katy, *is* it true? it can't be true." Katy burst into sobbings, and then for the first time I knew.

The remaining family members clung to each other and cried. Clemens held Livy in his arms for the last time. He remarked how beautiful, "young and sweet" she looked. In informing friends of her death, each time he repeated how death had seemed to rejuvenate her. "How sweet she was in death, how young, how beautiful, how like her dear girlish self of thirty years ago." To all, Sue Crane, Reverend Joseph Twichell, William Dean Howells, Clemens remarked how odd it was that Livy did not notice him touching her. She was "unresponsive to my reverent caresses—a new thing to me and a new thing to her; *that* had not happened before in five and thirty years." He also insisted that her death was a surprise. "I was not expecting this. In the last few days I was beginning to hope and half-believe, she would get well."

As a writer, the bereaved husband tried to find some solace in words. At 11:15 that same evening he wrote, "She has been dead two hours. It is impossible. The words have no meaning. But they are true; I know it, without realizing it. She was my life, and she is gone; she was my riches, and I am a pauper. How sudden it was, how wholly unexpected." He spent the night pacing—wandering from his room to gaze at her face.

Although Clemens insisted to friends and family that her death was unexpected, as all deaths are no matter how long the person lingers, he admitted in the passage he wrote a few hours after Livy's death that his desire for her recovery was only that, a wish.

> Poor tired child, how she loved her life, how longingly and eagerly she clung to it through all these twenty-two months of captivity and loneliness and bodily suffering, and how pathetically she searched our eyes for hope! And how these bitter months we lied to her loyally and said she would get well *sure*, when we knew in our hearts it would never be! Only four hours ago—and now there she lies, white and still!

Throughout Livy's final illness, husband and wife had "loyally" lied and put up a brave front to each other about her surviving. Eventually he would be able to admit to Twichell and others, "Deep down in our hearts we believed she would never get out of her bed again."

Only two years before, Livy had written a letter of consolation to a friend whose mother had died in which she had stated, "One of the hard things is that we go one at a time." In going one at a time others are left behind to cope. The importance of Olivia Clemens to her family can be seen in their reactions to her death. One of Clemens's pet names for her was "my dear little gravity" and for the Clemens family the name was appropriate. She was the center that held them together. At her death each drew into himself or herself with grief.

In his notebook Clemens chided himself, "I was full of remorse for the things done & said in these 34 years of married life that hurt Livy's heart." He blamed himself for staying too long in her room the night she died and for all the hurtful things, real or imagined, he said to her over the years. He was thankful for her release. He wrote Howells, "But how thankful I am that her persecutions are ended. I would not call her back if I could." The words "I wish I were with Livy" reverberate through his letters to friends. Clemens readily admitted that he felt tired and old.

He was not the only member of the family to feel tired and old. In the hours following her mother's death, Jean had her first epileptic seizure in thirteen months. Clemens paced until he was exhausted, yet he said of Clara, "It would break Livy's heart to see Clara." Clara lay sobbing under her mother's casket. When Katy could get her to go to bed, Clara insisted on lying in the bed her mother had died in. In a strange repetition of the ritual with Livy, Clemens was allowed to see Clara, who "keeps her bed & says nothing," only twice a day. As Clara's despair grew worse, "nervously wrecked by her mother's death," she would eventually have a breakdown and be "in the hands of a specialist" in New York. Clemens would not be able to contact her even by phone for a year. A year later Isabel Lyon accurately described Livy's death as "the great tragedy of this family."

The tributes to Olivia Langdon Clemens following her death give testament to a well-loved and respected woman. Howells declared, "She hallowed what she touched, far beyond priests." Clemens agreed with his adoration. "The family's relation to her was peculiar & unusual, & could not exist toward another. Our love for her was the ordinary love, but added to it was a reverent & quite conscious worship."

In his tribute, Twichell described Livy as "one of the loveliest and best of women. To an extraordinary grace of person and of manners she added an equal grace of universal kindliness and gentle good will. . . . A more right-minded woman could not be. In her domestic relations she was everything that is excellent; a perfect wife and mother. To her distinguished husband she was ever a good angel, and his intellectual companion and helpmate as well."

Sentiments expressed on the death of a loved one are often exaggerated, but for the life of Olivia Langdon Clemens enough superlatives could not seem to be found, nor were they mere outpourings of bereavement. Friends and family readily agreed with her husband that "she was the most beautiful spirit, and the highest and the noblest I have known. And now she is dead."

Yet every death begins with a life, and Livy's began in Elmira, New York.

CHAPTER 2

"A generous free household"

W hen Olivia Louise was born on the night of November 27, 1845, the Langdons were one of the most recent families to Elmira, New York. (By the time she reached the age of seventeen, they would be the most prominent.) Her father, Jervis, and her mother, Olivia Lewis Langdon, had only just arrived from Millport, Chemung County, New York. It was the last stop for the thirty-six-year-old Jervis on a journey he began at the age of sixteen. For twenty years he had moved from store to store among the hills and the pines in a one-hundred-mile area between Syracuse and Elmira on the road to prosperity.

New England had always been the home of the Langdon family. Among their ancestors they could claim John Langdon (1791–1819), a soldier in the Revolutionary War, a delegate to the Continental Congress, who also attended the Constitutional Convention and eventually became a governor of New Hampshire. Another Langdon served a term as president of Harvard. Jervis's immediate family was not so powerful or successful. Both his parents came from small farms. His father, Andrew Langdon, was born in 1774; his mother, Eunice King, in 1782. They married in 1804, and Jervis was born on January 9, 1809 in Vernon, Oneida County, approximately one hundred miles from Elmira.

As a boy, Jervis grew up on his family's small farm. His parents also managed a country hotel that Andrew Langdon feared would kill his wife with hard work. Ironically, Andrew died when Jervis was but three years old. In the spirit of the pioneer woman, Eunice was a tough survivor. Eunice Langdon Williams Ford would bear a total of four children and survive two more husbands and her own son, Jervis, before she died at the age of nearly ninety-one in 1873. She once described life as incessant work, and she obviously instilled the importance of hard work in her son.

Jervis remained on the family farm working and receiving the education available to anyone of his time and circumstances. When he turned sixteen, he went to work in a country store in Vernon and one in Ithaca, both owned by a Mr. Stevens. Stevens found the boy dependable and hardworking, and in two years he sent him to open a branch store in Enfield, another small neighboring village in 1827. For the next ten years, Langdon journeyed from Enfield to Salina, back to Enfield, to Ithaca, spending approximately two years in each town establishing a store's business and moving on to the next challenge. For the United States, it was the era of expansion. In an effort to speed settlement and economic development, the state of New York had undertaken internal transportation improvements. North of Syracuse, the Erie Canal, completed in 1825, connected the Hudson River with Lake Erie. South of Syracuse, the Mohawk and Genesee Turnpike stretched across New York to link Buffalo and Albany by land. As mobility became easier, building increased and the settlers needed stores. On July 23, 1832 Jervis married Olivia Lewis, the daughter of Edward Lewis, a farmer from Lenox, New York. The bride was twenty-two; the groom, twenty-three. That same year Andrew Jackson saw his reelection as a mandate to stop the influence of the Bank of the United States. Old Hickory's actions would have far-reaching effects on the lives of both Jervis Langdon and the father of his future son-in-law, John Marshall Clemens. As Jackson's administration removed its federal deposits, the bank began refusing loans, calling in debts. Credit dried up and many suffered. Clemens described it as the ruin of his father's fortune; "He suddenly woke up and found himself reduced to less than one-fourth." The contraction of credit at home and abroad plus the fall of cotton prices on international markets led to the Panic of 1837 and ended the feverish expansion and land boom. The subsequent depression forced young Langdon out of the store business and into lumber. John Marshall Clemens never recovered from the economic setback. Like Langdon, he also "kept store." But, unlike Jervis Langdon, in the words of Mark Twain, "Ill fortune tripped him." The only asset John Marshall Clemens counted on was one hundred thousand acres in Tennessee, now greatly devalued with no hope of developing its yellow pine, iron ore, and other minerals that would make them "rich next year." Judge Clemens lived another ten years and died believing, in Twain's words, the land "would soon make us all rich and happy." The Tennessee land remained an elusive specter of possible wealth that would even haunt Livy and her husband in the future. The experience would cause Mark Twain to write, "It is good to begin life poor; it is good to begin life rich—these are wholesome; but to begin it poor and *prospectively* rich! The man who has not experienced it cannot imagine the curse of it."

In Millport, Jervis Langdon moved closer to the possibility of being "rich next year." Out of the store business, for the years between 1838 and 1843, he became an agent and later partner of Mr. T. S. Williams, a dealer in lumber. After two more years in Ithaca, the young Langdon family moved to Elmira. Langdon established the firm of Andrus and Langdon to sell lumber. Chemung pine was in demand and could be transported by the Chemung Canal that passed through Elmira. He later acquired additional pine lands with rich deposits of coal underneath them in Allegany County.

Langdon moved his pregnant wife and nine-year-old daughter Susan into a home on the corner of Main and West Second streets. The house that was to be their home for the next two years was built by Anson C. Ely, a local builder and investor and one of the organizers of the Elmira Bank. Olivia, the first natural child of the Langdons, was born in this house. Susan had been born in Tioga

County, not far from Syracuse, on February 18, 1836 and adopted by the Langdons, who lived in Millport, prior to 1840 when it seemed to them that after four years of marriage they would probably have no children.

Home and business were not all that occupied Jervis and Olivia Langdon. They were so close as a couple that "no discriminating friend can describe or estimate either one without the other." Livy described the atmosphere of her home in her formative years as "a generous free household" in affection and ideas. So it was after only one year in Elmira that the broad-minded ideas of the Langdons caused them to become embroiled in a battle that could have seen them ostracized from the community. Along with forty others, the Langdons left the Presbyterian Church and founded, on January 3, 1846, the First Independent Congregational Church.

The issue was one that would divide the nation for many years—slavery. These forty opposed the proslavery attitude of their old church. In their new constitution in the same paragraph that forbade drinking, attending the theater, or parties, they intoned: "And no person shall be admitted to the church, or allowed to remain in it, who practices or approves of buying or selling human beings, or holding them in slavery."

Many of the founders of the church, including the Langdons, were abolitionists and workers on the underground railroad. William Lloyd Garrison, editor of *The Liberator*, former slave Frederick Douglass, and Gerrit Smith, abolitionist and philanthropist, were all guests in the Langdon home. When the stately Langdon home was razed in 1939, tunnels between Park Church and the home were discovered indicating the Langdon house to be a stop on the underground railroad. These liberal attitudes of the Langdons were instilled early in Livy and stayed with her. When Clemens was working on *Huckleberry Finn*, Livy told him, "I will give you a motto, & it will be useful to you if you will adopt it: 'Consider every man colored till he is proved white.' "

Park Church struggled under four pastors in four years until the church became firmly established under the leadership of Thomas K. Beecher from 1854 to his death in 1900. Beecher was one of the illustrious New England Beechers and a half brother of Harriet Beecher Stowe, author of *Uncle Tom's Cabin*. Once he was financially established, Langdon supported the church generously. He told Beecher, "My purse is open to you; you can do more good with it than I can." Langdon matched the funds for the new building that was finished in 1876. It became the first institutional church in the United States that included a kitchen, parlors for meeting, pool and billiard tables, and a theater for children's plays.

The unconventional "TKB" was what this congregation wanted. He insisted he was a "teacher," not a minister. He made no pastoral calls. Looking more like a workman than a pastor, he gave as much manual help as carpenter, painter, and paperhanger as he did spiritual to his parishioners. He was a writer and a scientist. His gospel was the love of God and the fellowship of man. His flock grew, and his church overflowed. This unorthodox man was matched only by his wife, Julia Ward Beecher. As energetic and headstrong as her husband, she taught Sunday school, and Livy was one of her pupils. A practical woman, Julia bobbed her hair in 1857 and wore flat heels. But most importantly, she instilled in her pupils a love of beauty, a sense of humor, an appreciation of the mind, and a celebration of the individual. Favorite texts of hers included Emerson and Whitman.

Friends described Langdon as an astute businessman whose "discernment was so ready and his insight so quick, his judgments intuitively formed." His quick intuition told him to dissolve his lumber business in 1855. He invested in a mill, but it burned in 1862. From yet another venture in lead, he turned to the coal that was needed to fuel the factories to fight the Civil War. From death and destruction Jervis Langdon and many others became wealthy. He bought mines in Shamokin, Pennsylvania; his holdings even stretched into Nova Scotia. He could boast that he forwarded the first load of anthracite coal to Chicago from Pennsylvania by canal.

While her father was establishing his business and acquiring his wealth, Livy was growing up in the home on East Union Street which her father bought in 1847 when she was two years old. It was valued at twenty-five hundred dollars. She lived in this house until 1862, when, in measure of her father's success, the family moved into a home valued at twenty-five thousand dollars. As a child she was probably largely unaware of her father's coalfields and what they bought. Her world consisted of her sister Sue, her brother Charles, born in 1849, her friends, her play, and her education.

A mother provided much of her children's early education in the nineteenth century. In a home where each evening was devoted to reading aloud, love of reading and the desire to read would come early in life. Mrs. Langdon taught her children to read widely in history, geography, mathematics, science, and literature. She instilled in them a love of learning for the sake of curiosity. All their lives, the correspondence between Livy, her mother, Sue, and Charles would be punctuated with comments on what they were reading or thinking. It is rare to find a letter of Livy's that doesn't include a recitation of her reading and her critical comments on it. Expressions like "What are you reading nowadays write and tell me all about it," filled her letters to friends and families.

Considering the liberal and well-read atmosphere of the Langdon home, it is no wonder that when the time came for their daughters to embark on their formal education, the Langdons chose the Elmira Ladies' Seminary under the supervision of Miss Clarissa Thurston. The Elmira Seminary, which became Elmira College in 1855, was established with the purpose of supplying young ladies with an education "which shall compare favorably with the best institutions for the other sex."

At the age of nine, in May 1855, Olivia became a day student in the preparatory department for the second school term of 1854–55. Sue had already received her certificate from what was affectionately known as "Miss Thurston's" in March of 1853. The catalog reads, "Except in rare cases, young ladies are not able to receive the full benefit of the course who commence it under the age of fourteen and graduate under the age of twenty." It also states that a young lady should obtain a "thorough knowledge of the branches of the preparatory department" before going on to start the college courses. Preparatory studies included such subjects as reading, orthography, mental and written arithmetic, geography, American history and grammar, Greek, and Latin before going on to the four years in the college course. Mrs. Langdon used the seminary as an extension of Livy's education, which continued at home. Livy, as well as many of her friends, would be in the preparatory department to gain "thorough knowledge" until she was old enough for regular admission.

The college catalog states the course of instruction was designed "for the purpose of affording a thorough and extensive education for Ladies, with special reference to the best practical preparation for the duties of life, and at the lowest cost." The training of a lady had to be "a thorough scientific as well as ornamental education" with emphasis on improving the "mind, manners and heart" for "mental and moral improvement is the great object in education." A lady must have "genuine courtesy which flows from a desire to render others happy, and which is the result of esteeming others better than ourselves." Her education was to prepare her for the care of husband and family and "by no means intended to serve as an incentive to a professional career."

The role of the upper-class Victorian woman was to adorn her husband's home and to one day also be an educator of her own children. So while it was "highly desirable that parents should make arrangements to give their daughters the entire course of six years, or at least of the last four years," few girls completed this course. In 1857 out of a total of 252 students, over half were in the preparatory department with only 10 seniors. Obviously, many left to pursue the career they were trained for—marriage—just as Livy's roommate, Ellen A. Park, left the college after only one year to marry in 1860.

At the age of thirteen, in the 1858–59 school term, Olivia became a resident at Elmira College although she only lived seven blocks from the school. In order to be admitted, Livy passed "a fair examination . . . in Spelling, Reading, Arithmetic . . . Modern Geography and the elements of English Grammar." Her father paid the ninety-five-dollar tuition fee that included room and board and some extras, perhaps to rent a musical instrument or for art supplies, since playing and drawing were refined skills admired in a young woman.

At the basis of her education was what Livy loved all of her life—reading and thoughtfully commenting upon it. "A habit of reading is also cultivated, no mere reading of stories, but of such authors as enrich the mind, refine the taste, and improve the heart." From home and school, Livy learned not just how to read but how to judge literary merit, how to discern a style, how to appeal to an audience: all the editorial skills her husband would call upon.

While a resident, she lived in the same building that housed the entire college, a four-story octagon with a cupola, and a three-story wing on both the east and west sides of the building. The central staircase was wide, to permit passage of the young ladies in their full skirts as they went about their daily activities. The college was proud of its accommodations for its young ladies. It boasted, "Nearly $80,000 have been expended upon the building, groups and fixtures. The Students' rooms are all handsomely furnished and neatly carpeted. They are also warmed with heated air from furnaces and lighted with gas. The entire income is expended upon the Institution."

The cultivation of a lady was more than reading, writing, science, and mathematics. It involved "the best development of the moral feelings and social virtues, with a special regard to the cultivation of a refined and elegant taste." A total environment was presented so ladies could cultivate both the "solid and ornamental branches" of their education to become well-rounded individuals. Young ladies were encouraged to take exercise "in the open air" by walking for a half hour each day when the weather permitted, "for the extensive grounds of the Institution afford ample opportunity." They were not to leave the grounds of the college without a chaperone. Students were expected to keep their rooms neat and tidy in order to pass daily inspections and "to perform a portion of the domestic labor necessary . . . in the varied duties which the general care of the building requires." But these "varied duties" were not to exceed one hour a day, for that work, after all, was left to another class, the domestics. Livy and her classmates only needed enough manual labor to build character, "a daily practical lesson in human industry." The kitchen and the storerooms were off limits.

As a boarding student Livy furnished her own towels and bedding, napkins, clothing, umbrella, and overshoes all clearly marked with her name. She was also required to bring her own dictionary, modern atlas, and a Bible.

Religion was stressed as part of a young lady's development. The Bible was required because "the Scriptures are the great source from which lessons of instruction are drawn, and to which each one is referred for the standard of duty." The college endorsed "sound piety and good taste attached to the sphere of woman." Students were expected to attend church each Sunday morning and evening. They must also know their scripture well enough to recite a lesson. While no denomination was stressed, the Sabbath was sacred. "Young ladies are not allowed to visit each others' rooms, nor indulge in light and trifling conversation, or anything which may disturb those who may desire to keep their Sabbath as a day of serious meditation, reading and devotion." Neither were Livy and her fellow students to "make or receive calls on the Sabbath."

The year that Olivia lived on campus was an exciting one in learning for young women. The observatory, complete with telescope, was opened. The first graduating class of seventeen women received their baccalaureate of arts, a degree the college boasted to compete with any in the United States.

Livy's classmates included young women who would also be a part of her life outside school. Ida Clark would marry Livy's brother Charles. Emma Nye would die tragically in the home of the newly wed Samuel and Olivia Clemens in Buffalo. Alice Hooker, Clara Spaulding, Emma Sayles, her doctor's daughter, would all remain lifelong friends and correspondents.

Records indicate Livy was a resident student at Elmira College only for the second term of 1858–59. By the time the first term of 1859–60 came around, she was living at home again and attending school as a day student. Sometime around the age of sixteen, her public education, her life, and her body would be paralyzed by a fall on the ice.

CHAPTER 3

"Quietly and steadily"

On November 12, 1863, when Samuel Clemens had just begun to publish in Nevada under the name of Mark Twain, Olivia Langdon began a commonplace book, her personal journal of quotable literary passages.

The commonplace book was a "common" part of the young, educated nineteenth-century woman. It was not a diary of daily events, but a hope chest of words—a place to write down ideas, to attach newspaper clippings, letters or other memorabilia, to copy quotations to reinforce her upbringing and to act as guidelines for the future. In her own hand Livy expressed her reasons for keeping her commonplace book.

> *In reading authors, when you find*
> *Bright passages that strike your mind*
> *And which perchance you may have*
> *reason*
> *To think on it another season:*
> *Be not contented with the light*
> *But take there down in black & white;*
> *Such a respect is wisely shown*
> *That makes another's strengths your own.*

This unidentified quotation could well serve as a purpose for all commonplace books.

As the nation endured the grinding to the end of the Civil War, "Livie L. Langdon, Elmira N.Y.," as she signed her name inside the front cover, was living in the self-centered, sheltered world of the nineteenth-century Angelic, Beautiful Invalid. Grant's siege of Vicksburg ended with its fall in July as did Lee's push north at Gettysburg. Lincoln delivered his famous address on November 19. Livy would turn eighteen on November 27, 1863.

While other girls of her age and time were writing in their commonplace books of taking their proper place in society through marriage and family, Livy was plagued with physical ailments. According to Twain's *Autobiography*, "She became an invalid at sixteen through a partial paralysis caused by falling on the ice." Livy lay on her back in the darkness of her room for two long years. Her only attempts to sit up were through the aid of a tackle that hung from the ceiling over her bed. Each attempt left her nauseated, dizzy, weaker. A myriad of doctors attended her over the frustrating two years of her confinement. Nothing seemed to work, but in the nineteenth century Livy was suffering from a prevalent malady.

It was known by many names: nervous prostration or exhaustion, hysteria, neurasthenia. Dr. George Miller Beard studied the disease and described it in his book *American Nervousness: Its Causes and Consequences*, published in 1881. Beard characterized it as a peculiarly American illness that resulted from the increasing pace of life in the nineteenth century. Some of its manifestations included a partial or complete paralysis, headaches, depression, anorexia nervosa, lethargy, insomnia. It was a frustrating malady, for the symptoms often "simulate so perfectly other diseases to deceive for a time the best physician."

In men and women it struck those "among the well-to-do and the intellectual." In a society that encouraged hard work and being a success, it was an acceptable illness for men of the middle class struggling to get ahead. Beard, as well as many others in the nerve doctor business, had suffered from it himself. The majority who succumbed to this sickness were, like Livy, educated middle- to upper-class women, who Beard and others felt used too much mental energy. Modern life was too demanding on delicate women.

These were not just the views of a condescending male doctor reinforcing the Victorian patriarchy. Dr. Rachel Gleason, a much-respected Elmira physician, also suffered from what she called an "over-strained" brain. Rachel Brooks Gleason earned her medical degree in 1851, just two years after Elizabeth Blackwell became the first woman physician in the United States. Gleason, along with her husband Silas, also a doctor, opened their sanatorium and health resort in Elmira in 1852 to treat those who suffered from various nervous maladies.

Gleason gave health lectures to the young ladies at Elmira College. Her books on medicine and female maladies were part of the Langdon library, and she attended Livy at the birth of her children. Gleason believed that "the fast ways of the American people, with their hurried lives, late hours, and varied excesses, wear upon the nervous system of all, especially that of sensitive, impressible women. Those who are brilliant and fascinating early become frail, freaky, fidgety—a condition difficult to cure, but which could be prevented by leading a quiet life, with more of simple, useful work, of which this world furnishes an abundance." The problems of Livy's social class were even compounded by "anxiety as to dress, social position, calls and company, [that] wears one more than needed work."

Gleason agreed with her colleagues, male and female, who blamed nervous disorders on too much thinking by frail young women. Gleason writes in her book *Talks To My Patients,* published in 1870, "Growing girls are proverbially weak and sensitive." Because of this sensitivity, "mental application also, close and long-continued, results often in invalidism." Overtaxing the mind with too much study could cause permanent damage through exhaustion which condemned the young girl to "life-long dullness." "In others, the mental burns more and more brilliantly, and the body dies or falls into incurable invalidism. Our modern excellent educational advantages furnish specimens of both classes, but mostly of the latter." Too much thought, according to Gleason, weakened the body and made it susceptible to other illnesses "which proved fatal, simply because the long course of study had so enfeebled the system that it had little power to resist disease or sufficient recuperative force to rally even from slight sickness."

The disease of frailty has always been with us, but it became a high art in Victorian times that saw women as weak, childlike, to be lifted onto a pedestal. Delicacy went with refinement. Mark Twain wrote his fiancée that he wanted nothing to offend her delicacy, for "it is a woman's chief ornament." Nervous exhaustion was not a problem for immigrant servant girls, black women, or other lower-class working women who were not expected to be frail. After all, it took money to be sick and thus idle.

Cures varied. Gleason recommended a balanced diet, rest, moderation in physical and mental exercise. She and her husband later popularized her "water cure" for nervous disorders and other illnesses in their home down the hill from the Langdon summer home at Quarry Farm.

Beard also advocated rest, massage, diet, exercise, and electricity. This was the time of Thomas Edison, and his inventions influenced all scientists. If a too-active life drained the body of electricity, surely it could be restored through the use of electricity.

By 1873, Dr. Silas Weir Mitchell's rest cure was the standard cure for neurasthenia. His cure also incorporated rest, massage, electricity, and isolation. Mitchell recommended a female patient be isolated in bed for six weeks, visited only by her doctor and her nurse to feed and massage her. Any intellectual activity was forbidden—no reading or writing, not even sewing. The purpose was to build the patient's fat and blood. Physicians believed "it takes much blood, bone, and muscle to effect all these rapid changes of growth" so the young woman "needs nourishing food, moderate exercise, and freedom from mental excitement."

Mitchell prized himself on suiting the individual cure to the patient. He took one of his female patients, languishing from paralysis, for a carriage ride. Once they were a distance from her home, he stopped the carriage and forced her to walk home. She did and was cured. Another paralysis victim refused to leave her bed. She did when Mitchell, in exasperation, began to remove his clothes and threatened to get into bed with her. These were the rare exceptions, for the majority of his patients were not malingerers but sufferers who hoped the rest cure would work for them.

Why did any intelligent young woman succumb to this mysterious malady? Livy may have been reacting to the growing pressures of her own sexuality and ambivalence concerning her intelligence, her place in society, and the changing role of women. Illness made Livy the center of the family's attention, as it would later do so when she was a married woman and mother. Whatever the causes, which remain as deep and hidden as the recesses of the mind, the pain and paralysis were real enough to Livy and her family.

Finally, as a last resort, in the fall of 1864, at the suggestion of Jervis's nephew Andrew, the Langdons in desperation paid Dr. James Rogers Newton a sum of fifteen hundred dollars to try to cure Livy. In Mark Twain's recounting of Langdon's words, "You have tried everybody else; now try Doctor Newton, the quack." While he considered the man a quack, Andrew Langdon was impressed that he had seen him cure a crippled Elmira man.

According to Twain, Newton pulled back the shades, letting light into the room for the first time in two years, and said, "Now we will sit up, my child." The tackle over the bed had long been abandoned by this time. Then with a prayer, Newton aided Livy in walking a few steps. Twain's rendition of Newton's final diagnosis is, "I have reached the limit of my art. She is not cured. It is not likely that she will *ever* be cured. She will never be able to walk far, but after a little daily practice she will be able to walk one or two hundred yards, and she can depend on being able to do *that* for the rest of her life."

How he "cured" Livy is not known. Gleason believed that "many women who have been confined to the bed for months will walk without the least protest, under the influence of a positive person for whom they have respect." Newton advocated the basic theory behind the cure that Beard popularized. Twain writes that Newton explained "perhaps some subtle form of electricity proceeded from his body and wrought the cures." Livy's illness was gone as quickly as it had appeared, according to Mark Twain.

Livy's mother writes of a much longer recovery, of delicate health for her daughter that continued on to her twenty-second birthday, only a month before she would meet Samuel Clemens at a Christmas reunion of *Quaker City* passengers that included her brother Charles.

Olivia Lewis Langdon's entries record the surprise and delight of her daughter's slow but steady recovery. For February 11, 1865, "This morning Livia breakfasted with the family. The first she has done so in *three years*." In May and June of that year she is being attended by the family doctor Sayles, but also still being seen by Doctor Newton as well. Twain may have remembered Newton's cure of Livy as complete in one session, but the diary entries show Newton would continue to treat Livy and remain in touch with her by letter. Livy's mother records on June 3, 1865, "He offered surprise at the improvement in Livia. I hope he will add still more to her strength." A year later her mother is still writing with surprise at her daughter's growing strength. April 23, 1866: "Yesterday Livia got out of her chair, walked to the bureau and back and sat down again without help—It seems almost more than I can realise [sic] that my child can once more walk." She also records that Livy is getting out of the house to visit friends and to attend "family worship for the 1st time in 6 years." Each step of progress was difficult and accompanied by minor relapses. April 5, 1866: "She enjoyed it [calling on her friend Clara Spaulding] but was very tired." April 12: "Livia seems quite over done today."

Delighted with his daughter's improvement, even if it was very slow, Jervis Langdon gave her a "beautiful watch & chain" on May 3 to celebrate her ability to walk again. Olivia Lewis Langdon records writing to Dr. Newton and then a few days later she writes, "On the 6th of June my dear boy left home with his father for New York expecting to sail for Europe on the 'Quaker City' on the 8th." It was 1867, three years after Mark Twain states that Newton cured Livy.

MARK AND LIVY

All through her bedridden illness and slow recovery, Livy wrote in her commonplace book. Because she could not venture out, her education and religion came to her. She was tutored by Darius R. Ford of Elmira College. Thomas K. Beecher and his wife Julia provided spiritual education through their visits.

The selections in Livy's commonplace book are sporadically dated, so it is difficult to ascertain what was written when. Roughly, she kept her book about seven years from when she was nearly eighteen through twenty-five years old.

The quotations she jots down come from the library shelves of her family. She documents the wisdom of English writers John Milton, Jane Austen, Charles Dickens, Robert Browning, and William Thackeray interspersed with that from Americans Henry David Thoreau, Ralph Waldo Emerson, Henry Wadsworth Longfellow, Oliver Wendell Holmes, and Nathaniel Hawthorne, as well as such diverse sources as Margaret Fuller, Daniel Webster, Horace Greeley, and those of Henry Ward Beecher. Generous segments from Shakespeare also fill her pages.

Many are unidentified selections that tell much of Livy's thoughts and feelings at this stage in her life simply because she felt strongly enough to want to record them. Typical are the following maxims that read like proverbs from a nineteenth-century *Poor Richard*. "Patience is genius, greatness the fruit of indefatigable labor, and success in life the result of purpose and persistent industry." "A good jest in time of misfortune is food and drink. It is strength to the arm, digestion to the stomach, courage to the heart. It is better than wisdom or wine." "Opportunities, like eggs, must be hatched when they are fresh." "The bread of life is Love; the salt of life is Work; the sweetness of life Poesy; the water of life Faith." This final remark is attributed to Anna Brownell Jameson, a popular British author of the time, and taken from her commonplace book.

All the entries attest to Livy's sheltered background, her intelligence, her feeling of her role in the world and her religious faith—quotations that admonish her to have an inner and outer beauty. "Improve your physical condition. Educate your intellect—Expand and purify your affections—Cultivate your spiritual nature—

Be healthy—Be wise—Be loving—Be spiritually minded—Be beautiful."

Whatever influence Samuel Clemens did or did not have on her faith over the years of their marriage, the words recorded by the young woman in her commonplace book show a devout and orthodox, even if untested, faith. "Our brains are seventy-year clocks. The Angel of Life winds them up once for all, then closes the case, and gives the key into the hand of the Angel of Resurrection." "Run a hem of prayer around each day," she reminds herself sometime in February 1870. She married Clemens on February 2 of that year.

Untested may very well be the word for the reason behind many of her choices of quotations. Many entries make a sharp delineation between black and white. The pains of life would shade areas gray for her in years to come. From *Oldtown Folks*—"Whenever the wandering Demon of Drunkenness finds a ship adrift—no steady mind in its sails, no thoughtful pilot directing its course—he steps on board, takes the helm, and steers straight for the maelstrom." And she included these thoughts from Horace Greeley:

> In the ever proceeding warfare of Good against
> Evil, Right against Wrong, Truth against
> Error, there can be no real defeat, no
> absolute discomfiture, only postponement,
> repulse and the ill-successes of a misdirected
> attack,—an unwisely planned maneuver. . . .
> Happy they who learn in childhood, and
> treasure through after trials and temptations,
> the grand lesson of the age—the physolophy [sic]
> of living to noble ends.

Livy's entries in her commonplace book reveal an ethical if inexperienced mind. Yet this young woman's genteel upbringing displayed in her pensive smile and quiet demeanor would attract the "wild humorist of the Pacific slope."

CHAPTER 4

"Twenty-two yesterday! Growing old fast!"

L ivia, as her family called her, had at twenty-two become a beauty, a delicate, sheltered blossom to rival those that flourished in the Langdon greenhouse. Brunet hair framed her face and accented her dark eyes. All of her life, people would remark on her slight bemused smile and her manner of ducking her head before she burst into "the heart free laugh" of a young girl. The gentleness in her face emanated from an inner beauty and quiet purpose that considered others before herself.

Although she was thought frail by her family, she never used her health as an excuse for sympathy. Her concern, along with that of her parents and sister, was for the development of her younger brother, Charles. At eighteen, the heir to the position of managing the Langdon coal had not yet shown sufficient interest in it to please his parents.

Charlie completed his formal education at the Gunnery School for boys. Jervis Langdon, ever mindful of his social position and what he didn't have growing up but could now afford, wanted to send his son on a "grand tour," or a trip abroad, the standard finishing school for wealthy young men in the nineteenth century. Early in 1867, after consulting with Thomas K. Beecher, the Langdons decided Charles should travel to the "Holy Land, Egypt &

elsewhere." Captain Sturges was secured as his chaperone in April. His worried mother records in her diary, "On the 6th of June my dear boy left home with his father for New York expecting to sail for Europe on the 'Quaker City' on the 8th." Bad weather delayed departure for two days.

Livy summarized the family's feelings in a letter to her friend Alice Hooker. He would naturally be missed, "But still we are all glad to have him go, hoping he will return much improved in many ways—I told him that I expected him to return a gentleman." This trip as well as a subsequent one Livy described as her father's way of getting his son to learn despite his "inability to study."

The future of the Langdon family seemed as settled, opulent, and comfortable as the mansion they occupied on Main Street. Charles would join his father's business after his excursion to Europe. Sue had married Theodore Crane in 1858. Livy told her friend Alice that her main hope at twenty-two was not marriage, "But if I only grow in Grace and in the knowledge of our Lord and Saviour I am content—." Livy would be the unmarried sister to remain at home to care for her parents as they grew older. Jervis Langdon sometimes joked he would probably die if Livy ever left home so certain was he of her fate.

The pattern of her life seemed ordered and secure. Her gradually restored health allowed her to take carriage rides with her mother, to visit with her friends, and to have them visit her. Reading—talking and writing about it—was her passion. While it was a standard practice in Victorian life to read by yourself and aloud with others for entertainment, for Livy it was the main outlet of her energies. Describing what she was reading, with whom, and her opinions of the works were the predominant subjects of her letters. She and Clara Spaulding enjoyed L. Muehlbach's *Frederick the Great and His Court*. "We became very much excited over some portions of it." Certain evenings and afternoons were devoted to reading with certain people. "We read King Henry V last evening—Mrs. Corey reads with us on Thursday evening."

Within a month of her twenty-second birthday, and Livy's certainty she would not marry, she met her future husband at a reunion of *Quaker City* passengers held in New York at the St. Nicholas Hotel. Mark Twain wrote in his autobiography thirty-nine years later that he had actually seen her before December 27, 1867. "I saw her first in the form of an ivory miniature in her brother Charley's stateroom in the steamer *Quaker City*, in the Bay of Smyrna, in the summer of 1867, when she was in her twenty-second year. I saw her in the flesh for the first time in New York in the following December." According to his autobiography and Paine's biography, Clemens loved her from that first glimpse of the photograph. He had to meet her.

On New Year's Eve, Clemens joined the Langdons for dinner and then attended a reading given by Charles Dickens, a particular favorite of Livy's. Clemens was not as enthusiastic as Livy about Dickens's performance. He found the literary giant to be arrogant and rather boring. He reported in his newspaper, the *Alta California*, that the evening was of even higher culture for him, continuing his image of the western ruffian, because he had been in the company of "a highly respectable young white woman."

New Year's Day, Livy and her friend Alice received callers at the home of Mrs. Barry, a family friend and acceptable chaperone. Clemens wrote his mother, "I anchored for the day at the first house I came to—Charlie Langdon's sister was there (beautiful girl) & Miss Alice Hooker, another beautiful girl, a niece of Henry Ward Beecher's. We sent the old folks home early, with instructions not to send the carriage till midnight, & then I just staid [sic] there and deviled the life out of those girls. I am going to spend a few days with the Langdon's [sic] in Elmira, New York, as soon as I get time."

In one week he had been in her company three times, but does not mention her by name. The young woman, he states forty years later, who "was never out of my mind" from the moment he supposedly saw her portrait, is not mentioned again in his correspondence for nearly seven months.

Livy may not have been contemplating marriage, but her future husband had been for a long time. In January 1862 he vowed to his sister-in-law Mollie that he would never marry until "I am a rich man." He desired enough money to have servants "to leave my wife in the position for which I designed her, viz: as a *companion.*" He already knew the type of woman he wanted, a helpmate as well as someone who would love him. To his friend Will Bowen he expressed his fears in a letter dated August 25, 1866. "Marry be d—d. I am too old to marry. I am nearly 31. I have got gray hairs on my head. Women appear to like me, but d—d them, they don't love me." Shortly before he met Livy he tells Mrs. Fairbanks, "If I were settled I would quit all nonsense & swindle some [poor] girl into marrying me. But I wouldn't expect to be 'worthy' of her. I wouldn't *have* a girl I was worthy of. *She* wouldn't do. She wouldn't be respectable enough."

Samuel Clemens admired women all his life. He agreed with the popular Victorian belief that man was rough and crude, woman from her pedestal was gentle and pure. Man needed, in Huck Finn's words, the "sivilizing" influences of women for they upheld the values of the community. He related to all women in the same way that began with his mother, Jane Lampton Clemens. Clemens, the eternal little boy, would request reform from a woman, promise to be better, change for a while, then relapse into his old ways so he could be scolded, and then the process could begin all over again.

Jane Clemens was the first woman to "reform" Samuel Clemens long before there was ever a literary twin named Mark Twain. Because his mother administered the discipline, did the pleading and praying, Clemens naturally came to associate reform with women. He said of his mother, "My mother had a good deal of trouble with me but I think she enjoyed it." Throughout his life she made him take oaths, thinking that might keep him out of trouble for a while. In a particularly poignant story told after the death of his father, she asked him "to promise me to be a better boy. Promise not to break my heart." This story, as related by Paine, similar to the story of Livy and the miniature, may or may not be true, but Jane Clemens in all probability asked young Sam to be a "better boy" many times.

The first woman following his mother to whom Clemens appealed to civilize him was Mrs. Mary Mason Fairbanks. Like her fellow passenger on the *Quaker City*, she was writing letters to be published. Only her letters would be in her husband's newspaper, the Cleveland *Herald*. Although at thirty-nine she was only seven years his senior, her bearing and demeanor and interest in Clemens and the younger passengers on board, including Charles Langdon, made it seem natural for him to refer to her as "Mother" Fairbanks. She remained Clemens's confidante for thirty-one years until her death in 1898.

Mrs. Fairbanks offered a new dimension to Clemens's relationship with women. She could not only civilize his manner, but offer valuable advice on his writing. He described her in a letter to his family: "She was the most refined, intelligent, & cultivated lady in the ship, & altogether the kindest & best. She sewed my buttons on, kept my clothes in presentable trim, fed me on Egyptian jam, (when I behaved), lectured me awfully on the quarter-deck on moonlit promenading evenings, & cured me of several bad habits."

Clemens created a role for Mrs. Fairbanks to play, just as he created a role for his mother. Mrs. Fairbanks would willingly play that role, whereas his mother did not realize evidently she was a pawn in her son's game of transgression, regret, reform, and an inevitable slipping back into doing as he pleased.

Clemens thanked and praised Mrs. Fairbanks for helping him get his travel letters to the *Alta California*. He praised her copy-reading done in an "efficient, tyrannical, and overbearing fashion." Clemens cast Mrs. Fairbanks in the role he was to create for Livy—the tyrannical woman bossing a henpecked man. Over the years Clemens wrote a number of letters to Mrs. Fairbanks thanking her for reforming and refining him and encouraging her to supply more of the same. "Don't be afraid to write sermons—I am perfectly willing not only to receive them but to try to profit by them." Yet part of the game of his asking for correction was his ability to slip back. In a letter to Livy, he says, "I stopped chewing tobacco because it was a mean habit, partly & partly because my mother desired it. I ceased from profanity because Mrs. Fairbanks desired it. I stopped drinking strong liquors because you desired it." For his entire life Clemens would continually give up smoking, swearing, and alcohol without success.

On the same date that he first informed his mother of Charlie Langdon's sister, January 8, 1868, he wrote to a young lady with whom he had been friendly on the *Quaker City*. Emma Beach was the seventeen-year-old daughter of publisher Moses Sperry Beach. The mode of his courtship he would repeat with Livy—reform me, I am unworthy man, you are woman. He responds to Emma almost in rapture. "Your reproofs are so honest, & so pleasant, withal, that I really can't help feeling a strong desire to deserve more of them! But I will conquer it and try to behave myself." He ends the letter with, "Come, Miss Emma, send me some more reproofs, & upon my word I will do all I can to profit by them—."

He also reports to Emma that he received a "scorcher" of a letter from Mrs. Fairbanks condemning his use of slang, or any word she felt was inappropriate. "I know I never, never, never shall get reformed up to the regulation standard." Clemens's letters to Mrs. Fairbanks are full of his asking forgiveness for using slang. He would be sorry and then proceed to use it again. Apparently not yet thinking of courting Livy, he asks Emma, "If you will help me, now, I will go to church every Sunday for a month—& I believe steadily continue reforming."

Whether Clemens had or had not seen and immediately adored Livy in the form of a miniature or loved her the moment he met her, Clemens remembered it that way. Their relationship, their marriage of thirty-four years, was a succession of events that Clemens remembered one way, often varying from what really happened. So long in love with love, he fell for an image at some point—the image of an ideal woman. Livy, raised in a world of Eastern respectability that could smooth out his western rough edges, was close to that ideal.

Clemens was in his own words "too busy" until August 1868 to accept the Langdons' invitation to Elmira. On the twenty-fourth of the month, Charles, informed by telegram of Clemens's delay, took an old friend and rode the Erie railway to Waverly, New York to meet his new friend and *Quaker City* confidante. Clemens had mistakenly taken a slow train called the Cannonball. Charles, knowing the propriety of his family, was horrified to see his friend in "a yellow duster and a very dirty old straw hat," but Clemens assured him he had more presentable apparel with him. Much to Charlie's relief, they arrived late, giving his friend time to buy a proper hat and change his clothes before meeting the family the next day.

Clemens was like no guest who had ever stayed in the Langdon home. He adopted young Charles on the trip to Europe and the Holy Land because of the young man's immaturity and inexperience. Charlie was fourteen years younger and had seen little beyond New York. Charlie warmed to Clemens because of his humor and his easygoing manner exemplified in his slouch and drawl. What attracted Charlie on board the *Quaker City* also piqued the curiosity of Livy. Here was a man who had been raised on the frontier, left home at fourteen, piloted on the Mississippi, mined in Nevada, wrote in California. He was now well-known as a humorist and lecturer and soon to publish a book.

The Langdons and their home were certainly unlike anything Clemens had ever known. These pillars of a community of fifteen thousand lived in a three-story home with grounds that covered an entire city block. Three sets of gates opened automatically, triggered by the weight of horses, to carriages as they approached. A tribute to the architecture and style that became known as the Brown Decades, the house was decorated with elaborate figures in the carpeting, wallpaper, and on the ceilings. Huge chandeliers hung from the high ceilings of each room. Sumptuous curtains and plush upholstery gave the home the palatial yet somber, heavy look that the wealthy of the time so desired.

Yet the Langdons were never as smug as their surroundings. Sam Clemens was overwhelmed by their affectionate nature toward each other. They conversed and laughed, read and sang together in the evenings. Years later Clemens would write Sue Crane that he always associated the song "The Sweet By and By" with Livy. It was playing when they met, and they used to sing it in the evenings in the Langdon home.

His own family had maintained an "atmosphere of reserve. . . . I never knew a member of my father's family to kiss another of it except once, and that at a deathbed." During Clemens's visit a cousin of Livy's, Hattie Lewis from Illinois, was also staying with the Langdons.

> My cousin Olivia and myself felt a little nervous about enter-
> taining an unmarried man who had written a book! At this time
> he had written The Jumping Frog. We wondered how he would
> look: how he would act: would he be funny all the time? and
> must we try to be? etc. as young ladies will. I really felt that I
> had one advantage over my cousin, but only one. She was rich,
> beautiful and intellectual, but she could not see through a joke,
> or see anything to laugh at in the wittiest sayings unless ex-
> plained in detail—I could. . . . I soon discovered that my quick-
> ness at seeing the point of a joke and the witty sayings that I
> had considered irresistible were simply nothing in comparison
> to my cousin's gifts. Mr. Clemens evidently greatly preferred
> her sense to my nonsense.

Setting down her account after the event, Hattie Lewis remembered that she felt Clemens and Livy "would be a most suitable
match." She curtailed her visit so the two could spend more time
together. She hinted to Livy that she was certain Clemens would
propose. Hattie may have had a selective memory in recounting
how she and Clemens feigned being in love prior to his formal
engagement to Livy in order to squelch the stories of Elmira's
gossips, for she was disappointed in his interest in Livy and not
her.

Clemens had been invited for one week. At first his hosts were
delighted with his humor, his unusual experiences that he described in his fascinating stories. Later Livy admitted to him that
during his first visit they began to wish he would leave. At the
end of the week, he confided to Charles, "I am in love—in love
with your sister, and I ought to get away from here." Charles was
aghast that such a worldly and experienced man desired his sister.

Young Langdon was not the only one shocked. Clemens abandoned his reserve, and disregarding all proprieties, proposed to
Livy. She promptly refused. She probably was not in love with

him yet, but part of the ritual of proper courtship of the time was to refuse the first proposal. Livy was the epitome of this upper-class late-nineteenth-century woman, which was part of Clemens's attraction to her. She had done the expected thing. The ritual of courtship was a strict one, and Clemens had violated the rules of the game. He may have expected a refusal, would have been equally shocked at an acceptance, but he was upset by her actions. Livy allowed him to hope and granted his permission to write to her as one of the roles she knew—he could write to her as a brother would to a sister.

In a letter to "My Honored 'Sister' " written after her refusal and on his last night in Elmira, he poured out his love. "For I do not regret that I have loved you, still love & shall always love you. I accept the situation, uncomplainingly, hard as it is." Thus began a courtship that would run to nearly two hundred letters before they were married and a series of love letters that would expand their married life during their separations. Livy would one day describe them to their daughter Susy as "the loveliest love letters that ever were written." Clemens appealed to Livy in the most sympathetic way he knew, the only way he knew, his urgings that she reform him so that he might not become a "homeless vagabond" forever. From the same letter of September 7, 1868:

> I ask that you will write to me sometimes, as to a friend whom you feel will do all that a man may be worthy of your friend-ship—or as to a brother whom you know will hold his sister's honor as dearly as his own, her wishes as his law, her pure judgments above his worldly wisdom. . . . My honored sister, you are *so* good & so beautiful—& I am so proud of you! Give me a little room in that great heart of yours—only the little you have promised me—& if I fail to deserve it may I remain forever the homeless vagabond I am! If you and Mother Fairbanks will only scold me & upbraid me now and then, I shall fight my way through the world, never fear. . . .

Livy was to carry on in the role of reforming him as Mary Fairbanks had consciously begun and his mother unconsciously before her.

In this first letter, Clemens established the techniques of his courtship of Livy. He recited his great love, but vowed he was unworthy of her. After expounding on his love for her, he states that he will never mention it again and calls Livy his "sister" to reassure her after his preceding outburst of love. Clemens, the little boy inside the man she would call "Youth," appealed to her open, generous nature. Livy has a duty to write him, to lecture him, he reasons. It is the least she can do.

Livy replied and sent a picture of herself and news that he was in her prayers. She also consented to a visit from him at the end of September. He is touched by her prayers. "I will so mend my conduct that I shall grow worthier of your prayers, & your good will & sisterly solicitude as the days go by."

He spent a day and a night with the Langdons in Elmira. Then an accident allowed him more time with Livy.

> Mr. Clemens spent two days here on his way back to Hartford from St. Louis, he intended only to remain one day, but as he and Charlie started for the Depot, they were thrown out of the back end of the wagon (it was a democrat wagon and the seat was not fastened) both striking their heads. Charlie's head was quite badly cut. Mr. Clemens was stunned—It did not prove to be serious in either case—We all enjoyed Mr. Clemens' stay with us very much indeed.

Clemens did not see the accident so matter-of-factly. Years later in his autobiography he described it as "one of those cases so frequent in the past centuries, so infrequent in our day—a case where the hand of Providence is in it." The happy accident gave him three more days and the advantage of being nursed by Livy. "It pushed my suit forward several steps," and it earned a return invitation during his November lecture in Elmira.

The extra time with Livy made Clemens feel he could go beyond the brother-sister pose only to be slapped back in writing by Livy. He wrote her from Hartford apologizing for his "hot-blooded heedlessness." Ever mindful of what would impress Livy and her parents as to his sincerity in being a more acceptable suitor, he mentioned that he had made a new friend in Hartford where he worked on revising his travel letters from the *Quaker City* voyage into a book. The Reverend Joseph H. Twichell, the popular minister of the Asylum Hill Congregational Church, was as enchanted by Clemens's unorthodox behavior, attitude, and humor as the Langdons had been. Clemens also was as attracted to Twichell's eastern decorum as he had been to the Langdons'. They got along so well that Clemens went home with Twichell from the church sociable where they met to continue their visit. The conscious writer in an attempt to reach his audience, Clemens wrote Livy of how he then attended church the next day and went with Twichell to the alms house. "I have not had anything touch me so since I saw the leper hospitals of Honolulu & Damascus."

While Clemens proceeded with his letters to his "honored sister" as not to alarm Livy and convince her and her family of his suitability, he was not so restrained in his purpose to others. He admitted to Samuel Webster, his friend, that "I'll harass that girl and harass her till she'll *have* to say yes!"

Clemens was at the Langdon door again November 21 with the words, "May the prodigal have some breakfast?" Livy attended his lecture "The American Vandal Abroad" in Elmira, Monday evening the twenty-third. To further ingratiate himself to the family, Clemens was foregoing his usual $100 lecture fee to benefit the Volunteer Fire Company of which Charlie was an active member. The public paid from $.35 to. $.75 to hear him promote his forthcoming book. Clemens felt confident enough in his feelings to push his suit. But Livy, fearful of her feelings and her parents' disapproval, tried to avoid him for several days. Clemens was not so easily put aside. "Wednesday night she said over & over & over again that she loved me but was sorry she did & hoped it would yet pass away—Thursday . . . said she was *glad & proud* she loved me!" Clemens returned to New York the next day fearing the gossips already had enough to besmirch her "sacred name." Admitting her love had been difficult for Livy. She was exhausted, for she had eaten or slept little in forty-eight hours as she agonized over how her decision would affect her family.

Livy's parents agreed to an engagement, but they insisted it be secret until they were more certain of their prospective son-in-law.

They were worried their daughter's health and happiness might be trifled with by someone who was only interested in her inheritance. Livy's share of the Langdon fortune approached a quarter of a million.

Mrs. Langdon expressed her concerns to Mrs. Fairbanks. "I cannot, and need not, detail to you the utter surprise and almost astonishment with which Mr. Langdon and myself listened to Mr. Clemens' declaration to us, of his love for our precious child, and how at first our parental hearts said no, to the bare thought of such a stranger mining in our hearts for the possession of one of the few jewels we have." While convinced Clemens was "a man of genius" and "affectionate," Mrs. Langdon requests from Mrs. Fairbanks, "your opinion of him as a *man*; what the kind of man he *has been*, & what the man he now is, or is to become." Her main concern is if he intends to "enter upon a new . . . Christian life." At the same time, Clemens is telling his sister Pamela Moffett, "When I am permanently *settled*—& when I am a Christian—& when I have *demonstrated* that I have a good, steady, reliable character, her parents will withdraw their objections, & she *may* marry me—*I* say she *will*—I intend she *shall*—."

At the Langdons' request, Clemens left them with a list of references, people he had known out west, that they could contact as to his character. While he remembered in his autobiography that he supplied the names of "six prominent men, among them two clergymen," they did not write complimentary letters. Such unflattering phrases as describing Clemens as a man who will make "trivial" use of his talent, "born to be hung," "fill a drunkard's grave" horrified the Langdons. In his autobiography Clemens described his meeting with Langdon asking, "What kind of people are these? Haven't you a friend in the world?" From the letters it seemed he didn't, so Langdon exclaimed, "I'll be your friend myself. Take the girl. I know you better than they do."

Clemens described later when Langdon heard him speak admiringly of the man who had hired him for the *Territorial Enterprise*, Joe Goodman. "Why didn't you refer me to him?" inquired Langdon. Clemens didn't because "The others gave me all the vices;

Goodman would have given me all the virtues." Clemens actually had given Goodman as a reference, but his positive comments were outweighed by the negative ones collected.

Despite their doubts, it was obvious to the Langdons that their daughter was in love. Livy confided to Alice Hooker, "that a great satisfying love, has slowly, gradually worked its way into my heart—into my entire being." Also Jervis Langdon's health was starting to fail. He would be dead within the next eighteen months. In his devotion to his daughter, he certainly wanted to see her happily settled.

Livy's faith in the man she loved helped to convince her family of Clemens's desire to begin a new life. She also believed in her role to help him achieve that new life. Livy disclosed to Mrs. Fairbanks that she was humbled by "Mother" Fairbanks passing the mantle and responsibility of reforming her future husband to her. She writes that she is "proud that you should feel that I might help Mr. Clemens—Humbled when I remember how much I must strive to do, as a Christian woman." For once she worried, and others did not, that her health wouldn't allow her to be a good wife, but she could rely on "a strength from above." She is concerned about her fiancé's image as the "Wild Humorist of the Pacific slope." "I want the public . . . to know something of his deeper, larger nature—I remember being quite incensed by a lady's asking, 'Is there anything of Mr. Clemens except his humour?' "

Clemens could happily exclaim to his family, "This is to inform you that on yesterday, the 4th of February, I was duly & solemnly & irrevocably engaged to be married to Miss Olivia Langdon, aged 23 1/2, only daughter of Jervis and Olivia Langdon, of Elmira, New York. *Amen.* She is the best girl in all the world, & the most sensible, & I am just as proud of her as I can be." It was not entirely unexpected by his family for he had told his sister Pamela the previous December that he intended to marry, but he demanded they not tell "*any* one—I make no exceptions."

Livy had to wait until the twentieth for her engagement ring. Clemens requested that Mary Fairbanks have a plain gold band made in Cleveland, sized from an old ring of Livy's. When the ring was crafted and engraved with the date of their engagement, Mrs. Fairbanks sent it "express" to Elmira to Clemens in time for him to place it on Livy's finger while he stopped there during his continuing lecture tours. As with most engaged couples, they were beginning with very little. Livy called the ring "the largest piece of furniture in the house." Clemens complimented her remark as "a burst of humor worthy of your affianced husband."

Both realized it would be a while before they married. Clemens wished to save enough money to keep Livy in the style to which she was accustomed. Livy also knew he wanted a more secure situation. "Of course, every thing in the future is very uncertain as Mr. Clemens is not yet settled anywhere, but he is very tired of the wandering life that he has been leading."

Fortunate are those in the first flush of love. More fortunate are those who have never been disappointed in love, for they believe they can be and are everything to the beloved. Clemens needed "a darling little mentor" to attempt to reform him. Livy needed "a dear little man" to care for.

CHAPTER 5

"As happy as a queen"

An engagement is the period of preparing for a marriage. It involves the planning of a ceremony, but it is also the time when two individuals become a couple. Physically, Clemens had lectures to give and a manuscript to prepare for publication. Livy had a wedding to plan and a household to set up. But spiritually, each had an image of what a husband and wife should be. Happily for both, the other was malleable, pliably in love.

Now that Livy was to be a part of his life, Clemens escalated his efforts to make her his paragon of perfection. For Clemens, Livy "fills *my* ideal of what a woman should be in order to be enchantingly lovable." The Livy addressed by Clemens in his love letters during their year of engagement seems too good for this world, but then that is the way he wanted to see her. The traits attributed to her were real, but carried to an adoring extreme. Livy was a woman he loved and admired, but Clemens wanted to transform her into an earthly goddess to be worshipped. He addressed her as a "precious little philosopher," "little saint," "princess-darling-idol," "darling little mentor."

Livy objected to being put on such a high pedestal, but there was little she could do but accept the situation. In Clemens's mind,

Livy was the woman to worship, a woman to save from his past and to preserve his future. In the letters following their engagement, Clemens emphasizes his need for her reform and her goodness.

> I grow prouder and prouder of you day by day, as each new evidence comes that there is none like you in all the world. If ever a man had reason to be grateful to Divine Providence, it is I. And often & often again I sit & think of the wonder, the curious mystery, the *strangeness* of it, that there should be only *one* woman among the hundreds & hundreds of thousands whose features I have critically scanned, & whose characters I have read in their faces—only *one* woman among them all whom I could love with all my whole heart, & that it should be my amazing good fortune to secure that woman's love. . . . I have found you at least, & in you I can discover *no* blemish. It is strange, it is very strange. The hand of Providence is in it. When I cease to be grateful, deeply grateful to you for your priceless love, my honored Livy, I shall be—dead. Never before, Livy— never before.

She remained his "Human Angel," his "Dear Gravity" all of her life. Clemens provided the code of conduct for Livy, so she could live up to his ideal embodied in the names he gave her. One way to preserve Livy's purity was through her reading. If she wished to read *Gulliver's Travels*, he offered to mark the sections fit for her and to remove any offensive parts for "portions of it are very coarse & indelicate." Neither should she read *Don Quixote* or Shakespeare until "some hand has culled them of their grossness." She had already read the works he found offensive and, somehow, still managed to be for Clemens "as pure as snow, & I would have you always so—untainted, untouched even by the impure thoughts of others." She, in her perfection, could mete out the reforms he desired so much.

This Victorian view of men and women was summarized in a popular marriage manual of the time.

> Few women understand at the outset that in marrying, they have simply captured a wild animal . . . the taming of which is to be the life work of the woman who has taken him in

charge. . . . The duty is imposed upon her by high heaven, to reduce all these grand, untamed life-forces to order . . . to make them subservient to the behests of her nature, and to those vast undying interests which, to these two and to their posterity, center in the house.

Both Livy and Clemens believed it was her "life work" to "tame" him. As the moral vessel, the Victorian woman was responsible for refining men's actions; thus it was her job to detect any improper actions on his part and to eliminate them.

In the bloom of love and in the desire to please his prospective in-laws and his fiancée, Clemens urged Livy's reforms. Changing his smoking habits, which Clemens suggested early in their courtship, is typical. He had given the practice up for his mother and Mrs. Fairbanks. He would give it up again for Livy, but not without an occasional protest even if Livy was worried about his health.

> . . . I shall treat smoking just exactly as I would treat the forefinger of my left hand: If you asked me in all seriousness to cut that finger off, & I saw that you really meant it, & believed that finger marred my well-being in some mysterious way, & it was plain to me that you could not be entirely satisfied & happy while it remained, I give you my word that I would cut it off. . . . Now there are *no* arguments that can convince me that moderate smoking is deleterious to me. . . . But there is one thing that will make me quit smoking & only one. I will lay down this habit which is filled with harmless pleasure, just as soon as you write me or say to me that *you desire it*. It shall be a sacrifice—just the same as if I simply asked you to give up going to church, knowing that no *arguments* I offered would convince you that I was right.

The message is ambiguous to his spiritual earthly angel. He wants to be reformed, but not really to give up smoking. All of their married life he alternately smoked and gave it up. A year after his marriage, he writes to Twichell, "Originally, I quit solely on Livy's account (not that I believed there was the faintest *reason* in the matter, but just as I would deprive myself of sugar in my coffee if she wished it, or quit wearing socks if she thought them immoral,) and I stick to it yet on Livy's account, and shall always continue to do so, without a pang." Clemens probably wished that Livy would declare socks and sugar immoral, so he could have the pleasure of giving them up only to take them up once again. For Clemens there was always pleasure in the forbidden, or partially forbidden.

He could always tell Livy, "I stopped chewing tobacco because it was a mean habit, partly & partly because my mother desired it. I ceased from profanity because Mrs. Fairbanks desired it. I stopped drinking strong liquors because you desired it." And she could smile knowingly in realization that her "Youth" would relapse and want her to scold yet again.

During their engagement, Livy's fiancé commuted to her from Hartford where he worked on his proofs of *The Innocents Abroad* with his publisher, Elisha Bliss. Completing a lecture series, he stayed in Elmira from March until mid-May, becoming a part of the family. By November 1869 Mrs. Langdon could remark of the man she once thought of stealing their family jewel, "Now he seems so incorporated into our whole being that I seem hardly to remember when it was not so." Clemens felt confident enough in his reforms and place among the Langdons to lecture young Charles on his wild oats and to become part of the decision to send him abroad yet once again to seek maturity. Clemens believed what cured him would help Charlie. "I suspect that the most promising course will be to set Ida to reforming him." Charlie eventually married Ida Clark in October following his sister's wedding.

The closest Clemens ever came to being a Christian was during his engagement period to Livy and certainly at the desire of her parents to see him nearer to their ideal of a perfect son-in-law. Being a Christian was their chief criterion for him beyond his caring for Livy and providing for her. In a letter to Mrs. Langdon just following his engagement, Clemens works yet again at convincing her of his changes. "But now I never swear; I never taste wine or spirits upon *any* occasion whatsoever; I am orderly, & my conduct is above reproach in a worldly sense; & finally, I now claim that I am a Christian."

MARK AND LIVY

His plans for the future included buying a share in a newspaper to "instruct & elevate & civilize the public through its columns, & my wife (to be) will superintend the domestic economy, furnish ideas & sense, erase improprieties from the manuscript, & read proof. That is all she will have to do."

Livy's desire as a good wife was to help her husband in his career by providing a comfortable home for him. It was her personal desire, and also his, that she edit his works. Clemens appreciated her intelligence and her good judgment as a reader in helping him to "erase improprieties from the manuscript" in order to reach the middle-class reading public he so wished to court. "I take as much pride in her brains as I do in her beauty, & as much pride in her happy & equable disposition as I do in her brains." He would keep her pure by censoring what she read; she would keep him a popular writer by editing what he wrote. There were already rumors that his forthcoming book was blasphemous. If Livy approved, it would be acceptable for the type of reader she and her family represented—those of this genteel tradition who bought the books. Clemens described her role in his autobiography.

In the beginning of our engagement the proofs of my first book, *The Innocents Abroad*, began to arrive and she read them with me. She also edited them. She was my faithful, judicious, and painstaking editor from that day forth until within three or four months of her death—a stretch of more than a third of a century.

Livy's role as editor may have been certain but the other part of their planned life, finding a newspaper, was not. By mid-April, where the couple would live and where Clemens would work was still not settled, and it worried both of them. Clemens felt guilty about taking Livy away from her adoring family. "I feel like a monstrous sort of highwayman when I think of tearing her away from the home which has so long been her little world, her shelter, her refuge." Livy worried about her health allowing her to be a good wife. She was no stronger in the six months that they had been engaged, and she was very sensitive about it despite her fiancé's confidence that he could make her "well and happy" in their own home.

The couple attended a wedding of particular importance to Livy at Nook Farm in Hartford. Her dear friend Alice Hooker married John Calvin Day on June 17, 1869 with Livy serving as a bridesmaid. To please Livy and her family, Clemens had tried to become closer to the Hookers when he was in Hartford. Isabella, Alice's mother, was a sister to the Langdons' pastor Thomas K. Beecher. They were not Clemens's kind of people, no matter how much the Langdons wanted him to call on them in Hartford. "I am afraid I never shall feel right in that house, though I let my trust & confidence go out to them as I seldom do with new acquaintances, & they responded by misunderstanding me." He admits that he likes them only because "Livy darling" does and will risk her wrath. So if he can't get along with them, she must "Scold away, you darling little rascal sweetheart." The Hookers never really approved of Clemens. Livy had delayed telling her oldest friend Alice of her engagement until Jervis Langdon let it slip in a letter to Alice's father a month after her formal engagement. A serious, to the point of bizarre, woman, Isabella Beecher Hooker took her feminism and spiritualism to the extreme in her belief that not only was "TKB" her brother, but so was Jesus. Such a person could not appreciate Clemens's sense of humor; it seemed a lack of respect to her.

Clemens had approached his old Cleveland friends, Abel and Mary Fairbanks, following his secret engagement in November 1868 to purchase part of their *Herald*. It was now June 1869. He and Livy had completed editing *The Innocents Abroad* in May. They were both ready to get on with their plans, and the Fairbankses' delays irritated him. When at the suggestion of Jervis Langdon, Clemens demanded a price, his irritation turned to anger. They would sell one-fourth of the paper for fifty thousand dollars. Now Livy's apprehension turned to relief. Her future husband could find an editor's chair closer to Elmira. She did not wish to leave her friends and family nor to be that close to Mrs. Fairbanks. Livy was Clemens's editor now.

MARK AND LIVY

Buying a newspaper costs money; more than Clemens had. All his life when he needed money, Clemens could turn to the grueling schedule of the lecture tour, or as he described it, being "banged about from town to town." In frustration he considered touring in California but had no real desire to leave his fiancée. Nor did Livy want him to go. By the time he received the price for the paper from Fairbanks, it was too late to head west. Through Livy's intervention with her father, Clemens agreed to take a loan of $12,500 to buy one-third of the Buffalo *Express*.

The fortune of the future Clemenses changed in August, so Livy could make definite wedding plans. Clemens took possession of the *Express* on August 14 as Livy wrote her friend Alice after several letters of uncertainty "so Buffalo is to be our home—." *The Innocents Abroad* was published at the end of July and by early August was on its way to becoming a best-seller. His royalties amounted to nineteen cents a copy and sold eighty-five thousand copies in sixteen months.

Now a newspaper editor, he could further promote his own book. "I am so grateful to Mr. Langdon for thinking of Buffalo with his cool head when we couldn't think of any place but Cleveland with our hot ones" wrote Clemens to Livy from Buffalo. During the week he boarded with the McWilliams and on the weekends made the hundred-mile trip to Elmira to be with Livy. Although he was separated from her during the week, Livy's influence stayed with Clemens through her letters. He will wear a flower in his buttonhole even though he feels only a fellow "who had a weak spot about his head somewhere" would wear one on the street. He is faithfully reading his Bible and praying before he goes to bed.

They were settled enough to announce their wedding date as being close to the one-year anniversary of their engagement. Livy writes the Twichells, " . . . and if life and health are continued to us we shall probably be married the first week in February." The date seemed "so far away and yet so near."

Livy's prenuptial jitters were allayed by her friends. She thanks the Twichells for their kind words, for there is "plenty to tell them of the changes and trials that come after marriage, trying to make them think that they will never be quite as happy again." She writes Alice, "I know that I am happier now than when Mr. Clemens and I were first engaged, yet I was happy enough then, I thought—" She hopes love will grow and in the same letter to Alice, she appreciates her good words on marriage. "I am glad you have tried it and I say 'Verily it is good' I hate to hear the whining of married women."

After two months, missing Livy and bored with newspaper routine, Clemens took a leave of absence from the paper in October to stay in Elmira. His pretext was to prepare for his upcoming lecture tour. Delivering sixty lectures on this tour, he would spend weekends with Livy and the Langdons when he could.

While Clemens was delighted with his prospective in-laws, Livy was trying to understand hers. She intervened for them with her father when Orion, Pamela, and their mother hoped Langdon would develop the fabled Tennessee land, always the hope of wealth for the Clemens family. Clemens agreed to give up all his claim to it, but Langdon did not buy the land. Even Livy did not like to press this issue with her father, writing her love, "But if you think that I better bring it before him again, I will do so—." She did not, and the Tennessee land remained only an illusion of wealth.

The Clemens family, back in St. Louis, were a bit awed by the prospect of Samuel marrying an heiress. Livy was adamant that they attend their wedding although Pamela felt out of place. *"Don't let your sister stay away from our wedding because she fancies her clothes are not fine enough—We want her, and her daughter here we don't mind about their clothing."* Livy offers her assistance, "We will be the more economical in our way of living, I will look out that I get few dresses and gloves and the like, and we shall be able to help them on."

With the popularity of his book—twelve thousand sold in December—and his growing notoriety as a speaker, Clemens was delighted to be accepted so by Hartford society that Charles Dudley Warner wanted him to sell out his newspaper interest in Buffalo and buy a share in the Hartford *Courant.* Even the Hookers requested "that we take an ownership in that paper." It pleased him to tell Livy of this sweet, "unchristian" revenge. "All I should get for it would be, the pleasure of living in Hartford among a most delightful society, & one in which you & I both would be supremely satisfied." As much as they both may have desired a newspaper in Hartford, Jervis Langdon advised against it when Livy asked her father to help them again. Clemens couldn't yet afford to make the move.

Livy spent her twenty-fourth birthday buying what her father called her "trowsers" in New York. Jervis Langdon, tired of business and in declining health, found great joy in his daughter's upcoming wedding. He reveled in admiring all the clothes she bought. Langdon's involvement, Clemens recounted, "so touched Livy with this loving unbending to her little womanly affairs that she could not tell me of it without moistened eyes." Part of Livy's trousseau purchased in New York included several suits of silk, cloth, satin, and velvet in gray, purple, and white. The bill presented to Mr. Langdon from Madame Fogarty on January 15, 1870 totaled $513.50.

Livy spent Christmas with her family while Clemens continued to lecture. He celebrated Christmas by reminding her of her reforming influence on him. "It is just a year to-day since I quit drinking all manner of tabooed beverages. . . . But all that goes to *your* credit, not mine."

Clemens concluded the last lecture of his tour by informing Livy in a letter, "This is the last long correspondence we ever shall have, my Livy—& now on this day it passes forever from its honored place among our daily occupations, & becomes a *memory*." For the previous year, they had written each other daily when separated. Livy, too, felt this was a "memory to be laid reverently away in the holy of holies of our hearts" for she wrote on the envelope of this letter, "184th—Last letter of a 17-months' correspondence." Livy was ready to begin her new life when Clemens ended his lecture tour and returned to Elmira on January 21 to await his wedding.

CHAPTER 6

"The clouds will come."

Livy and Clemens had hoped to have a "quick" and "quiet" wedding "with only relatives and particular friends present." But Livy's parents were far too prominent to settle for a simple wedding for their last daughter at home.

Nearly one hundred people filled the Langdon parlor on Wednesday evening, February 2. The Fairbankses, Beechers, Hookers, members and friends of the Langdon family, and notable citizens of Elmira witnessed the ceremony performed by two ministers—Thomas K. Beecher and Joseph Twichell. Clemens's sister Pamela Moffett and her daughter Annie attended while his mother, Jane Clemens, did not. Clemens had sent the fare for all of them to journey to New York, but Jane had not been present at the weddings of Pamela or Orion because she couldn't afford it. Now she didn't wish to show favoritism toward her last child to marry.

As with all weddings, Livy and Clemens had made other compromises besides acquiescing to a larger guest list than they originally planned. Livy had suggested they be married February 4, the one-year anniversary of their engagement. She, aware of her husband's desire to start marriage in as little debt as possible, insisted her engagement band would also serve as her wedding ring. It would take little effort to change the engraved date inside the ring. The wedding date was changed to the second because the fourth of February was "too near the end of the week for Mrs. Langdon's housekeeping convenience."

The time of the wedding had to be set at seven, not eight, in the evening because Thomas K. Beecher was due back at Park Church, across the street from the Langdon home, for an eight-o'clock meeting. Despite the changes in plans, Livy married her Youth in her white dress with long white gloves that nearly reached her delicate shoulders. Following the wedding service, bridge, groom, and guests sat down to a supper of boned turkey. Congratulations were accepted and toasts were made with non-alcoholic beverages in the temperance-conscious Langdon home. The bridge and groom had the first dance of the evening. After that Livy danced with her father, and then all the guests joined in.

The only wedding trip the couple had planned would be to their new home in Buffalo, as Clemens said, "for neither of us are fond of traveling." It would also cut down on expenses. The morning of his marriage, Clemens had received a royalty check of four thousand dollars for three months' sales of his book. The check added to his optimism that he could be out of debt in one year.

The afternoon following their marriage, Livy and her new husband left on their honeymoon journey for Buffalo. Clemens had asked J. D. F. Slee, Jervis Langdon's Buffalo coal manager, to find suitable lodgings for them in which to set up housekeeping. It should be a boardinghouse "of as respectable a character as my light salary as editor would command." They traveled to Buffalo in a private car supplied by another Langdon business associate, the president of Pennsylvania Northern Central. Also on the train were the Langdons, the Beechers, the Fairbankses, and Pamela and Annie Moffett.

They all arrived in Buffalo at nine in the evening, to be met by Slee who provided horse-drawn sleighs to take the entire wedding party to the boardinghouse. Livy and Clemens's sleigh got sepa-rated from the others as they rode through the ice-covered streets of Buffalo. Exasperated at the cold and concerned that the bride and groom should reach their home first so that they could greet their guests, Clemens grumbled to Livy over Slee's incompetence in selecting a home so difficult to find.

The driver finally stopped at 472 Delaware Avenue. On viewing the three-storied brick home on the fashionable street, Clemens remarked to Livy, "People who can afford to live in this sort of style won't take boarders."

The house was ablaze with lights and warmth as the other members of the wedding journey, who had already arrived, greeted the newlyweds at the door. Clemens was dumbfounded, nearly irate, that Slee would, "put us into a boarding-house whose terms would be far out of my reach." Livy's reply was, "Don't you understand, Youth. . . . It is ours, all ours—everything—a gift from father!" Livy later remarked that telling her new husband this gave her "an intoxicating rush of pleasure" greater than when she finally said she'd marry him. Her acceptance of his proposal "was little or no suprize [sic]" but the house was totally unexpected.

Jervis Langdon presented his new son-in-law with a deed. Clemens wrote in his autobiography, "There was a conspiracy— and my bride knew of it, but I was in ignorance." The "conspiracy" included not only the house, but furnishings, a cook, housemaids, horse and carriage with a coachman in uniform, plus a generous check to keep the household running. Livy, with the aid of her father's funds, had spent her hours separated from Clemens in planning and decorating this home. Jervis Langdon willingly financed the project because of his desire to keep his daughter in the style in which she had grown up. Livy, despite her sympathies with her new husband's plans to be out of debt, only knew how to live in a large house with servants. With this seemingly generous gift, Livy and her father committed Clemens to a way of life that he had always wanted but had been willing to wait for.

Mrs. Fairbanks recorded this "first-class swindle" for her faithful readers in an article that began, "Mark Twain's wedding day ended with a genuine surprise party, if a correspondent of the Cleveland

Herald can be trusted." She described how Clemens was so over-whelmed with gratitude that for once he seemed to be without words. Controlling his tears, he said, "Mr. Langdon, whenever you are in Buffalo, if it's twice a year, come right here. Bring your bag and stay overnight if you want to. It sha'n't cost you a cent!" Whether or not the correspondent could be trusted to guard the privacy of old friends, Mrs. Fairbanks described for her readers the house with its predominant blue satin furnishings with touches of scarlet as a "little sanctum." She saw the whole incident as "a delicious bit of romance." So did Livy, for she saved this clipping and pinned it in the back of her commonplace book.

In Clemens's mind, this latest episode added to what had seemed to be the impossible—marrying Livy—and it gave his new life an unrealistic quality. Again and again, he would describe the early days of his marriage as a "Fairy Land," an "Aladdin's palace" inhabited with his princess.

The correspondence from the couple to those outside their dream castle in the first six months of their marriage bubbles with their contentedness in good-natured teasing of each other, family, and friends. Clemens loved to invent stories depicting his sweet, shy princess as a wicked witch maintaining their home.

In a letter to Mrs. Fairbanks, Clemens gave a fanciful description of his tyrant Livy. Livy read the letter and commented upon it.

But there is no romance in this existence for Livy. [False]

She embodies the Practical, the Hard, the Practical, the Unsentimental. She is lord of all she surveys. She goes around with her bunch of housekeeper's keys (which she don't know to unlock anything with them because they are mixed,) & is overbearing & perfectly happy. When things don't go right she breaks the furniture & knocks everything endways. You ought to see her charge around. When I hear her warwhoop I know it is time to climb out on the roof. But law me, *you* know *her*.

Because Mrs. Fairbanks did know Livy and the playful Clemens, this letter was meant to charm all involved.

In a letter to Livy's parents, Clemens described his wife's cooking. Because they had a cook, the story would amuse his in-laws all the more. Again, Livy comments on his tale.

> . . . this morning she had a mackerel fricassed [sic] with pork & oysters [False] and I tell you it was a dish to stir the very depths of one's benevolence. We saved every single bit of it for the poor.

Later, on March 3, 1870, he commented on Livy's bookkeeping, and again she had to come to her own defense.

> I am very glad to begin to see my way through this business, for figures confuse & craze me in a little while. I haven't Livy's tranquil nerve in the presence of financial complexity—when her cash account don't balance (which does not happen oftener than once [False] a day) she just increases the item of "Butter 78 cents" to "Butter 97 cents"—or reduces the item of "Gas, $6.45" to "Gas, $2.35" & *makes* the account balance.—She keeps books with the most inexorable accuracy that ever moral man beheld.

> [Father it is not true—Samuel slanders me—].

The humorist was entertaining his own in-laws with exaggerated stories of his wife's bookkeeping when in reality they would know their daughter was levelheaded and thorough in any task she approached.

The princess was also happy in their fairy tale. "I wish I could remember some of the funny things that Mr. Clemens says and does and besides these funny things, he is so tender and considerate in every way."

But the responsibility of running the palace was solely hers, and she approached it in an organized and serious fashion. "I enjoy house keeping very much indeed, yet I am not settled and regulated as I want to be and shall be," she confides to her friend Alice. Housekeeping for Livy included overseeing the servants, approving menus, shopping, paying bills, and decorating the house. Their servants had come from her parents' home, so she knew them well. Ellen and Patrick McAleer would serve the Clemenses for many years. The housemaid Harriet could not get along with

Ellen, so Livy decided it was "best a change be made" and discharged her. Ellen contacted another servant of the Langdons to replace Harriet. This action angered Livy; she would run her own home, hire her own servants without the aid of a servant, who still considered her a little girl, or her mother. "The girl that I am going to have comes well recommended." The thought of replacing Harriet made Clemens "shudder." "But I had rather discharge a perilous & unsound cannon than the soundest servant girl that ever was." Clemens would write; Livy would provide a background of details in which he could create.

Livy also handled the money. In examining the books, she determined that their living expenses averaged fifty dollars a week. A modest amount considering that the running of her father's home averaged about seven hundred dollars a week. Royalties from *The Innocents Abroad*, about fourteen hundred dollars a month, were to go toward paying the debt on the purchase of the *Express*.

The Langdons remained generous to their daughter and son-in-law, providing them with money to fix their home as they pleased. Clemens thanked them for a check for one thousand dollars. "I am beginning to yearn to furnish the billiard-room & make it lovely—& just as soon as I break down Livy's sensible prejudices about one's spending money while one is still in debt you will hear of the upholsterers & carpenters being at work in the sky parlor."

Except that Livy was now the lady of the house, her routine did not vary too much from when she was a girl in her parents' home. Visitors came and went—the Twichells, the Slees, Pamela and Annie Moffett, the Spaulding sisters. She was "at home" on Thursdays to receive callers. As was the custom, she went out paying calls to others on their days at home. She admitted her nervousness the first time she did this without her mother or sister at her side. "I felt a little desire to see familiar . . . faces the first day that I went out to make formal calls." She records with horror and amusement for her friend Alice that at the first home she stopped at, when the servant answered the door "[you] find that you have . . . no possible idea of the lady's name, so you hand your card in silence, and while your card is being taken to the lady of the house you look at your list to prepare yourself to address her by name when she enters."

Livy also called on and left her card at the wrong house. "I think I shall get the name of leaving my cards at strange houses in rather a peculiar way, if I am not careful—" She confides to Mrs. Fairbanks that she could use some mothering in getting over her blunders of calling. "Mr. Clemens is splendid to laugh it off with, but then when it comes to his giving me any practical advice in these matters I find him a little incompetent."

Making calls on strangers and attending another church made her sometimes miss Elmira. After letters to her parents insisting she was not homesick, she writes, "I came about as near having a touch of homesickness this morning in church as I have at any time—I thought of you in church, with the Spauldings sitting in front of you, all listening to *our* teacher—and I thought that I should like to be there with you—" She misses the female companionship so abundant in her youth, for she repeats in her letters to her girlhood friends, "I wish we could have one good long visit."

Livy's and her husband's daily routine, modeled on her family's, included saying grace before meals in addition to other prayers and Bible reading. They arose at nine in the morning and were in bed by ten in the evening after dinner and reading aloud to each other. Poetry was a favorite but so were biographies, novels, history, science. Very much in love, Livy pampered her husband with "affections in kisses and caresses and in a vocabulary of endearments whose profusion was always an astonishment to me." Clemens wrote that all this attention "broke upon me as the summer waves break upon Gibraltar."

Clemens had grown tired of the newspaper business during his engagement. Now he rarely went to the *Express* office, and then only to deliver the articles he wrote at home. He also began a series of articles for *Galaxy* magazine for twenty-four hundred dollars a year and had plans to begin another book. In his contentment he considered traveling to England, to California, and the Adirondacks with the Twichells, but not as a lecturer. "I guess I am out of the field permanently," he wrote Redpath. "I am making more money than necessary, by considerable, and therefore why crucify myself nightly on the platform?" But more importantly, Clemens had no desire to leave his "lovely" wife and home.

Their happiness seemed complete. Livy, the once prostrate invalid, became pregnant within three months of her marriage. The thoughtful person knows that happiness can be fleeting—hard to find, it can easily disappear. When she had not yet been married a week, Livy asked her parents, "Don't fail to make mention of us in your prayers." Her reasoning was simple. "We need the prayers . . . more now in our great joy, than we shall when days of darkness and trial come to us." In her flush of newlywed bliss she admitted, "Of course I cannot but expect that the clouds will come some time, but I pray that when they do I may be woman enough to meet them."

The dark clouds gathered over her father. His ever-worsening nervous stomach from years of fretting over his business ventures became so threatening that his doctor sent him in March to the South for relaxation. He wrote the happy couple from Richmond, Virginia assuring them that "I have thrown off all care." Heavy on his mind was his daughter. "Samuel, I love your wife and she loves me. I think it is only fair that you should know it, but you need not flare up. I loved her before you did, and she loved me before she did you, and has not ceased since. I see no way but for you to make the most of it."

After six weeks Langdon returned to Elmira. He was suffering from stomach cancer, and by June he required round-the-clock nursing. Clemens and Livy returned to Elmira to take their turns at his bedside. Livy and her sister Sue sat with him for seven- to eight-hour stretches as the hot summer proceeded. They waved a palm-leaf fan over their dying father to stir the air in an effort to ease his pain. Clemens did his vigil at midday and from midnight to four in the morning. As cancer patients often do, Jervis Langdon rallied briefly in July, only to succumb to the disease and die with the words, "Beecher, I'm going home . . . and I'm almost there," on the afternoon of August 6, 1870. "Truly a great light went out of our house—" wrote Livy.

Livy was devastated and exhausted. "He was my back bone . . . what energy I had came from him." His body was laid out in the parlor where only seven months before he saw his daughter married. All of Elmira mourned the passing of the man who by creating his own estate of one million dollars had also brought prosperity to the community. Thomas K. Beecher gave a funeral oration for him at the Elmira Opera House on August 21 to accommodate those who could not fit into the Langdon home for the private services Monday after his death.

After twenty years of wandering New York to finally make his fortune and home in Elmira for twenty-five more years, Jervis Langdon was laid to rest in Elmira's Woodlawn Cemetery. The practical Langdon would have recognized that as the land was too hilly to farm and without lumber to cut or coal underneath it to develop, it was most suitable as a cemetery.

In her commonplace book Livy wrote above a newspaper clipping of a poem, "Father died August 6th 1870." The poem was "God is Love" by John Greenleaf Whittier. She noted on the clipping, "sent me by Father 29th 1870 May." It was his favorite poem that he had often recited in his final illness. To comfort herself in her grief, she recopied in her own hand the poem that included the lines:

> *I long for household voices gone,*
> *For ravished smiles I long,*
> *But God hath led my dear ones on,*
> *And He can do no wrong.*

Livy and Clemens returned to their Buffalo home to put their lives together and prepare for the birth of their first child. The storm clouds followed them. Livy required medication to sleep. In September her mother came to visit to share in their mourning. Emma Nye, an old school friend of Livy's, stopped to visit on her way from South Carolina to take a teaching post in Detroit, Michigan. Clemens had hoped the visit would cheer Livy, but Emma soon fell ill. It was typhoid fever, the disease that knew no social barriers, but would take thousands each year due to drinking water or eating from dishes contaminated with human waste. The German scientist Karl Eberth would identify the deadly bacteria as salmonella typhosa in 1881 and lay the blame for its growth on the poor sanitary facilities of the nineteenth century that allowed raw sewage to collect in drains, the perfect place for the bacteria to grow.

Too soon, Livy and Clemens were nursing another severely ill person, this time in their own home. Little could be done to aid the patient but bathe her in an attempt to reduce her temperature. In delirium ravings, as was common with high fevers, "dear Emma" died in their bedroom September 29. Her body was removed for burial to Elmira.

Livy's exhaustion turned to a numbness of body and soul. During her father's illness she could not even think of herself having a baby. "I try to picture it to myself, but I cannot at all realize it." In October she nearly miscarried. Clemens blamed Livy's dashing in the carriage pulled by a galloping horse over the cobblestoned streets of Buffalo to take another visiting friend to the train station. The doctor confined Livy to bed downstairs in the library. By November 5 Clemens felt Livy had improved. In fact, the doctor said she could go out for brief periods. Two days later, Livy gave birth to a four-and-a-half-pound boy, born a month prematurely. They named him Langdon Clemens.

Despite the fact that Clemens didn't think his frail son would live five days, he announced his birth to friends and family in a manner suitable for Mark Twain. In his own paper, the Buffalo *Express,* he stated in the announcement that his son would soon, unlike his father, go out on the circuit to lecture on milk. To the Twichells little Langdon wrote (with his father's help), "I have had wretched health ever since I made my appearance . . . I am not corpulent, nor am I robust in any way." Langdon also wrote to "Granny Fairbanks" and his great-grandmother Eunice Ford in Elmira. Through Twain's humor is the message that the baby is not healthy. Nothing fits the new baby, "I am only 13 inches long." He is often ill and cranky. "They call it *colic* & give me some execrable medicine.—*Colic*. Everything is *colic*."

Young Langdon described his mother as "bright and cheery, and I guess she is pretty happy, but I don't know what about. She laughs a great deal, notwithstanding she is sick abed." Livy remained bedridden—this birth seemingly the final strain in her life that had become an endless series of stresses. Within a week she was up to care for the baby until exhaustion would send her to bed and the cycle would begin again.

By January Livy could write, "Mr. Clemens, baby and I are alone again, our lives are very quiet happy lives even in spite of the great sorrow that is almost constantly present to us—" Her mother returned to Elmira after a two-month visit, her sister Sue had already returned shortly after Langdon's birth. Part of Livy's daily routine now included taking Langdon to Buffalo General Hospital to a wet nurse. "I have had a great aversion always to wet nurses, but all told me that I could not nurish [sic] him myself . . . so after much battleing [sic] I yielded." The whole process only added to her depression. She wrote Alice, "It is about the forlornest place that ever you saw, but you know we can do almost anything for the dear little one." Her lack of concentration would not allow her to read or write much—"I find hands and heart so full that I seem to have little leisure—"

By February the listlessness, lack of appetite, headaches, and insomnia that Livy attributed to her grief and her weariness from birth complications took a turn for the worse. The doctor recognized her high fever and the telltale rose spots on her stomach as the first signs of typhoid. As was the course of the disease, the fever brought on deliriums until it broke or the sufferer died. As with Emma Nye, twenty-four-hour watches were necessary to try to keep Livy's temperature down with wet compresses. Sue Crane came from Elmira with Dr. Rachel Gleason to nurse Livy. Sue was relieved by Clara Spaulding when it seemed to Theodore Crane, Sue's husband, that she had constantly been in Buffalo nursing her sister. Typhoid could be deadly even to the healthy and strong.

Somewhere in Livy's weakened condition was her desire to live. Clemens thought she was dying. "Sometimes I have hope for my wife,—so I have at this moment—but most of the time it seems to me impossible that she can get well." But by mid-March she could sit up several times a day and she tried walking with Clemens holding her up.

Buffalo had become a city of clouds for Livy and Clemens. In the midst of his wife's illness, Clemens put up the house and his share in the Buffalo *Express* for sale on March 2. Perhaps a change of scenery would help them both. In ten days they would go to Quarry Farm, the home of Sue Crane, in the hills above Elmira. In his despair he was willing to risk moving Livy even though the only way she could travel was prostrate on a mattress. "We leave for Elmira as soon as she can travel, & the agents may take their own time about selling the house." He would sell the house for twenty-five thousand dollars that only a year ago had brought him such pleasure, and eventually he sold his share of the newspaper at a loss of ten thousand dollars.

Clemens had all but stopped writing. He had nursed his wife nearly round the clock for the past six months; his son was sickly and seemed to cry constantly. All he wanted to do was to get out of Buffalo or he would "butt my frantic brains out and try to get some peace." He gave up writing for the *Galaxy* in April. He had begun *Roughing It* prior to Jervis Langdon's illness and subsequent events had given him little time or inclination to work on it. He vowed he would stay at Quarry Farm "until I finish the California book, say three months." Keeping to his schedule, they left by train for Elmira on March 18.

Quarry Farm had been in the Langdon family since 1847, when out for a drive one summer evening Jervis and Olivia Langdon stopped to water their horses at the hillside property. They were enchanted with the small farmhouse and seven acres that overlooked the mists of the Chemung River and the lush slopes surrounding Elmira. They purchased it from the stonecutter owner for their summer home because secluded in the hills it was cooler than the city next to the muggy river below. Over the years the home would be enlarged, and they would expand the land to 250 acres.

Jervis Langdon left Quarry Farm to Sue Crane at his death. Clemens often walked the two and a half miles from the downtown Langdon home up East Hill to this summer house, stopping to rest and visit at the Elmira Water Cure run by Doctors Silas and Rachel Gleason and at the home of Reverend Thomas K. and Julia Beecher. The Langdons had debated on several names for their summer retreat, until Beecher recommended Quarry Farm because of an abandoned quarry on the property. For Mark Twain, it would always be "Go-as-you-please Hall." On this acreage in years to come, he and his family would celebrate some of their happiest times, and here in this hideway from the world he would write some of his greatest works.

In the isolation of Quarry Farm, life's cares, like Elmira, were far away and down below and could not harm them anymore than the twinkling lights of the city at night. The hushed peace and quiet contentment of the rustling pines would soothe and heal the battered bodies and souls of Livy and her husband who had endured so much in their first year of marriage.

CHAPTER 7

"I believe my heart prays."

Spring regenerated the hillsides of Elmira. Sunshine, blossoms, gentle breezes helped to restore Livy and her husband. Once totally prostrate, she could now walk a few steps holding onto a chair. After a year of ever-worsening strains on Livy's health, Clemens once again could call her "bright and cheerful." Her strength improved enough that in April they planned a trip to Cleveland to visit Mary Fairbanks. Clemens's confidence in his work returned. "My stock is looking up." By May he felt his book was half done, and he started to receive offers to write and to lecture. His writing went so well that he gave up the Cleveland trip for fear "I couldn't dare make another break in my work lest I fail entirely."

Livy spent her days with Sue and the new baby, her time punctuated by visits from her mother, the Gleasons, and the Beechers from down the hill. As her strength improved, she began to read again and could go out for carriage rides "to take the air."

Joe Goodman, Clemens's former Virginia City *Enterprise* editor, was also a guest at Quarry Farm. Goodman had been one of those acquaintances from whom Jervis Langdon had requested a letter of recommendation before agreeing to his daughter's engagement. Goodman inspired his old friend with memories of their western days to include in Clemens's new book. More importantly, Goodman praised the manuscript pages he read, giving Clemens the desire to finish the book.

Livy became pregnant again in July, and Clemens's book neared completion. It was time they found a home of their own again. Before their wedding, they had leaned toward living in Hartford, but the purchase of the Buffalo *Express* prevented that. Clemens had written Orion before they moved to Quarry Farm, "I shall not select a new home till the book is finished, but we have little doubt that Hartford will be the place." They would rent a house until they could build their own, perhaps several years in the future. "I mean to take my time in building a house and build it *right*— even if it does cost 25 per cent more."

Unlike Buffalo, Clemens and Livy had only pleasant memories associated with Hartford. Livy's friend Alice Hooker Day lived there along with her parents John and Isabella Beecher Hooker. For Clemens, the Twichells and his publisher Elisha Bliss were there. After all their problems, they looked toward a pleasant beginning in Hartford. The first anniversary of her father's death left Livy worried about the future. Her own health was still shaky, and worse, the pale Langdon was not thriving. At nine months he could not sit up without support and showed no inclination to even begin standing, let alone walking. Clemens wrote her from Hartford where he was looking for a house for them, "But let us hope & trust that both you & I shall tend him & watch over him till we are helped from our easy-chairs to the parlor to see his children married."

Clemens chose to rent John Hooker's home on Forest Street where he had once stayed. Hooker in 1851 had purchased a tract of land consisting of one hundred wooded acres at the edge of the city of Hartford, founded by one of Hooker's ancestors in 1636. He selectively sold portions of his Nook Farm to those he wanted as neighbors, at first primarily his relatives and his wife's intertwined in family trees through marriage among sisters, brothers, cousins, and friends. This group included Senator Francis Gillette, whose niece Lilly would marry George Warner, brother of Charles

MARK AND LIVY

Dudley Warner. Isabella had two sisters who both lived at Nook Farm: Mary and her lawyer husband Perkins and Harriet Beecher Stowe and her husband Calvin.

Since they had lost money on the sale of their Buffalo home and the newspaper, a move would cost the Clemenses more than they had in their bank account. Clemens once again turned to the lecture circuit, which, like drinking, smoking and swearing, he would give up all his life, only to turn to each again in necessity. All summer, as he and Livy recuperated, he had worked on platform presentations and even reported to Mrs. Fairbanks with enthusiasm, "I have written a lecture which I just know will 'fetch' any audience I spout it before."

Clemens settled his wife, child, and servants into the Hooker rented home on October 1, 1871. He left Livy to unpack the furniture that had been in storage. On October 16 Clemens opened his winter lecture series in Bethlehem, Pennsylvania.

Livy did not wish her husband to leave but knew the state of their finances. She felt utterly alone with the burden of running the household and caring for Langdon. Nearly a year old, Langdon seemed to cry constantly from his never-ending cold. He only ceased and slept when given laudanum. He cut one tooth but that appeared to be the only normal thing about his development, for he was still not speaking, even though Livy liked to think that he had a "speaking face." Daily she pursed her lips and made sounds of "pet pet-i-pet" to get Cubbie, as she and Clemens called Langdon, to speak. Eventually he had two teeth and could say "Pa," but he never walked. Langdon could respond as Livy writes her husband, "He laughed until his little shoulders shook—oh I do love the child so tenderly, if anything happens to me in the Spring you must never let him go away from you, keep him always with you, read and study and play with him, and I believe we should be reunited in the other world—" In the spring, she would have her second child. Livy was not just being a harbinger of doom, for in the nineteenth century and considering her previous problems, childbirth was a life-threatening experience.

Langdon's health was precarious; he seemed close to death several times. At one point during Clemens's lecture tour, Livy called him home by telegram only to send another one on its heels stating Langdon was better, "no need of coming." Understandably, Livy hoped her next child would not be so delicate.

Despite the separation from her husband and the problems with her son, Livy found solace in being a mother. Upon visiting a friend of hers who was depressed about being twenty-six, Livy informed her absent husband, "I told her if she had a little one she would not feel so." Having just turned twenty-six herself, "I never think about feeling badly to think that I am growing older—I hope that age will make me more worthy of the respect of my husband and children—I do long . . . to be worthy of such a dear sweet baby as mine is, I hope that as he grows older I shall be thoroughly in sympathy with him in all ways—"

Livy's worry was not in growing older but in growing away from her faith. It weighed heavily on her mind in the hours she spent alone in the winter of 1871. It burst out in words searching for affirmation from her husband who always had a doubtable faith. "Do you pray for me Youth? Oh we must be a prayerful family—pray for me as you used to do—I am not prayerful as of old but I believe my heart prays—" Attending Twichell's church accentuated her anguish. "Mr. Twichell's prayer touched me and made me cry, he prayed particularly for those who had fallen away and were longing to come back to God—Youth, I am ashamed to go back, because I have fallen away so many times and gone back feeling that if I ever should fall, grow cold again, it would be useless trying, because I never could have more earnest and prayerful and at times heart broken determination to keep by the truth and the right, and strive for God's spirit—it would seem if I did not remain steadfast after such times I never could." Livy's perspectives had changed and it tormented her. "If I felt toward God as I did toward my husband I should never be in the least troubled—" Her attitude was "almost perfectly cold . . . toward God."

Each act of faith that once brought comfort now bothered her. On seeing the congregation at communion, "My heart sank because I do feel so unfit to go to the table of communion, yet cannot bear to go away from it." Heaven to her had become a *"thoroughly united loving family—"* So she prayed for her little family, "Oh a Father and Mother do have so much to pray for, so very much that they need guidance in—"

During her husband's absence and her spiritual doubts, Livy occupied her mind by staying busy. She engaged tutors to help her study German and French. She continued her reading, but missed discussing it with her husband. She wished he could mark her pages as he had done when they were courting. She enjoyed his "nice sweet things in the margin." From Elmira came a steady string of visitors: her mother and sister, her friend Clara Spaulding. Thinking of the future passed the time the quickest for her. So she set to investigating lots they could buy in Nook Farm and in "drawing a plan of our house" that they would build.

Running the home she presently occupied often distressed her. She agonized over dismissing the cook. "Youth in certain things you must teach me a 'don't care' spirit, as regards cooks and the like. . . ." Her husband's "don't care" attitude because of his involvement in his career left the daily concerns of money to her.

Although Clemens regretted leaving "all the weight of housekeeping on your shoulders," Livy didn't mind handling the finances and the business correspondence. It gave her the opportunity to set to calculating their finances, so they could live without the extensive lecturing that demanded his long absences. "I *can not* and I *will not* think about your being away from me this way every year, it is not half living." If it was necessary to cut expenses to be together, "We will change our mode of living—"

She figured twenty-nine thousand dollars would be needed to buy land, build a home, and furnish it. If they waited until they could afford it, that would be eight years until the copartnership of her father's coal company ran out and she would receive a lump settlement. Consulting with Charlie, she found her own income included "from three to five hundred dollars a month." If Clemens were to lecture just one month and only in New England, so he would not be far from home, that would make two thousand dollars. She continued her calculations deciding that his regular writing would bring in another three hundred dollars a month. Livy would happily "live in a small cottage and keep one servant" to be together and to save for their own home. "We need now the comfort of a convenient home, while our babies are young and needing care—"

Clemens concluded what he called "the most detestable lecture" series with the largest portion of the eleven or twelve thousand dollars he earned going toward his debts and the expenses of his touring. He had "less than $1500 to show for all that work & misery."

Still, 1872 was a new year that promised to treat them better than 1871. Clemens had a new book out, *Roughing It*, and they would soon have a new baby. Livy and Clemens left for Elmira where in the big Langdon house downtown, Olivia Susan was born on March 19. Livy had chosen the name, for all along she said this baby would be a girl.[1]

Clemens records that from the beginning, "The new baby flourishes, and groweth strong and comely apace." At nearly eighteen months old, Langdon still was not walking. Clemens characterized him as "white as snow, but seems entirely healthy, & is very fat & chubby, & always cheerful & happy-hearted—can say 'Pa' & knows enough to indicate which parent he means by it (which is Margaret the nurse)."

In May, Clemens and Livy felt confident to leave their two babies in Elmira under the care of the children's nurse, grandmother, and aunt. Along with Jane Clemens, they made their long-delayed visit to Mrs. Fairbanks in Cleveland. On their return May 14, Langdon again had the cough that he seemed to have been born with. As careful as his parents were, Langdon must have recovered enough for Livy to resume her practice of taking him out with her on her morning drive. One morning his father took him, and it

[1]At Susie's birth, she made the fourth Olivia Langdon—Livy, her mother, and a niece named Julia Olivia Langdon. This tradition of repeating names in the Langdon family remains. At present there is a fifth-generation Jervis and a sixth-generation Olivia.

would haunt Clemens all his life. From Mark Twain's *Autobiography*:

> I was the cause of the child's illness. His mother trusted him to my care and I took him for a long drive in an open barouche for an airing. It was a raw, cold morning but he was well wrapped about with furs and, in the hands of a careful person, no harm would have come to him. But I soon dropped into a reverie and forgot all about my charge. The furs fell away and exposed his bare legs. By and by the coachman noticed this and I arranged the wraps again, but it was too late. The child was almost frozen. I hurried home with him. I was aghast at what I had done and I feared the consequences.

One consequence was that Clemens would henceforth blame himself for Langdon's death, caused by diphtheria, the disease that took so many children in the nineteenth century and for which no antitoxin would be developed until 1890.

They immediately returned to Hartford, where on June 2, Langdon gasped and died in his mother's arms. Like the grandfather he never knew, he was laid out in the Langdon parlor and buried in Woodlawn Cemetery. Before his burial, a death mask, as white as his face had been in life, was cast. Livy placed it in the green box that held her and her husband's most prized possessions, their love letters.

For the third time in two years, death had touched Livy—her father, her friend, and now her son. "I feel so often as if my path is to be lined with graves," she said. Rather than endure this pain again, she wished she would die before her sister and her husband.

CHAPTER 8

"I feel so incompetent."

As was to become their yearly practice, Livy and Clemens felt the need to get away that summer. Their main concern was to protect Susie from the heat that "wilted Hartford children away like a simoon." Livy, as she had done only a year before, oversaw their packing with an infant in her arms. Clemens's brother Orion and his wife, Mollie, would watch their home in Hartford during their absence. In July they left for New Saybrook, Connecticut, soon to be joined by Mrs. Langdon, where all could enjoy the cool winds off Long Island Sound.

Distraught over Langdon's death, Livy ignored the social convention of replying to the letters of condolence they had received. While they lodged at a hotel called Fenwick Hall, she often remained inside because it pained her to see people from Hartford who reminded her of Langdon's death. "Seeing the others with their children does make me so homesick for Langdon—it seems as if I could not do without him—" she writes Mollie. Each person's grief is unique. Clemens's letters of this time radiate with the news of their living "Muggins." "Susie is bright & strong & we love her so that no sacrifice seems too much to make for her."

Livy's mental distress again manifested itself in physical ailments. Her back bothered her. Clemens felt water would soothe her backache and get her out of her room and her depression, for hydrotherapy was the cure-all of the nineteenth century. Livy wrote Mollie to send her a bathing suit and a wrapper so she could swim and take sitz baths.

Each partner fretted over the other. Livy worried that as in the first year of their marriage, personal calamities would prevent her husband from writing. She readily agreed to his traveling to England to lecture, to protect his copyright on *Roughing It,* and to gather material for another book. "England is a subject that he will get inspired over—" she informed Mrs. Fairbanks. She would miss him, but "my Susie does comfort me so wonderfully, in the absence of her Father and brother—sometimes the desire is almost stronger than I can bear to see the dear little son and daughter together, and I feel sure that I shall have that joy someday." Her husband's voyage abroad was for him but also for herself. She needed her own time to mourn and to heal.

Clemens left August 21 for his first of many trips to England. Livy decided to stay in New Saybrook until she was certain the summer heat had subsided in Hartford. "I do not intend to run any risk with the baby." Mrs. Langdon remained with her daughter and granddaughter to keep them company.

Once back in Hartford, in an effort to keep her mind away from past griefs and toward the future, Livy continued planning their new home while she waited for news from her husband. Clemens was clearly as delighted with the English as they were with him. His letters to Livy, while admitting that he missed her and Susie, contain none of the acute dissatisfaction and forlorn quality of those written home during his lecture tour the previous winter. He visited the traditional tourist haunts of the Tower, St. Paul's, Westminster Abbey, Oxford, Warwick Castle, and Stratford-upon-Avon. He looked forward to his next trip when she could share these experiences. "You will heartily enjoy your English welcome when you come here."

When not sightseeing, he was feted by many, including the nobility, the Sheriffs of London, and the Lord Mayor. He gave speeches, and the introduction of his name brought "a storm of applause." He proudly reported to Livy that the Lord High Chancellor of England told him "when affairs of state oppress him & he can't sleep, he always has my books at hand & forgets his perplexities in reading them!" All the celebrated adoration left little time to take notes for the satiric travel book he planned. "Time slips relentlessly away & I accomplish next to nothing. Too much company—too much dining—too much sociability."

In the almost three months he was away, Clemens was so used to Livy handling the details of running a home that his one domestic consideration he places in a postscript. She is to order coal when she needs it. The former coal baron's daughter had long past ordered and paid the seven dollars per ton.

During Clemens's absence, Livy began to socialize again. She attended the women's luncheon parties of Nook Farm and the Ladies' Auxiliary of the Monday Evening Club of Hartford, the discussion group to which Clemens belonged. While ladies were tolerated at the Monday Evening Club, it was generally accepted that this was a forum for men to examine the ideas of the time. The ladies formed their auxiliary so they too would have an atmosphere for intellectual stimulation. The topic most often discussed in both male and female circles was woman's suffrage.

So, for Livy, Livy's mother, Harmony Twichell, Susan Warner, and other Nook Farm women during the fall of 1872 the conversation centered on the retirement of the eccentric Isabella Beecher Hooker from the feminist movement.

Isabella had become a feminist after she met Anna Dickinson in 1861. Anna was a popular orator on the subjects of abolition and women's rights. During the Civil War, at the height of her celebrity, she lectured in support of the Republican party and the Union. Anna was the first woman ever to speak publicly in Hartford, and she did so on behalf of Abraham Lincoln.

Dickinson had informed Isabella Hooker of the work of Susan B. Anthony and Elizabeth Cady Stanton. Isabella had found her cause. In 1869 she organized the first women's rights convention in Hartford. Isabella considered it so successful that she wanted to move into the national fight. By 1871 she hoped to become the leader of the National Woman Suffrage Association. She called a convention in Washington, D.C., but she was upstaged by the leadership of Susan B. Anthony and the charisma of Victoria Woodhull, who eventually became a third-party candidate for president. Isabella's retirement from the feminist movement in favor of the more powerful and persuasive seemed in order.

Livy informed her husband of Isabella's decision, and his response is characteristic of his attitude toward this woman whom he never understood. "For all these long months . . . [she] has been blandly pulling down the temple of Woman's Emancipation & shying the bricks at the builders." Both Livy and her husband had long supported women's rights, since it had been Livy who converted her husband to the cause.

At first Clemens opposed and abhorred the idea of delicate, pure women lowering themselves to vote with men. In 1867, in the *Alta California*, he had humorously declared that the idea of women voting would be "time for all good men to tremble for their country." While Samuel Clemens held women in high esteem, no one was safe from being a target of Mark Twain's humor. Later in the same article he declared his true concern about giving women the vote.

> I never want to see women voting, and babbling about politics, and electioneering. There is something revolting in the thought. It would shock me inexpressively for an angel to come down from above and ask me to take a drink with him (though I should doubtless consent); but it would shock me still more to see one of our blessed earthly angels peddling election tickets among a mob of shabby scoundrels she never saw before.

When Clemens met his own "earthly angel," Livy convinced him that because women were of finer material than men they should be allowed to vote and correct society's flaws. A constant topic during their courtship was that Livy often felt she wasn't doing enough to right the wrongs of the world. She admired the courage and determination of Anna Dickinson, who had spoken out in favor of abolition and Abraham Lincoln. This brought Dickinson into contact with the abolitionist Langdons. It must have seemed to the frail Livy confined to her bed that here was an intelligent girl almost her age who was doing something to help others. Livy's lack of involvement in society's problems still bothered her when she became engaged. Clemens wrote Livy not to be so troubled. "Do that which God has given you to do, & do not seek to improve upon his judgment. You cannot do Anna Dickinson's work, & I can freely stake my life upon it, she cannot do yours—"

Clemens supported women's suffrage in various ways. In a speech to the Hartford Monday Evening Club he stated: "All that we require of a voter is that he shall be forked, wear pantaloons instead of petticoats, and bear a more or less humorous resemblance to the reported image of God. . . .We brag of our universal unrestricted suffrage but we are shams after all, for we restrict when we come to the women." Despite his dislike of Isabella Hooker, he did agree in the 1880s to speak at her rallies and to lend financial support to the cause of votes for women. From his notebook come the words that summarize his thoughts: "No civilization can be perfect until exact equality between man and woman is included."

Clemens's joy that "Mrs. Hooker's solemn retirement from public life is news which is as grateful as it is humorous" didn't last long, due to an event that would soon shock and divide the Nook Farm community. At a meeting of Boston spiritualists, Victoria Woodhull accused the titan of American Congregationalism Henry Ward Beecher of adultery with the wife of his associate Theodore Tilton. Elizabeth Tilton admitted the truth to Susan B. Anthony and Elizabeth Cady Stanton. By September 1872, feminism had become hopelessly embroiled with sensationalism and spiritualism. Woodhull and her sister Tennessee Claflin published accounts of the Beecher-Tilton scandal in their newspaper *Woodhull and Claflin's Weekly* in November 1872. They were promptly jailed for obscenity. Isabella quickly came out of retirement to declare her brother guilty.

Harriet Beecher Stowe and Mary Beecher Perkins, unlike their sister, supported their accused brother against the dubious reputation of Victoria Woodhull, who advocated and practiced free love. The family split spread into the community, and Mrs. Hooker found herself alone. When Clemens returned home in late November, he made his stand by saying Livy would not visit the strong-willed Mrs. Hooker, and he would tell Mrs. Hooker so even if she still was his landlady. The scandal continued for three years, ending in an acquittal of Beecher by a hung jury in July 1875 after Tilton sued Beecher for alienation of affection. Clemens and Twichell attended the trial and heard Beecher testify in April 1875.

It was a tense Christmas at Nook Farm in 1872. Holidays held obligations as well as pleasantries. Clemens recalled in his autobiography that Livy "always devoted two or three weeks to Christmas shopping and was always physically exhausted when Christmas Eve came." She not only shopped for family and friends, but wanted to give to the less fortunate in the community.

The busy social atmosphere of Nook Farm could take its toll. With the constant round of parties, dinners, receptions, Clemens did little actual writing here during the fall and winter seasons. Livy confided to her mother in January 1873, "I get a little homesick to see you once in a while; tonight I should like to put my head in your lap and cry just a little bit, I want to be somebody's baby—" Caring for a husband, house, servants, and a baby caused her to admit, "Sometimes I would like to lie down and give it all up—I feel so incompetent for every thing, I come so very far short, yet I think I do try earnestly every day."

Their added responsibilities included a lot they had just purchased for twenty thousand dollars on Farmington Avenue next to the home of Calvin and Harriet Beecher Stowe. Livy wrote her sister Sue, "Mr. Clemens seems to glory in his sense of possession; he goes daily into the lot." But glory is not free. "Now that we have bought the lot he feels anxious to make all the money that he can, but knows that he will make more in the long run by writing than by lecturing, but it is a great temptation to him when they offer him such enormous prices—"

Fortunately, Clemens felt inspired to write to make the money they needed. Livy described her husband as "perfectly brim full of work" with a project that began over dinner one night with Charles Dudley and Susan Warner. The men were complaining about the quality of novels their wives and others read.

> The wives naturally retorted that the proper thing for the husbands to do was to furnish the American people with better ones. This was regarded in the nature of a challenge, and as such was accepted—mutually accepted: that is to say, in partnership. On the spur of the moment Clemens and Warner agreed that they would do a novel together, that they would begin it immediately.

From the beginning of *The Gilded Age*, it was a collaboration for husbands and wives. Livy and Susan would act as an audience adding their editorial comments to their husbands' efforts. Twain handled the satire; Warner conceived the melodrama. This division of labor led Twain to think after the book was completed that "in the superstition that we were writing one coherent yarn, when I suppose, as a matter of fact, we were writing two *in*coherent ones."

This novel introduces one of Twain's better-known characters, Colonel Sellers, but it is primarily the story of Laura Hawkins. While her narrative was worked out jointly, she is typical of Twain's women characters and perfectly acceptable for a Victorian audience. Laura has had a hard life, and circumstances force her to act as she does. She is an orphan, five years old when she comes to the Hawkins family. As she matures, she decides to go to St. Louis to earn money to help her family until the Tennessee land can be sold and the family fortune made. (Clemens at least found a value for the Tennessee land in his writing.) When it is discovered that Laura is not Hawkins's daughter, she is ostracized by society and loses her true love. Her harsh treatment causes her to say, "I *do* begin to despise this world."

In genteel, sentimental fashion, Warner has her seduced and abandoned. Twain picks up the thread of the story to make her a Washington lobbyist. His high regard for women and his readers' propriety would not allow him to make her a prostitute, as some female lobbyists were. He makes her sophisticated, promising much, captivating her admirers. "Her wealth attracted many suitors. Perhaps they came to worship her riches, but they remained to worship her."

Warner handled the section on her murder of Selby, her trial, and acquittal. Livy and Susan decided Laura's end. Warner and Twain both read their conclusions to their wives. Clemens described it to Mrs. Fairbanks:

> They both pleaded so long & vigorously for Warner's heroine, that yesterday Warner agreed to spare her life & let her marry— he meant to kill her. I killed my heroine as dead as a mackerel yesterday (but Livy don't know it yet). Warner may or may not kill her to-day (this is in the "boss" chapter.) We shall see.
>
> P.S.—(Night) My climax chapter is the one accepted by Livy & Susy, & so my heroine, Laura remains dead.

Laura is hissed from the lecture platform, followed and cursed by an angry mob.

> "If I could only die!" she said. "If I could only go back, and be as I was then, for one hour—and hold my father's hand in mine again, and see all the household about me, as in the innocent time—and then die! My God, I am humbled, my pride is all gone, my stubborn heart repents—have pity."

Laura dies bravely of heart failure affirming the characteristics Clemens and his reading audience most admired in women. She longs for her home and her honor, to uphold their moral values.

While Clemens and Warner wrote *The Gilded Age*, Livy worked with the New York architect Edward Tuckerman Potter on their new home. Potter, in his architect's plans, used Livy's sketches of how she wanted the rooms laid out to overlook various parts of the Connecticut countryside. Surely it is no accident that the house resembles a riverboat with the pilothouse porch on the third floor extending westward toward a small river, sometimes called the Park River or the Riveret or Little River.

Livy admired Potter's flamboyant originality that was unlike his quiet manner. He did not design the Clemenses another staid, square, wooden Hartford home, but a house reflecting the author's personality and success. Potter incorporated turrets and spires in brickwork laid in a myriad of angles and projections. This showplace of Hartford opulence would be a home for entertaining guests as well as raising a family. Neighbor and lawyer Charles Perkins was left to intercede between the mild Potter and the intimidating builder and his carpenters when the Clemenses sailed for England.

In April Livy took Susie to see her mother in Elmira while Clemens polished his novel manuscript. Husband and wife had just had their first true taste of an extended, calm family home life that winter of 1873. The results showed in their faces and their activities—Livy with her house, Clemens with his novel. Livy told her mother, "Mr. Clemens was never so good and lovable as he is now, we were never so happy together it seems to me—"

Olivia Langdon at about fifteen years old.

Livy as a young woman, about nineteen years old. At sixteen she slipped on some ice and was mysteriously paralyzed.

Mark Twain and Charles Langdon, Livy's younger brother.

Livy at twenty-four years old, the time of her engagement to Samuel Clemens.

Olivia Lewis Langdon, Livy's mother.

Jervis Langdon, Livy's father.

The palatial Langdon home in Elmira, New York. Livy grew up in this home, in which the house and grounds covered an entire block.

The home in Buffalo, New York, which Jervis Langdon purchased and furnished for the newlyweds.

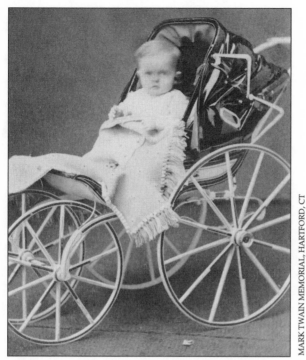

The sickly Langdon Clemens, who died at twenty-two
months old.

Mark Twain with Clara and Susy, 1877.

The "curious house that Mark built" as it looks today.

Clara, Livy, Jean, Clemens, Susy and Hash on the Ombra, 1885.

Clara, Clemens, Jean, Livy and Susy on the Ombra of their Hartford home.

Livy, Clara, Jean, Clemens and Susy in Hartford.

Jean at eighteen with her dog, The Professor.

Susy Clemens as a student at Bryn Mawr, about 1890.

CHAPTER 9

"I feel so rich and thankful for you."

In May of 1873 the Clemens party sailed on the *Batavia* for England. Their group included Livy's old school friend Clara Spaulding, a young man named S. C. Thompson to act as secretary for Clemens, as well as a nurse, Nellie, for fourteen-month-old Susie. On this first voyage for all the women, they got seasick, even little Susie.

Clemens, now with Livy at his side, took up the social whirl he had left off in the fall of 1872 by setting up their court in a suite of apartments at Langham Hotel in London. The introductions they made that spring are a list of eminent Victorians—Lewis Carroll, Herbert Spencer, Robert Browning, Ivan Turgenev, Anthony Trollope, Wilkie Collins, John Millais. Livy, the avid reader, was thrilled to speak with so many writers. She was even more pleased with the high regard in which they held her husband. He was not just a humorist, as his audience at home considered him, but a literary figure. After so many prominent personalities, Livy only regretted not seeing the celebrated medium Mr. Home who, it was reported, could float out of a window. She also had hoped to meet Thomas Carlyle, whose words she had copied down in her commonplace book. Both men were too ill to either fly or visit.

Livy wrote her sister, "There is so much to write about that it makes me feel as if it was no use to begin." The hectic schedule again prevented Clemens from seriously gathering notes, but even more importantly, he was so fond of England and the English that he felt no sting to write a satire. Clemens didn't need a secretary; he gave Thompson one hundred dollars to return home.

Between the rounds of receptions, dinners, and attending the theater, Livy enjoyed shopping for her new house and for her family. She wanted to purchase a sealskin coat as requested for her mother-in-law, gloves for Pamela, a cloak for Annie, and dishes for herself and her mother. The responsibilities of home never far from her mind, she wrote Mollie to contact a woman who had worked for the Hookers in the continuing quest of finding a cook to suit her mother, who was a "particular eater."

Their London lifestyle was expensive, and Livy began to worry they would run short of money. "The trouble is that the kind of things that we want are intrinsically good and so are not so very cheap." She asked her mother to place another fifteen hundred to two thousand dollars in their overseas account. The building of their Hartford home concerned her, and she requested that Charlie, who was paying the bills in their absence, inform her of progress in the construction. "I feel quite in the dark as to matters there and think I may discover myself a little short. . . . It is a great temptation to spend money over here, it seems as if there were so many things that it would be an advantage to get here." All depended on the cost of the house in Hartford, and she couldn't be certain of this until it was finished. "If I was *sure* our house would not exceed $20,000 or $25,000 I would spend more here."

Livy, always a private person, preferred the company of her own family or a few close friends. When Clara Spaulding went to the Continent for six weeks, Livy began to grow tired of the demanding social schedule and all the attention that Clemens wallowed in. They canceled their London engagements and set out for Scotland.

By the time they reached Edinburgh at the end of July, Livy collapsed with exhaustion from "six weeks of daily lunches, teas and dinners." Knowing no one in the city, Clemens remembered it was the home of Dr. John Brown, the author of the popular dog story *Rab and His Friend*. The doctor was still practicing medicine, and Clemens gained not only a physician to attend Livy, but a friend. Brown spent every day of the next six weeks with the Clemenses. The doctor with his "sweet and winning face" had a personality loved by all dogs, kittens, and children. He quickly became the "worshiper and willing slave" of Susie Clemens.

At sixteen months, Susie was all that Langdon never was, which made her even more precious to her parents. Brown called her Livy's "ludicrous miniature—and such eyes!" He gave her the name Megalopsis, Greek for big eyes. Her father called her Modoc in an attempt to describe her hair, which reminded him of the Indian tribe at war in California. She acquired that name when they met Joaquin Miller, the author of *Life Among the Modocs*, in London. She was standing, jabbering, bright and alert. Daily she played the game of "bear" with Dr. Brown. Susie hid and "sprang out from behind the sofa and surprised the Doctor into frenzies of fright, which were not in the least modified by the fact that he knew that the 'bear' was there and was coming." For young children, the more repetitive the game, the more delight; Susie would dissolve in laughter at the doctor's feigned fright.

While they did some sight-seeing and attended social affairs, the quieter life of Edinburgh left Clemens with time to write and to read to Livy in the evenings, but he was impatient to see more foreign lands. Livy regretted leaving Dr. Brown and his sister. Any separation from people she cared for bothered her because "we shall probably never see them again." Nevertheless, from Edinburgh they traveled on to Glasgow and Belfast, back to England and spent two weeks in Paris.

Livy had vowed that upon returning to London she would live as "cheaply as possible so that I can have the money to spend." But once back in London, the Clemenses were plagued with money problems resulting from the Panic of 1873. After the theater one evening, they were horrified to learn that their bankers had stopped payment on their account. Clemens spent a sleepless night blaming himself. He worried what Charlie would say about him for not withdrawing their money from the banking firm of Jay Cooke and Company.

The business expansion in the United States that followed the Civil War tapered off during Grant's second term as president. Cooke and Company overspeculated in financing the Pacific Railroad, had to declare bankruptcy, and took nearly five thousand businesses down with it. The result was the Panic of 1873. Livy and Clemens felt the consequences of it in London and at home. A drop in prices, labor unrest, and a depression that lasted until 1879 affected the Langdon coal business. Livy lost money and her income fell. During that sleepless night, Clemens and Livy, like others "seriously inconvenienced," counted their money. If their bankers didn't resume payment, Clemens could lecture to "get money to pay our debts and get us home—" "Lecturing is what Mr. C.[lemens] always speaks of doing when their [sic] seems any need of money."

So Clemens began speaking before the very appreciative British audiences. Pregnant again, Livy was tired and depressed about their money situation. She missed her mother, brother, sister. "I do think you are just about the dearest people in the world." Uneasy at five months of building without her aesthetic or monetary supervision, Livy wanted to see how her house was progressing. The London fog made her feel "almost as if the end of the world had come." While she couldn't bear another month in London, she knew Clemens must stay to protect his copyright of *The Gilded Age* and to lecture to acquire "'a more enviable reputation.'" "His reputation will be better for his staying and lecturing." Even "blue and cross and homesick," she considered staying not for the money, but for his sake.

Clemens resolved the situation by taking Livy and Susie home. They landed in New York on November 2. At Livy's request, Charlie was there to help them through customs. Clemens immediately returned to London to continue his triumphant three-month lecture series. But the adoration of the crowds did not soothe his loneliness. He missed his wife and daughter acutely. The same "dreadful fog'" that had shrouded Livy in sadness now enveloped her husband. What had been so pleasant before was now empty. He waited for her to appear in their hotel room, he gazed at her picture, lingered over old letters from her, and noticed women who reminded him of her. Praise was hollow without her. "I made a speech which was received with prodigious applause— but I thought if Livy were only here, I would enjoy it a thousand times more." Clemens realized "what an access of love, a bit of separation brings." Livy was the more demonstrative in expressing love and "one gusher usually silences another—but an ocean is between us, now, & I *have* to gush." As absence from a loved one often causes, Clemens vowed he would express his love more when he was with her again. "I *do* feel it, even if I don't talk it." For now all he could say was "My own little darling, my peerless wife, I am simply mad to see you." When they would be reunited, he reminded her several times, "Expedition's the word. . . ." Expedition, their private word for lovemaking.

Clemens sailed for home on January 13, 1874 after advising Livy in a letter of the homecoming he wanted.

> Livy, my darling, I want you to be sure & remember to have in the bathroom, when I arrive, a bottle of Scotch whiskey, a lemon, some crushed sugar, a bottle of *Angostura bitters*. Ever since I have been in London I have taken in a wine glass what is called a cock-tail (made with those ingredients) before breakfast, before dinner, & just before going to bed. . . . Now, my dear, if you give the order *now*, to have those things put in the bathroom & left there til I come, they will *be* there when I arrive. Will you? I love to write about arriving—it seems as if it were to be to-morrow. And I love to picture myself ringing the bell, at midnight—then a pause of a second or two—then the turning of the bolt, & "Who is it?"—then ever so many kisses—then you & I in the bathroom, I drinking my cock-tail & undressing, & you standing by—then to bed, and—everything happy & jolly as it should be. I *do* love & honor you, my darling.

Time and the familiarity of marriage changes all relationships. The fiancé who once gave up hard liquor to impress his girl and her family is now telling his wife of four years to have a drink mixed for him.

Once reunited with his precocious Susie and his affectionate Livy glowing in her fourth month of pregnancy, Clemens had no desire to leave them despite the temptations of Redpath's money. Clemens told his wife, "There isn't money enough in America to hire me to leave you for one day." But the truth was, there never was enough money for the Clemenses, so Livy persuaded him to give talks occasionally during February.

In March, Clemens and Charles Dudley Warner collaborated again—this time to extend Hartford hospitality to Boston. Clemens and Warner met William Dean Howells, Thomas and Lilian Aldrich and James Osgood in Springfield, Massachusetts and rode by train with them on to Hartford, wherein a show of eastern respectability and prosperity, the group was greeted by Clemens's uniformed coachman and butler. Clemens had been friends with Howells since 1869 after requesting to meet the man who wrote the favorable review of *Innocents Abroad* in the *Atlantic Monthly*. Their forty-one-year friendship supplied Clemens with an invaluable editor and Howells an indefatigable champion. Aldrich was the editor of Boston's weekly magazine *Every Saturday*. Osgood was Clemens's publisher.

Lilian Aldrich was dubious about this invitation to Hartford. Two years previously, her husband had invited Clemens home unannounced to dinner. The casual western attitude that had puzzled yet eventually charmed Livy and her mother mortified Mrs. Aldrich. His drawl, his shuffle, his eccentric mannerisms and dress (sealskin hat and coat, gray jacket accented with a purple tie) convinced her he was drunk. She did not offer him dinner. When Clemens left, she castigated her husband for bringing such a man home. It was then she learned her visitor had been Mark Twain.

His identity did not change her attitude toward him. The incident hardened his feelings toward her. The morning after their arrival Lilian overheard a conversation Clemens had with her husband. Clemens complained that the Aldriches had made so much noise in the night that they had disturbed Livy whose bedroom was one floor below. Such were Livy's winning ways that no one wished to trouble her especially in pregnancy. The Aldriches inquired as to her health at breakfast. Puzzled, she exclaimed, "I have no headache," and that their rooms were in another part of the house. "If you had shouted we should not have known it."

Clemens was always painfully aware that he was a western outsider in eastern society. He wanted acceptance by all that the eastern seaboard represented, whether in his courtship and marriage to Livy, or his writing and literary reputation. Yet inexplicably, he often repelled any approval he gained by his actions.[1]

Clemens seemed determined to irritate and to prove Lilian Aldrich right about his unorthodox character. After dinner he went out at midnight, in his sealskin coat and cap, to buy more ale. At the saloon he had a drink, but forgot the ale and his hat. The butler had to be dispatched to fetch both. Upon his return, Clemens, determined to be outrageous, put on his white slippers which clashed with his evening clothes and sang Negro spirituals and danced. Mrs. Aldrich recalled, "He twisted his angular body into all the strange contortions known to the dancing darkies of the South." Livy could only exclaim what she always did when her husband's behavior puzzled her, "Oh Youth!" Sometimes she said these two words in love and laughter. In this situation she could only look down at her hands with a slight shake of her head and make her statement in embarrassed bewilderment.

All during their thirty-four years of marriage, Clemens would later recognize his transgressions and regret how he hurt Livy.

> I was always heedless. I was born heedless and therefore I was constantly, and quite unconsciously committing breaches of the minor proprieties which brought upon me humiliation which ought to have humiliated me, but didn't because I didn't know anything had happened. But Livy knew; and so humiliation fell to her shore, poor child, who had not earned them and did not deserve them. She always said I was the most difficult child she had.

---

[1] Justin Kaplan's biography *Mr. Clemens and Mark Twain* explores these twin sides of Clemens's personality of easterner vs. westerner as symbolized in the title.

Like a little boy who never forgave a slight, Clemens proclaimed his opinion of Lilian Aldrich to be still unchanged in 1908: "I do not believe I could ever learn to like her except on a raft at sea with no other provisions in sight."

The rest of that spring was devoted to preparing for the birth of the Clemenses' third child. A new nursemaid was hired when Susie's Nellie left to tend a dying sister. It was a welcome departure to Livy who didn't have to dismiss her because "I know that she was disrespectful of me" in speaking to the other servants. Livy took an immediate liking to the new German nursemaid because she had experience with children and could also help Livy with her German lessons.

Just prior to Susie's second birthday, Livy, now nearing thirty, "barely escaped miscarriage." Due to all the complications of Langdon's premature birth, Livy was confined to bed. Once she was out of danger, Clemens moved his household to Elmira where their second daugther was born at Quarry Farm. The "New Modoc" arrived June 8. Nearly an eight-pound baby, she was born with a caul, said to indicate psychic powers. Clemens called her "the great American Giantress." When her father died in 1910, Clara Langdon Clemens would be the only surviving member of the immediate family. A second girl in the shadow of the adored Susie, Clara's name in her father's and mother's words, whether written or spoken, was always linked with her older sister's. Thus, it was Susie who gave Clara her nickname of "Bay" in an attempt to say "baby."

All spent the summer of 1874 at Sue Crane's Quarry Farm. With a houseful of children, servants, and relatives, Sue realized it was not an ideal atmosphere for a writer. For her brother-in-law, she built what Clemens described to Twichell as "the loveliest study you ever saw." It was a one-room octagon a hundred yards from the house next to the old quarry. With windows in each of the eight walls, it was complete with a small fireplace for cool mornings. If the day became warm, Clemens could open the door and windows for fresh air. "It is a cozy nest and just room in it for a sofa, table, and three or four chairs." For over twenty creative summers his schedule at Quarry Farm rarely varied. After break-fast, Clemens left the hubbub of the Crane house, strolled across the lawn, and climbed up the steps to his sanctuary. He labored steadily all day, not stopping for lunch, and rejoined the others for dinner. Each evening he read to his family audience his day's work. It was forbidden to disturb Mark Twain during the day. Samuel Clemens could summon or be summoned only by blowing a horn.

Also born that peaceful summer were two boys, as precious to their creator as his two daughters. Livy would remark years later that "Mr. Clemens thinks of Huck as he does of one of his own children." From his writer's pilothouse overlooking the Chemung River and its valley and Elmira, Mark Twain went back to another river, another valley, another village and began to write *The Adventures of Tom Sawyer*.

CHAPTER 10

"Show our babies and our new house"

For Livy, it had also been a productive, creative summer. While her husband wrote, she arranged the furnishings and decorating of her new home at 351 Farmington Avenue. In late August, she and Clemens made a trip to Fredonia, New York to visit Jane and Pamela. They had wanted to go on to Hartford, but returned to Elmira with Livy exhausted from preoccupation with readying their new house. Although delaying their move to Hartford, Livy rested until sufficiently recovered to travel to New York City. While Clemens coached actors in rehearsals of the dramatization of *The Gilded Age*, Livy bought more "'carpets and furniture."

When Livy first moved into the rented Hooker home in the fall of 1871, she had remarked that anyone could tell the house was built by a Beecher. "It's so queer." The description could well have applied to the home she so proudly and minutely planned into which she, her husband, two daughters, and servants moved on September 19, 1874. The builders occupied the first floor; the Clemenses occupied the second of three floors. Livy ran her unfinished home from the study, the nursery, and what would be her mother's bedroom.

Livy loved supervising the finishing details. She was "perfectly delighted with everything." She watched and advised the workers and decorators and enjoyed strolling from room to room each evening to inspect the day's progress. Her husband worried that she would exhaust herself, wanted to take over the supervision while she rested. But it was Livy's project. "I am a man who loathes details with all his heart!" Clemens informed his mother-in-law. He described his exasperation, "I have been bully ragged all day by the builder, by his foreman, by the architect, by the tapestry devil who is to upholster the furniture, by the idiot who is putting down the carpets, by the scoundrel who is setting up the billiard-table (and has left the balls in New York), by the wildcat who is sodding the ground and finishing the driveway (after the sun went down)."

That fall as Livy looked out from one of the third-floor balconies, she could watch the leaves turn to hues of orange and red to match the vermilion shades and angles of brickwork. The house seemed curiously to have always belonged amidst the shrubbery that Potter had also landscaped.

A visitor to the Clemenses' home, approaching it from Farmington Avenue up Asylum Hill, would first be struck by the gothic style of turrets, chimneys, gables, the colored roof tiles. The house today remains an affront, yet a delight to the eye that quickly learns to appreciate its unconventional symmetry. The back of the house faces the street. Why? Mark Twain would reply, "So the servants can see the circus go by without running out into the front yard." Livy built this house as a stage with her author husband as the chief entertainment. Much of it was designed to please guests in addition to the family. As the house sits on a gentle hill, it was Livy's design that guests and family would look out not at the street, but at the lovely grounds of Nook Farm and the Park River.

A porch curved around the front of the house. Potter elaborately used wood and railing in the "stick style" to rival his brickwork in creating an open, airy veranda or "Ombra." Upon entering the entrance hall, the visitor's eye would catch the dark, ornate woodwork and plush, heavy furniture and draperies, all elaborately patterned. Livy's taste, acquired from her mother, remained the epitome of style in fashionable eastern homes. Ladies' teas could be served in the drawing room that included a large, ceiling-high mirror that had graced their home in Buffalo. Off from the drawing room, the dining room featured a window cut into the chimney of the fireplace so the diners could watch flames and snowflakes at the same time. The centerpiece from their wedding table adorned the dining room table, set with delicate china and silverware inscribed "OLC."

In the library the Clemenses installed a fireplace purchased from Ayton Castle in Scotland complete with a coat of arms from the Mitchell-Innes family. The date of their home, 1874, was added to the fireplace. The overmantel was too large for the room so the top of it was placed above the door between the library and the dining room.

On a brass plate in the fireplace the words of Emerson are carved, "The ornament of a house is the friends that frequent it." The choice of this saying sets the tone of the house, for Livy incorporated many concessions to hospitality. She put a guest bedroom on the first floor off the library. Livy reasoned that guests would appreciate being away from the children's activities on the second floor. The bedroom had an adjoining bathroom with shower, monogrammed towels, and colored soaps. The shower, running water, and indoor plumbing were enough to make this house the showplace of Hartford. To further distinguish it, the house contained twenty rooms, thirteen fireplaces, seven bathrooms with sinks matching the rugs and drapery. The plumber Robert Garvie believed they were the first of their kind in the country. The rooms in this mansion were connected by speaking tubes to summon servants. The price tag for having people ride by just to admire your home could be steep: the Clemenses spent one hundred thousand dollars to build and furnish their house.

From the library, family and company could step into a small greenhouse of sunlight and plants complete with a trickling water fountain so even the outdoors could be enjoyed in bad weather. Mrs. Fairbanks once described the library as "always summer" because of this conservatory. Standing in it, one could look across the lawn to the home of Harriet Beecher and Calvin Stowe. Harriet had originated the idea of the conservatory in Nook Farm, and Livy liked it so much that she built one in her home. The conservatory made a perfect jungle for tiger hunts. Clemens, the faithful elephant, carried his daughters on his back in pursuit of George, the tiger and sometimes butler.

On the second floor were bedrooms for the family and a study for Clemens. It became a schoolroom for the girls when he found it too easy to lie down on the built-in benches along the wall rather than to work.

On the third floor was a special room Livy designed for her husband. It became Clemens's glory and joy of a hideaway—a billiard room and adjoining bedroom where he and his male guests could smoke, drink, cuss, and discuss without disturbing the rest of the family. The Clemenses' daughters thought it a perfect place for Rochester's insane wife from *Jane Eyre*. Clemens could walk out on one of the three balconies from this "study" and survey the countryside from this seat of prosperity, his American dream come true. In a poem Mark Twain published in 1877 in *The Travelers Record*, he described his home:

> *In his cozy, sunny and snug retreat,*
> *At once both city and country seat,*
> *Made up of bricks of various hue*
> *And shape and position, straight and askew,*
> *With its nooks and angles and gables too,*
> *The curious house that Mark built.*

Livy built and ran Mark's curious house, and for her, the house was never finished. Like raising her children, it was a lifelong occupation. Her pride was to buy for it, care for it, decorate and redecorate it during the seventeen years the Clemens family lived in it. Like a spoiled child, the house was demanding both monetarily and physically. They proclaimed love for their house but fled from its grasp on their money and time for long periods as if they had no control over it. When their happy memories were confronted with tragedy, and they could no longer bear to inhabit their curious house, Livy insisted only friends occupy it, and she agonized over selling it for seven years until it was sold in 1903.

Once settled in their new home, Livy urged her husband to begin writing again. His most productive times would always be at Quarry Farm, but he occasionally did some writing or revising in the Nook Farm home. He felt "I can write ten chapters in Elmira where I can write one here. I work *at* work here, but I don't accomplish anything worth speaking of." The *Atlantic* had published his "A True Story," which he had heard from the black cook Auntie Cord at Quarry Farm and written down that summer. This Civil War story of a slave mother's reunion with a long-lost son had been well received, so William Dean Howells wanted something for the January edition. Clemens told Howells, "Mrs. Clemens had diligently persecuted me day by day with urgings to go to work & do something, but it's no use—I find I can't." But he did. With Twichell's and Livy's encouragement he began his series on piloting and steamboating, "Old Times on the Mississippi." It was a subject he knew and loved and the first of the series appeared on time in January 1875.

Aware of her duties as the hostess for a famous husband, Livy began entertaining. With pride she extended an invitation to the Howellses "to show our babies and our new house." In March, a week prior to Susie's birthday, they came to visit for a few days. Livy immediately liked Elinor Howells because "she is *exceedingly* bright—very intellectual—sensible and nice." For all of Livy's concerns with fashion in clothes and homes, her first love was reading, and she preferred women who would discuss books rather than furnishings. To join the Clemenses and Howellses for dinner one evening, Livy also invited Joseph and Harmony Twichell, George and Lilly Warner, and Thomas and Mary Perkins. Impressed by the Clemenses' hospitality, Howells called them "whole-souled hosts, with inextinguishable money, and a palace of a house."

Susie celebrated her third birthday that March 19 in style. Livy recorded it in detail for her mother, who could not attend. On a table in the main hall were her presents: dolls from her mother that Susie shared with "Bay"; candy she gave out, including her own piece from her mouth to Patrick, the footman; a silver setting from her grandmother to be built upon in gifts as she got older until she had a full set for her own household; a golden ring, silver thimble, and Bible from the servants; a Noah's Ark holding two hundred wooden animals from her father. The celebration delighted both mother and daughter, for Livy tells her mother, "Tonight she was so loving and sweet and said 'Mama you're so good to me, dear Mamma.' " Even Livy realized that so much repetition of Susie's charms might make her own mother feel she was "silly, but you know Susie is so large a part of my life and I am so desperately fond of her." Considering that a grandparent's tolerance for "these particulars" of grandchildren knows no bounds, it is a criterion by which to judge Livy's involvement with her children.

"Clara continues to grow in loveliness," she adds, so that not too much attention would be given to Susie's news. Because of Clara's wet nurse, Livy made the decision to stay in Hartford that summer. She had to refuse an invitation to visit Elinor Howells that she very much would have liked to accept. She couldn't leave because Clara's wet nurse was "tractable and good when I am in the house but . . . gets drunk when I go away." Clemens described Clara's fifth wet nurse (Clara had feeding problems from birth, physical reactions to anything but a "mother's" milk) as nearly six feet tall with "the appetite of a crocodile, the stomach of a cellar, and the digestion of a quartz-mill." The woman smoked, ate, and drank everything within her sight, "whooped like a Pawnee and swore like a demon." She nursed the baby "with a banquet of which ought to have killed it at thirty yards." Clemens delighted in his daughter taking nourishment from such an unconventional woman. Livy tolerated the woman while Clara flourished, knowing she would soon be weaned that fall at nine months.

Livy worried about the effects of the warm weather on the girls in Hartford. Hot weather particularly made Susie quarrelsome;

she had inherited her father's bad temper. On occasion she hit her younger sister with her toys. Until Susie was old enough to be reasoned with, Livy fretted about how to curb her daughter's tantrums. Biographies were always a chief source of information for Livy, so she looked to the written words of other mothers for advice. She wrote her husband that she found one source on punishing children she would share with him on his return from one of his journeys: "There is much in this life of Sara Coleridge that is suggestive on this subject—" The method recommended was a common one that Livy had not wanted to use—spanking. When coaxing, bribery, standing in a corner did not work, and Susie's tantrums got more frequent, it seemed that a session in the bathroom with a hairbrush or paper cutter was the only option. Clemens recalled that within the span of a year, "We had to whip her once a day, at first; then three times a week; then twice, then once a week; then twice a month." By then Susie was nearly five and her transgressions could be discussed with her.

Clemens went to Cambridge alone to visit with the Howellses and to attend the centennial of the Battle of Lexington. Clemens and Howells, through a comedy of errors, missed their train and could find no transportation to Concord because of the crowds. They had to return home, "uncentennialed" in Howells's words, where they tried to convince Elinor that they had been to Concord and returned. Clemens was pleased that she was not so easily fooled. The two men had such "a splendid good sociable time" talking that Clemens called it a "wise providence that thwarted our several ably-planned & ingenious attempts to get to Lexington." It was this type of close intellectual companionship her husband enjoyed that Livy craved so and often had to forego in caring for the house and children. Clemens could report to Howells that "my narrative has made Mrs. Clemens wish she could have been there." The comment has a poignancy to it, as Clemens thought her content with staying at home. Livy, knowing her role and responsibilities, never seemed to let him know how much she wanted friends. So she often remained behind, writing to her sister, mother, or women friends of her desire for conversation on books and ideas. In Livy's words, she was often on occasions like this "tied" to the house.

Livy was ill off and on that summer and fall and had to rest several days at a time. The cause was as elusive as always—exhaustion because of the heat, the children, the house, her husband—but genuine to the sufferer. Although Clemens compared moving his household to moving "a menagerie," he did so at the end of July to get Livy to the seaside at Bateman's Point, Newport. They stayed until mid-August. Howells, too, had taken his wife away for a few weeks. Elinor also suffered from frailty that sent her, in Howells's words, to "the habitual sick-bed."

It was not until October and Clara was weaned that Livy could join her husband in one of his visits to Howells. As delicate wives were another bond the two men shared, each could worry, in turn, that a visit to the other's house might help his wife but cause the other woman to "go correspondingly down, under the added burden of *her* cares & responsibilities." Both Clemens and Howells liked to present their gentle wives as domineering women to be feared. Clemens, as a humorist entertaining his good friend, enjoyed exaggerating his transgressions and Livy's attempts to transform him. After the visit to Howells he wrote on October 4, 1875:

Of course I didn't expect to get through without committing some crimes and hearing of them afterwards, so I have taken the inevitable lashings and been able to hum a tune while the punishment went on. I "caught it" for letting Mrs. Howells bother and bother about her coffee when it was "a good deal better than we get at home." I "caught it" for interrupting Mrs. Clemens at the last moment and losing her the opportunity to urge you not to forget to send her that MS when the printers are done with it. I "caught it" for mentioning that Longfellow's picture was slightly damaged; and when, after a lull in the storm, I confessed, shamefacedly, that I have privately suggested to you that we hadn't any *frames*, and that if you wouldn't mind hinting to Mrs. Houghton, &c., &c., the Madam was simply speechless for the space of a minute. Then she said:

"How *could* you, Youth! The idea of sending Mr. Howells, with his sensitive nature, upon such a repulsive or—"

RESA WILLIS

"Oh, *Howells* won't mind it! You don't know Howells is a man who—" She was gone. But George [the butler] was the first person she stumbled on in the hall, so she took it out on George. I was glad of that, because it saved the babies.

Clemens sounds like Tom Sawyer asking for permission before he takes action. When he doesn't, "Aunt Livy" gets in a tizzy, and he is punished. Like Tom, Clemens took his beating without a sound; he just hummed. Clemens liked to pose himself and Howells as boys pleading with their mothers, or rather wives, to be allowed to go out and play. In another letter to Howells, Clemens asked if his friend could get permission from Mrs. Howells to spend the night.

> Can't you tell her it always makes you sick to go home late at night, or something like that? That sort of thing rouses Mrs. Clemens's sympathies easily; the only trouble is to *keep* them up.

Clemens had finished *The Adventures of Tom Sawyer* that July after moving his study over the stable so he could write.[1] As was his practice since they were first engaged, he shared the book with Livy to edit as he wrote the manuscript. With Howells, he had found an additional editor. He passed the entire manuscript on to Howells for his comments. Clemens valued the advice of both his wife and friend, so when they suggested that *Tom Sawyer* be a book for boys and girls, he agreed. Publication of the book would be delayed until December 1876 by Clemens's publisher Elisha Bliss, who could not get the book out on schedule. At one point, so certain that it would soon be out, Howells published a favorable review of it in the May *Atlantic*.

Livy genuinely liked the Howellses, but she also liked the fact that her husband associated with the respectable eastern literary society represented by Howells and the *Atlantic Monthly*. The manuscript Livy wanted from Howells, for which Clemens "caught it," was a review of Clemens's *Sketches, New and Old* to appear in

[1]By 1877 he did his writing "in the billiard room—the very most satisfactory study that ever was. Open fire, register, & plenty of light."

the December *Atlantic*. She was pleased that Howells called her husband a *"subtile* humorist" with "a growing seriousness of meaning." Clemens told his friend, "You see, the thing that gravels her is that I am so persistently glorified as a mere buffoon, as if that entirely covered my case—which she denies with venom."

Livy turned thirty on November 27, 1875; her husband would be forty on November 30. With the peace of a secure home and love as they journeyed into their middle years, Clemens celebrated his wife's birthday and his love for her with a birthday love letter.

Livy Darling—Six years have gone by since I made my first great success in life and won you, and thirty years have passed since Providence made preparation for that happy success by sending you into the world. Every day we live together adds to the security of my confidence that we can never any more wish to be separated than we can imagine a regret that we were ever joined.

CHAPTER 11

"So desperately happy"

The United States celebrated its one hundredth birthday in 1876. For both Livy and her Youth it was a busy year. She remained occupied with her children, her home, and entertaining. Susie and Clara, now four and two, were going through their childhood diseases. Clemens remarked to Howells that plans had to be scheduled around their illnesses "because they always play such hob with visiting arrangements." Livy was often again at home while her husband went out.

May was a tense time for Livy as she nursed Susie through what Clemens called "the savagest assault of diphtheria," the same disease the frail Langdon had succumbed to four years previously. A visitor thought they might be overreacting. "However the little girl did not really seem very sick, so I could not help thinking they were unnecessarily excited. The effect on them, however, was just as bad as if the child were really very ill." Clemens recorded Livy's diligence as a nurse in his autobiography: "When our children were little she nursed them through long nights of sickness, as she had nursed her father. I have seen her sit up and hold a sick child upon her knees and croon to it and sway it monotonously to and fro to comfort it, a whole night long, without complaint or respite."

Unless she could take the children with her, Livy seldom ventured out of the house. Neighborhood visits were one thing, but she refused to sleep away from home. She once remarked to her husband that any extended visits would have to be postponed until "the children are old enough to release us from the bondage of our service to them."

Jane and Pamela came for their visit in June. Once they were gone, the Clemenses packed up "the menagerie" to spend another summer at Quarry Farm. The ten-hour train journey always tired Livy. This time Clemens hired a sleeping car. Although it was still hot, the privacy made for a much more tolerable trip. Livy could recline; Rosa kept the girls occupied; Clemens was away from other passengers. "She shall always go by special car, hereafter until we bust," Clemens vowed as much for himself as for his wife.

The girls continued taking turns being ill, and Clara again exhibited her propensity for accidents that in later years caused Clemens to say, "I don't believe God cares much about meeting her." At one week old Clara was asleep on a rocking chair. She landed on the floor two inches from an iron grate when her father "had forgotten her presence" and kicked the chair out of the way of an oncoming mechanical toy wagon. Another time, reminiscent of when Clemens took Langdon for a carriage ride and fell into a "reverie," he was pushing Clara in her baby carriage when he let go and gravity took the buggy and Clara downhill. The carriage upset, spilling Clara. Although her head was bleeding, she was not seriously injured. Livy's reaction is not difficult to imagine. Even as an adult, Clara's good luck or bad luck held, when she endured a carriage accident in which her head might have been crushed by the horse but she escaped without a scratch.

By August, with the children taking turns being ill, this time with whooping cough, Livy herself was laid up. Clemens reported to Mrs. Fairbanks that she couldn't venture from the hillside home into Elmira even once a week without then taking two days to recover.

At four, Susie may have inherited her father's temper and his flair for words, but she could also show a deep introspective side, similar to her mother's. Wearing some new shoes her father bought her that summer, but she didn't like, put her in a bad mood. So when her mother told her to say her bedtime prayers, "Now, Susie—think about God." Susie replied, "Mama, I can't with these shoes." After observing a fireworks display down in the valley of Elmira, Susie didn't want to give up her hillside seat and go to bed. "I wish I could sit up all night, as God does."

While the Clemens family faced these day-to-day dramas, Mark Twain occupied his octagonal study and continued work on another boys' book he called Huck Finn's Autobiography. He wrote Howells that, while he was nearly half finished, he had begun it, "more to be at work than anything else." At this point he reported, "I like it only tolerably well, as far as I have got, & may possibly pigeonhole or burn the MS when it is done." He set this potential kindling aside, not to work on it again until three to four years later and not to finish it until 1884.

In September all returned to Hartford where Clemens once again became involved in a collaboration. Collaboration, like lecturing, was an experience Clemens would vow to abstain from, but would be tempted because of the money. This time because the household expenses were "ghastly," he would write a play with his sometime friend, sometime editor, sometime rival, but always an ambiguity to him—Bret Harte. (In his autobiography, Clemens would describe Harte as "one of the pleasantest men I have ever known. He was also one of the unpleasantest men I have ever known.")

With all of Clemens's projects, on the surface this one seemed it could not fail. After all, wouldn't audiences clamor to see a comedy by two western humorists that included their well-known characters—Twain's Scotty Briggs and Harte's "Heathen Chinee"? Harte came to stay at the Clemens home in October while they worked on *Ah Sin*.

Clemens marveled at Harte's work habits under stress. One evening Harte came to dinner with a story due the next day. After dinner, Harte drank and talked until his host went to bed at one in the morning. With a bottle of whiskey, Harte worked the rest of the night, stopping only, Clemens recalled, for another bottle early in the morning. At ten the Saturday Morning Club met in the Clemens library. Clemens's fondness for young girls and Livy's desire that no young woman lack the companionship she did growing up because of her illness led them to form the Saturday Morning Club in 1876. Neighborhood young women of sixteen to twenty, excluded from the Monday Evening Club and their mothers' and aunts' auxiliary, read essays and discussed various topics. Clemens took great pride in being the only male member, but he asked Harte to share his story with this audience. Clemens read it aloud for Harte, who had drunk himself into such a stupor that he seemed sober. The young ladies were pleased. Puzzled as to how the story "Thankful Blossom" could be written under such "unpromising conditions," Clemens would later declare it one of Harte's best.

During his stay, Harte managed to add to his debt to Clemens, one that would one day reach three thousand dollars. But he incurred a higher personal debt that could not be repaid. While Harte was handsome and could be charming, Clemens could never understand the man's lack of charm toward his own wife and women in general. On Livy's instructions, Clemens ignored the venom that Harte passed as wit. When his guest included Livy in his remarks, Clemens could bear no more. From the *Autobiography*, as Mark Twain recorded his remarks in 1907:

> "Harte, your wife is all that is fine and lovable and lovely, and I exhaust praise when I say she is Mrs. Clemens's peer— but in all ways you are a shabby husband to her and you often speak sarcastically, not to say sneeringly, of her just as you are constantly doing in the case of other women; but your privilege ends there; you must spare Mrs. Clemens."

The exact insult does not survive, but Harte apologized, even if in a flippant manner, from New York, once the play was finished in mid-December. He promised to wear sackcloth, if it was fashionably cut, and ashes until Livy forgave him. Livy was always more forgiving than her husband. A year later, with the play in production and with Clemens still holding a grudge, Livy admonished her husband two days in a row to be "'civil as you can to Mr. Harte if he should come about—" The next day she writes, "Youth I want to caution you about one thing, don't say harsh things about Mr. Harte, don't talk against Mr. Harte to people, it is so much better that you be reticent about him, don't let anybody trap you into talking freely of him—" She reasons that they are happy and "he is so miserable, we can easily afford to be magnanimus [sic] toward him—"

Ah Sin opened in Washington May 7, 1877, moved to New York on July 31, closed in five weeks, and then went on the road. Despite Clemens's high hopes for the play, by October he called it "a most abject & incurable failure!"

Words often failed Livy's friends and neighbors in describing their admiration of and devotion to her. Livy deserved the high pedestal Clemens placed her upon if any woman did, but part of her charm was her unassuming manner that always considered others and placed their feelings and their comfort above her own. She practiced with great success the Biblical dictate of "Do unto others . . ." and the love emanating from her returned to her a hundredfold. Because of her, many doors opened to her husband at Nook Farm that otherwise might not have. A nature as generous as Livy's was sometimes needed to live in Nook Farm. It was such a close community that families did not lock their doors. Neighbors came and went through each other's homes without knocking, and all took pride in showing off the uniqueness of the Clemens's home.[1]

So it was Friday after Thanksgiving in 1876 that Isabella Beecher Hooker brought a friend to see the Clemens house. Isabella had recently and tentatively been readmitted into Hartford society after returning from Europe. Her husband, John, had hoped that her absence would allow others to forgive, if they couldn't forget, her role in the Beecher-Tilden controversy. Clemens, who had once forbidden Livy to associate with Isabella, now again had to be

---

[1]Livy and Clemens would surely be pleased by their open-door policy today—more than sixty thousand people a year tour their house.

tolerant for Livy's sake. Isabella remained Mrs. Langdon's friend and the mother of Livy's friend Alice Hooker Day, but she could never be Samuel Clemens's friend. Clemens, already in a touchy mood because he was working with Harte on *Ah Sin*, did not appreciate Isabella repeating gossip about him to him. The story going about the neighborhood was that once he had learned a certain lampshade to be cheaper than he thought, he no longer liked it. Her remarks made him defensive. He admitted he lacked decorating taste, but he justified his opinion by stating that expensive things were "worthy" of Livy. Isabella, sensing her host's anger at being talked about, tried to pass the incident off as a joke hoping that "one so given to joking" wouldn't mind. Livy, knowing her husband's dislike of Isabella, walked in and saved the situation by saying, "No matter how small the gift, the thoughtfulness & love make them valuable."

Isabella had seen Clemens and Harte working together in the billiard room. She perceived through her psychic powers that there was something wrong. Although she committed to her diary that perhaps she should warn the Clemenses of her feelings, she did not because she knew only Livy preserved their friendship that hung by a "slender threat." Isabella was not so cautious about revealing her other predictions. The spirits that supplied her with her information made it difficult for friends and family. She repeatedly told her son-in-law that because of him her granddaughter would not live to be eight. Eugene Burton forbade his mother-in-law to see her granddaughter Kathy. Aware of the difficult but hurtful situation for Isabella, Livy would relay information to her concerning "Miss Kassie" in passing conversation. John Hooker, Isabella's long-suffering husband, did not realize that the New Year's Eve party they were having to usher in 1877 was also to usher in a new order of government—her spirits told Isabella she would rule the world.

Nearly the entire neighborhood filled Isabella's parlor to await the coming of 1877. Unknown to them, and her husband, her medium friends filled the upstairs to await the coming of Isabella's regime. When midnight came and passed and guests came and went, traveling about the neighborhood wishing each other New Year's greetings, Isabella's daughter Alice let the secret out by loudly demanding to know what was going on in her mother's bedroom for there was the "queerest looking lot" sitting around a table attempting to conjure up the new order. In the confusion of celebrating people, the Clemenses would not find out what really had happened until later at the Warner residence, where they continued their festivities. Isabella took comfort in her embarrassment that Clemens, totally unaware of her predictions gone awry, had mistaken one medium to be a coachman. As bizarre as Isabella's traverses into the other world were, she was only an extreme example of a nation in the grips of spiritualism the latter part of the nineteenth century. The Clemenses had already expressed some interest in the subject that would grow after Susie's death when they would attempt to contact her through mediums.

On February 2, 1877 Livy and Clemens celebrated their seventh wedding anniversary by drinking wine from crystal glasses sent to them by Mrs. Langdon. While Livy was "wonderfully happy," the anniversaries of her engagement and wedding always depressed her, for they made her think of her father. Livy always felt that the occasion when he had left her and her new husband in Buffalo and returned to Elmira was the last time she had really seen him as himself.

One topic they discussed at their anniversary dinner over the wine was a proposed trip to Germany. Clemens wanted to leave that summer. Livy desired to visit Quarry Farm for the summer and go to Germany the following summer. She wrote her mother, "I don't know who will come out ahead." Then, confident of her power over her husband, she adds, "But I think I shall." And she did.

Clemens considered going to Europe for several reasons: to gather material for a new travel book and to relieve them of the burden of running their home. Entertaining was costly in money and in Livy's health. She fretted about the smallest detail being a reflection on her abilities as a hostess and her husband's position. She dreaded a visit from two English gentlemen, because she felt she did not have a "perfect" table. She described one week's "campaign" of social obligations to be attending a lunch party or two, giving a lunch party and a dinner, and receiving between twelve and fifteen calls, day and evening.

To facilitate this social atmosphere, the Clemens staff could number as high as six full-time servants and additional part-time maids, secretaries, governesses and nurses for the children. Their salaries totaled $1650 annually in the 1870s.

The turnover could be constant, especially with cooks. One stayed overnight, another lasted an entire week. Because her mother was a "particular eater," Livy, as any daughter, feared what she did would not meet her approval. Mrs. Langdon made such extended visits, anywhere from a few weeks up to six months, that when the Clemenses built their Hartford house a bedroom was planned especially for her. It was Livy's desire, she told her mother that when she visited, that "you can have just what you like to eat—"

Several devoted servants remained a part of the family for many years. Clemens's black butler and manservant George Griffin occupied his own room on the third floor. Clemens liked to say that George "came to wash windows and remained eighteen years." For the very reasons Clemens liked him, Livy disliked him—he gambled, he lent money at extortion rates, he lied for his employer by telling callers that Clemens wasn't at home when he was. George once told Livy, "Why, Mrs. Clemens, if I was to stop lying you couldn't keep house a week." A compromise was reached to please Livy. Clemens, on the third foor, would go out one of the three doors onto the porch so George, in good conscience for Livy, could say, "Mr. Clemens has stepped out." That summer from Quarry Farm Livy wrote her husband in Hartford, "I sometimes think George is utterly incapable of staying in that house & taking care of it—" Despite her discharging him at one point, Paine reports George served breakfast the next morning, explaining his presence, "I knew you couldn't get along without me, so I thought I'd better stay a while."

Rosina Hay, who would accompany them to Europe, had been

hired as a nursemaid in 1874 to care for the girls and to help Livy with her German. Patrick and Ellen McAleer, the footman and his wife, had come from the Langdon home and served the Clemenses for thirty-six years. Katy Leary would join the staff as a personal maid in 1880 and stay until Clemens's death in 1910. The gardener John O'Neill and his wife Ellen became caretakers of the Hartford home when Livy left it in 1891 never to return.

Both Livy and Clemens took a parental attitude toward their servants. Before Katy Leary's mother would allow her daughter to move to Hartford, Livy had to convince Mrs. Leary she would care for her, "as I would one of my own children." Livy supervised Katy's reading, discussing books with her and even scolding her when she read something Livy thought unsuitable. With great relish Clemens recounted to Livy when she was in Elmira of how a prowler turned out to be the lover of the housemaid Lizzy. In sneaking in and out of the house, the man set off the burglar alarm. Upon confronting the couple, Clemens insisted they marry even if the potential bridegroom refused four times. If the fellow thought he would get off the hook by finally agreeing, he was wrong. Clemens brought out Twichell, complete with a license to marry them. All the new husband could say was "But it was a put-up job." Clemens gave them a hundred dollars each to start their new life. Clemens later worked the details into a story he called "Wapping Alice."

The parental roles were sometimes switched as the servants cared for the Clemenses. Clemens often left instructions on his absences that someone was to sit with Livy if it should storm as she feared thunder and lightning and would take shelter in the closet. As Livy found it difficult to rest when her husband was away from home overnight, Clemens depended on Katy to keep her company.

In the country one seldom lacks for anything to do and so it was true of Livy, Susie, and Clara that summer while Clemens was at rehearsals of *Ah Sin*. Squirrels had to be supplied with nuts, birds watched as they hatched, dolls played with, flowers picked, sunrises and sunsets admired. Livy was teaching Susie to read and print but thought Clara would learn easily because she begged to study with her sister and was more patient. Livy wrote her husband, "Susie worked a long time today printing the letters to send to you at first she seemed to think that she was going to print the entire letter to you in a few minutes—but after she found how difficult it was she worked faithfully on it—"

Even though Susie was older and Livy could reason with her, the little girl still wasn't easily disciplined. Once Susie admitted the worst transgression in her mother's opinion, telling her a lie. Livy prayed with her for forgiveness at bedtime. "Susie don't you want to pray and ask for your self to be forgiven?" Susie reponded, "Oh one is enough."

Clemens returned to Quarry Farm, after *Ah Sin* seemed unsalvageable, to resume work in his study. He worked on "Some Rambling Notes" based on his Bermuda trip with Twichell that past May. Still trying to turn a profit from the stage, he wrote the play "Cap'n Simon Wheeler, The Amateur Detective." Livy would not allow her husband to title it "Balaam Ass," his first choice. At the urgings of Livy and her sister Sue, he started to think of a novel that would elevate his literary reputation. Even this novel about two look-alikes, a prince and an urchin, trading places, he planned to turn into a play.

Strikes in the anthracite coal mines hurt Livy's income and only made the need for additional income more accute. The depression that started in 1873 continued to worsen, causing workers to compete for ever lower paying jobs at longer working hours. Finally, a wage cut for workers on the Baltimore and Ohio line led to riots. Rutherford B. Hayes, president in 1877 and further distinguished by being Elinor Howells's cousin, dispatched federal troops to maintain order, and the nation witnessed some of the worst riots in the east, including Buffalo, close to the Langdon coal interests. In Pittsburgh, twenty-five were killed.

While these national disasters affected the Clemenses' bank account, a breathtaking rescue was the high drama of the summer. Just as Clara in her buggy had raced downhill the previous summer, East Hill again showed its treachery. After a visit to Quarry

Farm, Charles Langdon's wife, Ida, daughter, Julia, and nurse returned to Elmira with Ida driving a high-spirited horse. It was Livy who noticed the carriage careening downhill out of control because Ida's "horse is running away!" The family ran down the hill in a vain attempt to catch the buggy. When Clemens reached the bottom of the hill, he was certain "they can never pass that turn alive." John T. Lewis, the Cranes' hired hand, had been coming up the hill with a load of manure. In a show of quick thought and strength, Lewis turned his team diagonally across the road, stood in front of his team, and seized the runaway horse's harness. Clemens described it thus: "A miracle had been performed—nothing less." Livy was so upset at the near tragedy that she couldn't speak of the incident without her voice breaking. Neither could she sleep.

The Cranes gratefully rewarded Lewis by canceling four hundred of his seven hundred dollars' debt to them. (They later also canceled the additional three hundred.) The Langdon family always loved a party, with presents at a prettily decorated table with refreshments of sandwiches, punch, tea and cakes. This event served as a good excuse to celebrate, and so at supper with servants and the Cranes, Clemenses, and Langdons in attendance, Charles Langdon presented Lewis with a silver watch.

Livy, husband, and daughters left Quarry Farm that September 1877 to return to Nook Farm and the fall entertainments. A highlight was to be a dinner given in Boston by *The Atlantic* on the occasion of John Greenleaf Whittier's seventieth birthday, to be attended by "the largest literary billows," Ralph Waldo Emerson, Oliver Wendell Holmes, and Henry Wadsworth Longfellow. Howells would serve as master of ceremonies and Clemens would give an after-dinner speech. It seemed to both Livy and Clemens that Mark Twain, the western humorist, was at last an acceptable personage. On such an occasion Clemens couldn't help but let the Tom Sawyer side of him emerge even if he might regret it later.

Clemens's speech was actually a favorite device of his, the frame story. He informed his audience that when he was beginning to write in California, he knocked at the door of a miner's cabin where

he was told he had been preceded by three drunken literary men—
Emerson, "a seedy little bit of a chap"; Holmes, "fat as a balloon";
and Longfellow, "built like a prizefighter." Clemens continued
with the miner's rendition of their "queer talk," the three quoting
from their poetry. In the fashion of Scotty Briggs and the preacher,
the poets and the miner speak but neither understands the other—
elevated language versus dialect. It was a form of humor Clemens
would often use. For any student who has suffered through lectures on romanticism and transcendentalism, his speech is a rich
parody. But that evening and following, Clemens perceived that
the audience did not agree. The silence that followed his remarks,
Howells recalled as "weighing many tons to the square inch." The
silence only grew in Clemens's mind and Howells's until they
were blind, in addition to deaf, as to what really happened that
night. Warner tried to comfort Clemens by saying "Well, Mark
you're a funny fellow." In reality the world, or the program, did
not stop, there had been laughter and the festivities continued
until the end.

Clemens's imagined distress was multiplied by Livy's when he
related his version of the evening to her. She had been so proud
of her husband speaking before the very writers she venerated
and whose words filled the pages of her commonplace book.
Holmes's *The Autocrat at the Breakfast Table* had been the book she
and Clemens read together during their courtship. The more they
ruminated on that night—"which pretty nearly killed me with
shame"—the worse it got. Finally, he wrote Howells, "It seems
as if I must have been insane when I wrote that speech and saw
no harm in it, no disrespect toward those men whom I reverenced
so much." He had written his speech the day before the dinner
and not shown it to Livy. Although she had doubts as to the
"properest way" to handle the situation, Livy and Howells suggested Clemens write letters of apology to all three poets. In their
responses, both Longfellow and Holmes said that the newspapers
had made too much of the incident, and they were not upset.
Emerson's daughter wrote for her father, who in his age and poor
health hadn't heard any of the speeches. She wrote to Livy as one

woman aware of another's embarrassed sensitivity. The gesture showed great insight on Ellen Emerson's part, for Clemens had described Livy's distress as so great that "it is not to be measured."

Although husband and wife didn't speak of it because it "*scorches,*" the incident cast a gloom over the Christmas holidays, and it also affected his writing. In an effort to make up for the transgression, Livy had Clemens ask Howells not to print his story of the long-distance romance, "The Loves of Alonzo Fitz Clarence and Rosannah Ethelton," the first story to use the telephone as an integral part of the plot.

By February Clemens was getting a better perspective on it and could tell Mrs. Fairbanks that he intended no harm, "But nobody has ever convinced me that that speech was not a good one—for me; above my average, considerably." Twenty-eight years later, Clemens looked at the speech again and declared after reading it twice, "Unless I am an idiot, it hasn't a single defect in it from the first word to the last. It is just as good as good can be." He decided from his vantage point of twenty-eight years of writing and speaking that if it had failed, it was not the words but the speaker's lack of confidence in them, "for you can't be successfully funny if you show that you are afraid of it."

He was "afraid of it" for a while but then returned to work again on his "historical tale, of 300 years ago, simply for the love of it." He planned to publish it anonymously for he felt "such grave & stately work . . . [was] considered by the world above my proper level." So by February he had shared these secret portions of *The Prince and the Pauper* with the young ladies of the Saturday Morning Club.

In the first few months of 1878, Livy prepared their home to be left unoccupied for as long as two years. Clemens felt he needed an extended period to write because "a nine month vacation" each year in Hartford could not support them. Clemens told Mrs. Fairbanks, "I want to find a German village where nobody knows my name or speaks any English, & shut myself up in a closet 2 miles from the hotel & work every day without interruption until I shall have satisfied my consuming desire in that direction."

Livy had the furniture and carpeting crated for storage, which forced the family to again occupy a few rooms on the second floor. Right up until the day they left, Livy hurried to secure the house. Elinor Howells was in awe that she seemed so "calm & unruffled" despite all she had on her mind. She was so preoccupied with packing, leaving friends and relatives, that she couldn't sleep. She roamed the empty, "melancholy" rooms.

Leaving behind only "Patrick & the horses," Clemens, Livy, her friend Clara Spaulding, who had accompanied them to Europe before, Rosa, and the girls sailed April 11 on the *Holsatia* for Germany.

CHAPTER 12

"We dread changing our manner of life."

After a stormy two-week crossing, complete with seasickness and colds for everyone, the Clemens party landed at Hamburg to rest before going on to spend two months in Heidelberg via Hanover and Frankfurt. The beauty of Hamburg surprised Livy, since, of the friends she had consulted before her journey, only George Warner had praised the city. She also found the accommodations "charming" and the food "palatable." Livy wrote her mother that "my greatest anxiety just at the present is the fear that the children will be utterly spoiled by admiration that they receive." Livy never let Susie or Clara go out in less than perfect ruffled dresses in matching colors and shiny high-top shoes with manners to match. Few remarked about them in Nook Farm because everyone knew them, but on board ship and on the streets they stood out. Livy informed Rosa not to let people make such a fuss over the two girls. Even though people said, "Oh, what pretty children" in German, Livy knew when they learned the language the attention would not only turn but swell their heads.

And their mother and father planned they would quickly learn German. From the moment they landed in Germany, Rosa was required to speak only German to the girls. Susie, being Susie, rebelled, wishing that "Rosa was made in English." Clara, being

Clara, "scorned" the situation, knowing in her childlike practicality that adults, always desiring their own way, would have to communicate with her in some fashion.

Clemens and Livy believed that while cultivated young ladies knew French for diplomacy, German was the language of success. Its people, known for their hard work, had made Germany the leader in business, education, and intellectual activity. As with his first impressions of England, Clemens was enthralled with Germany and saw no faults. "What a paradise this is! What clean clothes, what good faces, what tranquil contentment, what prosperity, what genuine freedom, what superb government." Their parents felt Susie and Clara Clemens would be well equipped for the future with a sound knowledge of the German language and culture.

Although they had begun their studies before they left, the adults soon learned that the children picked up the language much more quickly. Susie wrote her Aunt Sue, "I know a lot of German; everybody says I know a lot." Although she had Rosa to help with the children, Livy believed that caring for the children made her "very much behind" in her studies as compared to her husband and her friend. In a month Livy stated, "If it was not for the children I should give it up because it seems a waste of time, yet I enjoy studying it." In another three months she gave up her goal of being able to read German works in the original and told her mother she was reading a translation of Schiller's *William Tell*. Livy wanted to attend church but didn't as "I think I should not understand anything of the service." Her husband's frustrations would be worked out in writing his book, and eventually he expressed them in a chapter called "That Awful German Language." Susie did become fluent enough to translate her mother's orders to the servants.

Settled at the Schloss Hotel in Heidelberg, Livy ran her three-room household as efficiently as she had in Hartford so her husband could begin work. "He has been making notes ever since we left home, so he has a good deal of material to work from." For his office Clemens rented a room in a house across the river from the hotel. Although Livy preferred the smaller hotel breakfast of rolls and coffee, she ordered for her husband much larger breakfasts of meat, potatoes, and eggs. She knew he could not work through lunch, as was his manner, without a substantial breakfast. Livy's duties varied little from one side of the Atlantic to the other. Once she saw that her husband could work, she turned to her daughters' education. Livy interviewed governesses and found a young lady who had taught in an English school to instruct the children for three hours each day.

Part of their education was to explore their foreign surroundings, or why go abroad? So reasoned the upper-middle-class Americans who "completed" themselves by taking their grand tours. Livy agreed. While Clemens wrote, she, Clara Spaulding, the girls, and their caretakers explored the castle on the grounds of the hotel. Similar to Quarry Farm summers, they picked flowers and played with the pets and farm animals—donkeys, goats, pigs, and chickens.

The physical exercise Susie and Clara indulged in daily delighted their mother. Children can be picky eaters, but compound that by coming from a family nearly obsessed with the quality of food and always worried about delicate constitutions. No wonder Livy was amazed at their increased appetite. Their boisterous good health had to be subdued each morning so their mother could sleep. Livy paid her daughters to play quietly and bribed them with candy not to argue.

Clemens, concerned first with his writing and hating small details, left managing the money to Livy. However, he sometimes took an interest in larger money matters. When he did, Livy deferred to his judgment, but he left day-to-day expenses to her. As were many Americans, and thus the reason they traveled abroad, Livy was pleased their money bought more in Europe. She recorded with pride that their rent and meals were a little less than $250 a month. She told her brother Charles, managing her money and the coal business back home, that she was "entirely satisfied" with the investments he made for her.

Maintaining money in Elmira was fine, but having her own

money in her purse was also very important. She wrote, "Mother, the money that you gave me does make me feel so rich. I feel on account of it some way taken care of by you, I feel so *much* freer because I have that money. I shall write you everything that I buy with it—" Periodically, throughout the trip, Mrs. Langdon would wire her daughter money. Often Livy's letters to her generous mother would contain words like "Oh, Mother you are too good to send us *so much money*, it is too much—you are so good to us—"

Although Livy could fill her time with excursions into town for shopping, museums, and concerts or taking carriage rides through the countryside of the Rhine Valley, it was not enough to occupy her. She felt relieved that she didn't have to entertain as Mark Twain's wife. "No one in the hotel knows who Mr. Clemens is— we are having as quiet a life as we could possibly desire." The quiet life left her with time on her hands. Money gave her something to do while her husband and children were busy. She shopped for her own home or herself. She bought a few hats, gloves, and dresses, but those made her feel too self-indulgent. She enjoyed buying for others for "it is a real pleasure to have errands to do." "Write me of something over here that you want me to do for you" she begs her mother as often as she thanks her for money. Livy found it particularly fun to shop "if other people are to pay for the things that I get—then there is no drawback to the buying."

Clara celebrated her fourth, what she called "my German birthday" in Heidelberg. As was Livy's and Clemens's practice, both girls got presents—dolls, books, cups, flowers. That afternoon they rode donkeys with the help of Rosa and the donkeys' owners up a hill that Livy determined to be steeper and higher than East Hill at Quarry Farm for a picnic of bread, butter, and strawberries.

Quarry Farm and home were on her mind. Livy once told her mother, "What an intense love of home I always had as a young lady—" All of her life, Livy was ready to travel but, having arrived, experienced true homesickness for her family, her culture, and her lifestyle left behind.

How I wish that we could see you all—I am glad our home is in America. I enjoy it as much as possible here but I should not like to think of living here always, of this being my home—I would rather live just where I do than any place that I know of—and I only hope that we shall always have enough money so that we can continue to live there.

The annual report from Langdon coal seemed to indicate there would be "money enough" as the company gradually recovered from the Panic of 1873 and the resulting labor unrest. Clemens felt optimistic enough to inform Howells that *"We've quit being poor!"* "We have more than income enough, from investments, to live in Hartford on a generous scale." Being able to live on Livy's inheritance would take some of the pressure off her husband to support them with his pen. Although he filled notebooks on this trip, he had not finished any of the six projects he had pigeon-holed. Years later he knew himself well enough as a writer to pronounce, "When the tank runs dry you've only to leave it alone and it will fill up again in time." Livy knew with six wells dry they might cautiously acquire a few more "necessities" for the Hartford home.

By August 1 they had moved on to Baden-Baden where Livy was again content "to know no one and be utterly unknown." At Clemens's expense, Joseph Twichell came to Germany to help him gather material for *A Tramp Abroad.* (Twichell became Mr. Harris in the book.) Together they would make a walking tour through the Black Forest and the Swiss Alps, but Clemens's rheumatism sometimes caused them to use carriage or train. Livy and entourage followed by rail. Clemens and Twichell walked to the top of the Rigi in the Alps. In their hotel, Clemens, who would have balked at being called a romantic, said they could contemplate "the eternal sublimities of the Alps." For Susie and Clara these sublimities included throwing rocks in Lake Geneva. For Livy it included exploring a glacier below the Grandes Mulets.

After six weeks, Twichell returned home, and the Clemenses sojourned down into Italy. Travel was not only broadening, but exhausting. From a woman who seldom uttered a harsh word,

Livy declared, "Oh how I do dislike the French—and I am more and more and more thankful that I am an American—I believe the old puritan education brings better men and women, than any of these looser methods—perhaps they were too severe, but they certainly leaned toward the wiser course." Weariness from "poor beds & poor food" had made her testy. Instead of reading, she and Clara Spaulding passed the time by torturing themselves with stories of the good food they'd enjoyed in the past.

Venice restored Livy's vitality. "It is so fascinating, so thoroughly charming." It proved to be a treasure trove for items to adorn her Hartford house. "We have bought several most beautiful pieces of wood carving & I am very anxious to see them in our house—" These pieces included a carved chest, a cabinet of drawers, and "a most wonderful old carved bedstead that was a great beauty—that we got for our room—" The bed came from an abandoned Venetian palace. It was elaborately carved black wood with cherubs and cupids laughing, dancing, singing, or reposing in deep thought. Clemens would later claim that since he had spent so much money on this bed, he wanted to admire the headboard, so he and Livy slept at the foot of the bed. In reality, Clemens slept fitfully, turning on the gas light to write or read at odd hours. The undecorated foot of the bed would be more comfortable to support his back during these activities. The four posts of the bed each contained a removable cupid. When one of the girls was ill, it was a special treat to occupy this bed and dress the pudgy cupids in doll clothing. To this day, one cupid is a shade lighter than the others—the consequence of too many doll baths.

Another Italian purchase became an integral part of the Clemens household and legend. They purchased a portrait of an unknown woman that Clemens said reminded him of Livy. Livy disagreed. Clemens in his autobiography said they called her "Emmeline" because "she looked just about like that." The name stuck, the whole family referred to her as Emmeline, and she still occupies the mantelpiece in the Clemens library. The name Emmeline had already graced chapter 17 of *Huckleberry Finn* when Clemens put the manuscript down in 1876. She was Emmeline Grangerford, the dead artist whose poems and sketches gave Huck Finn the "fantods" and who "with her disposition," he decided, "was having a better time in the graveyard."

Other knickknacks from the trip adorned the mantelpiece in Hartford to become part of Clemens's story repertoire. The story restrictions and requirements of the Clemens girls would tax even a creative genius like their father. They often asked him to tell a story using everything on the mantelpiece, starting with a picture of a cat in a ruff or collar and working his way through the bric-a-brac down to Emmeline at the other end. Jean, the youngest daughter, insisted on always having a much larger cat—a tiger—in each story. Each story had to follow this formula, but each story had to be different. For being an anonymous lady, "Emmeline" led quite a life as created by a father to entertain his young daughters.

Too many social obligations in Venice sent them on to Florence and Rome, where Livy continued sightseeing on her own. She believed "one ought to know no one when they are visiting picture galleries." Livy was enchanted with the culture Italy represented: the art museums where she spent four mornings a week, the gondolas of Venice, the ruins of Rome, the cathedrals, the opera. Clemens had not been impressed by these cultural artifacts on his first trip to Europe eleven years ago, and time had not improved them. He wrote Howells, "I *hate* travel, and I *hate* hotels, and I *hate* the opera, and I *hate* the old masters." And he didn't mind telling others of his opinions until at one point Livy chided him, "If you do not care for these masterpieces yourself, you might at least consider the feelings of others."

Livy informed her mother, "This Italy does tempt money so out of one's pocket—" Since items were about one-third to half of what they would cost in Hartford, the lure to overspend was hard to resist.

Livy kept meticulously detailed notebooks of her purchases whether for the house, the children, herself, or relatives. In the case of someone else's money, she wanted to make sure they got exactly what they asked her to spend: "Sue's $20 yet to spend," she noted. In order to accurately buy items to decorate her home, she filled pages before she left with notes of measurements and her ideas of accessories or furniture to fill certain spots on the floors or the walls. She wanted "glass transparency or something to hang in the north, northwest window." She recorded inches from doors to windows, windows to windows in each room, the length of hallways, the size of rugs needed, and on and on. In the dining room she measured fifty-three inches from door to window, fifty-five and one half from library to hall door. When the items were boxed to ship home she described the contents of each box, what the items looked like, their size and value. There were sixty-three presents she bought for family and friends. In Venice she spent $946 and $595; in Rome $416.90.

Overspending necessitated an economizing move to Munich. After a thirty-six-hour trip, they arrived tired, cold, and wet. Clara Spaulding commented on their good luck in traveling up to this point, "It seems as if some one person in the party must be the owner of Aladdin's lamp." It would seem that someone needed to rub the lamp in Munich; Clara and Livy cried when they saw their small, dingy rooms. They considered going on to winter in Paris. Livy had arranged the transportation and accommodations on this trip, sometimes a year in advance, so it was amazing that more mishaps had not occurred, or it serves as a tribute to Livy's organizational skills. After a night's rest and moving to larger, more convenient rooms, they decided to stay. Again, Clemens rented a room in which to work, but the words came haltingly. He described his work with frustration as "write and tear up."

With contacts from Lilly Warner, Livy secured teachers. Livy and Clara Spaulding occupied themselves with more German lessons from ten until noon each day. For additional practice they visited a German baroness "who has lost all her money," then went for drives and did errands. Drawing lessons filled their late afternoons and drawing practice their evenings. The girls continued their lessons. Livy found they could do all this and still take comfort in the fact "that we are living so much less expensively than at home."

Christmas in Munich had a storybook quality. Livy described,

"It is astounding to see how much they make of Christmas." "*Everybody* here has their Christmas tree, they are to be bought all the way from one foot high up to twenty feet." Then the evergreens were elaborately decorated with candles, paper chains, ornaments, hard candies. Snow was the final touch to the traditional picture. Susie and Clara were concerned, as children before and since, that Santa Claus wouldn't find them so far from home. When he did, he, of course, spoke German to them. It so impressed Susie that Santa could find them away from home that she had to write her cousin Julia in Elmira, who was skeptical about his existence anywhere.

Livy had planned for them to stay in Munich nearly five months, but she worried about the cold's effects on her daughters and a scare of what Clemens called the plague that their doctor assured them they need not fear. Livy confided in her mother, "I don't know what to do—I should feel so desperately to think that I was running any risk—" She and Clemens both felt Munich was a healthy place, so they stayed. Bay became ill. Clemens informed Howells, "We thought we were going to lose our little Clara yesterday, but the danger is gone, today, apparently." Clemens must have been exaggerating the malady as Livy only makes mention of Clara's stomachache.

From Christmas on, Livy's homesickness nipped at her soul with the cold. "I at once began to feel apprehension and to realize how far away from you all we are—" she wrote her mother. Her wedding anniversary, as it always did, touched off memories. Her married life had been happy save for "the two great griefs that have come into it." She was ready for home. The plans she shared with her mother were not of what she would be doing in France or England but when she got home. She wanted to complete her house, she writes but "[W]e have spent so much money I feel as if we ought perhaps not decorate at present—" Paris remained in which to buy presents, more for the house and things for herself and the children as they were all "rather destitute of clothing." The girls had had only one dress each since November.

Paris in the spring was a cliché even in 1879, but one Livy

couldn't resist. On February 27, "the tribe," as Clemens referred to his group, left for Paris. The extended European trek was beginning to take its toll. Livy was not the only one who was homesick. Clemens disliked the country and found its people rude. "France has neither winter, nor summer, nor morals." It did have plenty of dreary wet weather, however. Livy had observed of Italy, "In the countries where it is warmer they take so much less precaution against the cold that one suffers more than in a colder country." In Paris they had to have a fire every day even into June and July. Clemens grumbled about the price of firewood: "When I first saw the bill here I thought it was for carved furniture."

The cold and wet played havoc with Clemens's rheumatism, gave the girls colds, and aggravated Livy's aches and pains. Still, they resumed their daily routine—writing for Clemens; lessons for the girls; lessons and sightseeing for Livy and Clara.

The damp went to their bones and their money problems to their bank account. Paris was expensive, and Charlie sent word from home that the coal business was not recovering as he had first hoped, the labor problems in the mines had not subsided. Livy informed him to keep her securities the same "even if other investments should offer what seems to be better—" She wanted no speculation at this uncertain point. She mildly regretted the money she spent on furnishings in Venice, "but unless business is ruinous I think we shall be glad when we get home that we have got them—"

Decorating the Hartford house would have to wait. Livy recognized the drain it made on their resources. "I wish that we were living less expensively at home as well as here—when times seem hard I always regret that we have such an expensive establishment." She longed to confer with her mother as she continued to worry about "the prospect of not having money." "It seems to me that it is not so much because we cannot have the things that we want as it is that we dread changing our manner of life and how very foolish and weak minded that is in people as young as we are." Livy could always testify that she and Clemens brought their financial troubles on themselves. She knew they could rectify them by altering their lifestyle, and she felt pity for women who couldn't change. "I often reproach myself for liking them [luxuries] so well."

She knew she could economize in Paris. "I have no dress that I could wear if invited out in the evening—I intended to get one as soon as I got here but Charlie's letter has decided me not to." Her remedy was to refuse invitations or to have a six-year-old dress made over. What would her mother do? "Spending money on dresses seems the most uninteresting way that one can spend it—"

Livy and her husband could cut back, but the truth was, finances had to be very serious before they'd face the "dread" of changing. Mrs. Langdon again came to their economic rescue by offering her daughter a thousand dollars to decorate her house; this would free up money for them to spend in Paris. Livy refused halfheartedly. "I do hate to settle our house without decorating it—the white walls are not pleasant and it seems as if now when it is all torn up was such a good time to finish the inside." She wrote her mother that they would talk about it when she returned home: "At that time that you have a thousand dollars that you desire to part with, I think a thousand dollars would do all to the house that we should care to have done and I should be very glad to accept it."

The offer of the money eased Livy's mind about spending. She had dresses made so she could attend social functions. "We live in such a perfect whirl of people these days, that it seems utterly impossible to do anything." Clemens felt generous enough to offer to loan Mrs. Fairbanks a thousand dollars and to refer her to Charles Langdon for another thousand.

Despite the social whirl, Clemens worked on *A Tramp Abroad*, "six solid days every week—nothing short of it will ever finish this book." Livy encouraged his hard work and diverted visitors so he would not be interrupted. In the evenings he read passages aloud for her opinion. Reading aloud helped him to hear the rhythms in his sentences. Over the years of their marriage, Livy provided incidents and descriptive expressions that show her own literary flair and humor. One such incident started when Clemens arose early one morning because he couldn't sleep. He wanted to dress quietly in the dark and not waken his wife. He was completely dressed but for one sock. On hands and knees he crept around the floor looking for it. When he couldn't find it, his soft swearing became louder, but always in check because he didn't want to distrub Livy. Upon finding the rogue sock he rose in triumph only to hit his head on the washbowl. When Livy inquired as to what he was doing, he replied, "I'm hunting for my sock." She said, "Are you hunting for it with a club?" Clemens went to the couch and wrote down the incident, transferring the "adventure" from Munich to Heilbroon. He called the chapter "My Long Crawl in the Dark." The title is symbolic for *A Tramp Abroad*. He had long ago lost enthusiasm for it, but he knew he had to complete the book. When they left Paris, he would put aside his writing until they returned home to Quarry Farm that fall.

From Paris they toured through Belgium and Holland, landing in London on July 20. Livy's heart was cast west over the Atlantic. She wrote her mother that she would be looking for decorating ideas in England and would buy some stained glasss with the money she had left although "Mr. Clemens suggested that I reserve it to pay the duties with, now wasn't that like a man?"

Susie at seven and Clara at five were as different as Livy and Clemens. Both girls struggled to control their tempers. Susie was shy, "sweet and womanly." Clara was easygoing, independent, and forward. Susie's sensitivity showed in her face; Clara buried hers deep within. Clara had the intelligence and patience to learn but not the inclination while Susie's introspective side increased with her age. Livy informed her mother:

> Susie has little arithmetic lessons with buttons, adding and subtracting with the buttons, etc.—yesterday I said to her "Susie, next Winter we will study arithmetic together"— She said "Oh Mamma I know arithmetic, I have learned all the buttons."

Livy planned to teach Susie and Clara without the aid of governesses. "I have had such a long play time that I ought to be ready and able to do some good work."

After four weeks in England, they sailed for home on August 22 to arrive in New York September 3, 1879. Again, at Livy's request, Charlie met them to help get their twenty-two freight boxes and twelve trunks through customs. Reunions were their first obligations. They went to Fredonia to visit Jane Clemens and Pamela Moffet and then to Elmira. Livy was not unpacked when she began to hunt for an artist to fresco the Hartford house.

Despite the fact that Livy was happy to be home, she confided to her husband one evening, "I am low." Susie reproached, "Mamma I don't see how you can be low now you have come back to your beautiful home."

Susie was very perceptive. The beautiful, demanding home would have to wait a little while longer to be made even prettier. By her thirty-fourth birthday, Livy suspected she was pregnant again.

CHAPTER 13

"Women must be everything."

Livy could never sanction a house in disarray, and hers had stood empty nearly eighteen months. She had almost six thousand dollars' worth of European purchases plus furniture in storage to uncrate and arrange. No wonder she told her mother *"Everything every where* is confusion." Mrs. Langdon sent a generous check to help with the confusion, and Livy began to resettle her house.

She converted the second floor study that was once Clemens's office into a schoolroom and playroom for the girls. She engaged the Elmira decorator Frederick Schweppe to do the walls and ceilings. Clemens had moved his office from over the stable to his third-floor billiard room. Some of the items that had suited the stable needed a touch of refinement before Livy allowed them in the house. She hung a curtain over some crates that her husband turned sideways to use as "pigeon holes."

In the front hall she placed another of Clemens's joys—a music box he had had made in Geneva that cost four hundred dollars. While they ate in the dining room, they could listen to any of ten tunes of his choice, two favorites being "Pilgrim's Chorus" and "Lohengrin Wedding March." Clemens described it: "The sounds are more suggestive of the violin or a combination of violins (softly played) than anything else."

Overall, Livy was pleased with her purchases, even if she had to postpone decorating the walls of the house. "The new things look so pretty—There is so much fixing here and there that has to be done, that I am afraid when we get in the bills they will be pretty large, but I hope we shall soon be able to stop—"

Livy had to engage servants again. When the Clemens family had embarked for Europe, they left three people out of work. Although Livy intended on rehiring them on their return, even the faithful George had a long spell of unemployment. News of this troubled Livy abroad in Germany but she rationalized, "We keep some [servants] busy here so perhaps it is in a measure balanced." On their return, George returned, and even despite their differences Livy had to admit, "The house would not be at all natural without him."

Staffing the kitchen remained a problem. Livy found a cook but wasn't confident that she could do the work. She feared inviting guests to dine because "so much stress is laid now-a-days on fine cooking." Those who indulged in the dinners given by Livy never complained about the quality of the food or the setting of the table. A cut-glass bowl of flowers often adorned the center with flowers at each plate. The lit candelabra was silver. On the table were olives, almonds, bonbons, and decanters of wine. The courses consisted of a soup, a fish, then a meat, desserts of pudding or ice cream sculpted into flowers or angels washed down with champagne. The gentlemen would have cigars and brandy in the library; the ladies would have coffee or sherry in the drawing room. George and a maid served with gold and silver instruments. Not that Clemens noticed or enjoyed his food. He talked more than he ate, wandering about the room waving his napkin while he talked or helped George to serve, which worried Livy until she admonished Youth to sit down and eat. During dinners it irritated her that George, standing behind a screen at the kitchen door and waiting to serve courses, would laugh at the stories Mr. Clemens told to entertain his guests.

The responsibilities of entertaining weighed on Livy's mind, for autumn was the beginning of Hartford's social season. Mrs. Samuel Colt, the bejeweled widow of the firearms manufacturer, competed only with herself to stage more elaborate parties. Her dinners for two hundred guests swelled in the fall of 1879 to fifteen hundred invitations for one function. Only nine hundred were in attendance, two of whom were Mr. and Mrs. Samuel Clemens.

Entertaining on this lavish a scale could intimidate anyone. Livy confided to her mother about the Nook Farm standards, "I have felt rebellious about it ever since I came home." She had enjoyed her hiatus in Europe from the type of entertaining she perceived that Hartford demanded. It now seemed to her that perfect dinner giving with food daintily served and innovative house decorating were "being run to death."

> I told Mr. Clemens the other day, that in this day women must be everything, they must keep up with all the current literature, they must know all about art, they must help in one or two benevolent societies—they must be perfect mothers—they must be perfect housekeepers and graceful, gracious hostesses, they must know how to give perfect dinners, they must go and visit all the people in the town where they live, they must always be ready to receive their acquaintances—they must dress themselves and their children becomingly and above all they must make their houses *"charming"* and so on without end—then if they are not studying something their case is a hopeless one.

It is an accurate description of her role, and her dissatisfaction with the "perfect" and "charming" burdens she "must" endure that she allowed Hartford society to foist upon her. Although she boldly declared, "I am not afraid of Hartford people" when her sister-in-law Ida confessed her feelings of inferiority in the social milieu, Livy didn't stop worrying about cooks and decorating.

For Livy "the pleasantest work I do" was to give Susie and Clara lessons each morning. After breakfast and after she had given the servants their orders for the day, Livy and her daughters worked diligently in their schoolroom on the second floor. Their studies included German, geography, American history, arithmetic, penmanship, and English, with some extra diversions of tossing beanbags, gymnastics, and sewing. If they finished their lessons before twelve-thirty, Livy read to them. Bay, at five and eager to please, knew all the answers but often got her questions confused. When her mother asked, "What is geography?" she replied, "A round ball." When asked what was the shape of the earth, she replied, "Green."

On the next floor upstairs, Clemens labored to finish *A Tramp Abroad*. He had become so involved with it that he admitted to his mother he hadn't noticed that "Livy has been running down and getting weak, in consequence of overwork in re-arranging the house."

At one point Livy was so tired and depressed that she told her mother that only the children kept her from giving up house-keeping. Her daughters lifted her out of her lowest depths: "I do take much comfort with them this Winter." Despite Livy's protests that she wouldn't leave the girls in Hartford, Clemens took her to Elmira in January of 1880 for a few weeks' rest. He followed the advice of neighbor Mary Beecher Perkins: "You will never get any woman to do the thing necessary to save her life by mere *persuasion*; you see you have wasted your words for 3 weeks; it is time to use *force*; she *must* have a change; take her home & leave the children here." The nineteenth century was rampant with "musts" for women, and Livy tried to adhere to them.

As much as Clemens disliked working on *A Tramp Abroad*, he loved *The Prince and the Pauper*. He told Howells, "If I knew it would never sell a copy my jubilant delight in writing it would not suffer any diminution." Finishing *A Tramp Abroad* had been "a life-&-death battle" for him, and he vowed, "Next time I make a contract before writing the book, may I suffer the righteous penalty & be burnt, like the injudicious believer." He estimated that in his eighteen-month struggle he had written four thousand pages in order to get a little over half that to the publisher.

Clemens did not feel this pressure with his tale of Tom Canty and his look-alike, Edward VI. Now that Susie and Clara were old enough he included them as well as Livy in the evening reading sessions of his day's work. Livy adored the book, as Clemens told Howells:

I have even fascinated Mrs. Clemens with this yarn for youth. My stuff generally gets considerable damning with faint praise out of her, but this time it is all the other way. She is become the horse-leech's daughter & my mill doesn't grind fast enough to suit her. This is no mean triumph, my dear sir.

A Tramp Abroad was published a week prior to Susie's eighth birthday and sold sixty-two thousand copies in its first year, which was the best a Mark Twain book had done since *The Innocents Abroad*. Livy was again pleased when Howells praised what she called her husband's "strong points." Howells's review appeared in the May *Atlantic*, where he identified that Clemens's humor came from common sense, justice, "and a generous scorn of what is petty and mean."

Livy felt well enough to visit the Howellses in Boston before going on to Elmira in mid-June to await the birth of her fourth child. An alarm in early May caused them to summon the doctor, or as Clemens informed Howells, "The contemplated Clemens would have called before his apartments were ready." Clemens's use of the masculine pronoun and the fact he already had two daughters would seem to indicate his desire this time for a boy. Jane Lampton Clemens, named after Clemens's mother, made her entry at Quarry Farm on July 26. Clemens reported to Howells that "it is a girl again weighing seven pounds. That is a pretty big one—for us."

Jean, as she was called, was fated early in life not to be what her parents expected and later in life to be her parents' secret. No twins were on either the Clemens or Langdon side, but the father related to his friend, "The new baby is thoroughly satisfactory, as far as it goes; but we did hope it was going to be twins." The concept of twins was a permanent attraction for Clemens.

Elinor Howells in her congratulatory letter to Livy expressed her surprise that Livy had not informed her of the pregnancy during her April visit. This seems unusual, as Howells knew; and Livy would have been nearly six months pregnant. Clemens explained to Elinor that "we weren't certain; thought it was flesh, supposed it would wear off." Was he joking? Perhaps, or Livy did not want it disclosed. More likely Livy did tell Elinor, who misunderstood, for she remarked, "I am always in the wrong as to your intentions it seems." Ironically, Jean, who would have the most severe health problem of the three daughters, Livy pronounced as the "fattest healthiest baby we have had."

During the lying-in period Livy considered using some hair re-storer sent by Elinor Howells. Livy had fine hair, and pregnancy had thinned it even more. Instructions included washing the hair first with juniper tar soap, then rubbing a brown, smelly mixture into the part with a sponge, followed by a white tonic sprinkled all over the head. In the days of patent medicines, this was one of many potions she would try. In later years she would wear hair-pieces to cover thin spots.

Again Livy tried to breast-feed her child and was unable. A wet nurse was found, and after three weeks Livy was lifted into a chair and set out on the porch for some fresh air. In contrast, Elinor had related to Livy the incredible story of an Irish woman who was doing the wash three days after giving birth.

"Susie and Bay could not worship it more if it were a cat—and the same formula will fit my case," said Clemens of the new ad-dition. High praise indeed from a family of cat lovers. Clemens had once written Livy, "Next to a wife whom I idolize, give me a cat—an old cat, with kittens." The Clemenses loved all animals and had dogs, but cats always came at the top of the list. For Clemens, they were the symbol of independent survivors with good judgment. Dogs in their loyalty would remain with masters even if mistreated, but never a cat. As a mark of Jean's separateness as a young woman, she had a dog as a constant companion. Mark Twain would remark, "If man could be crossed with the cat it would improve man, but it would deteriorate the cat." The barn at Quarry Farm had a myriad of cat holes along the foundation to facilitate coming and going at feline leisure. Cats played an integral part in the bedtime stories Clemens composed for his daughters and were also a way of defining the various personalities in the Clemens family. At the demise of the kitten Motley, Clemens said Susie would wonder if the kitten had a soul and if her life had been meaningful; Clara would want a decent funeral for it. Other unique cats who deigned to live with the Clemenses were Fraulein, Sour Mash, Pestilence, Famine, Sackcloth, Ashes, and Stray Kitty. Livy once described her husband in a fit of temper as a spitting kitten. Susie once said, "The difference between papa and mama is, that mama loves morals and papa loves cats."

Livy resumed enforcing her daughters' morals as soon as she was up and about. Susie and Clara waited with anticipation for the highlight of their season—hay cutting. Livy agreed to allow them for the first time to ride in triumph on top of the hay wagon. Susie could not contain her excitement; it got the better of her, and in a fit of temper she hit Clara "with a shovel or stick or something of the sort." As was Livy's practice, she summoned Susie to discuss her transgression and to decide upon the appropriate punishment. Together they compiled a list of privileges, one of which would have to be forfeited. Livy asked her daughter, "Which one do you think it ought to be, Susie?" Susie chose to give up her planned ride on top of the world. She told her mother, "The other things might not make me remember not to do it again, but if I don't get to ride on the hay wagon I can remember it easily." In his autobiography Twain declared, "Susy's lost hay ride still brings *me* pang—after twenty-six years."

Susie's honesty—something Livy cultivated so deeply in her children—could wound. Livy asked if Susie had missed her during the birth of their new baby sister, for Susie had been ill and isolated from mother and baby for a few days. Whether out of jealousy or anger at separation from a mother she worshiped, Susie replied negatively. "I had Aunt Sue and Rosa with me all the time; and they talked; and Papa read to me a good deal—no, I did not miss you, Mamma." Clemens wrote that this truthful remark hurt his wife, "broke her heart a little." Livy realized she had asked for this sting of honesty from her insistence on truth from a child too young to temper it with consideration.

That summer Livy hired a housemaid, a young Irishwoman who would have been up the same day she gave birth if required of her. Katy Leary too was a native of Elmira, but from a background vastly different from Livy's. From a poor family, she had begun her life in service as a seamstress. Livy interviewed the seventeen-year-old woman in the downtown Langdon home. When Livy came through the library door in her white silk dress, Katy's first impression was, "She startled me with all her beauty—she was like an angel, almost." Katy's favorite word to describe Livy would always be "wonderful," for from the first "I felt like she was something from another world." Livy hired Katy because she was impressed by Katy's two requests—a room of her own and permission to attend Sunday mass.

The turning of the leaves signaled the return of Clemens, Susie, and Clara to Hartford. Livy and baby stayed on a bit longer that October at the farm. Ulysses S. Grant would visit Hartford October 16 to campaign for Garfield for president. All the houses and streets vied with each other in their decorations to greet the former general and president. The Clemens house sported flags on the balconies, along the Ombra and down to the street plus shields, signs of welcome, and even a set of armor. As elaborate as this sounds, Clemens, knowing Livy's sense of decorum, wrote her that he felt it necessary to draw the line at having a banner declaring " 'The Home of Mark Twain' in letters as big as your head."

Clemens admired Grant and agreed to speak at a Republican rally to be held October 26 at the Hartford opera house. More importantly, he basked in Grant's presence. After his imagined fiasco of the Whittier birthday dinner, it had been a banquet for Grant that gave him a comparable imagined triumph. The Army of the Tennessee had honored Grant in Chicago at a reunion the previous year, November 1879. Clemens was the last to speak before six hundred guests, or as he told Livy, he was to "hold the crowd." He finally rose to speak at two in the morning. His topic was a response to the toast of "the babies" because he believed responding to "the Ladies" was overdone.

> We haven't all had the good-fortune to be ladies; we haven't all been generals, or poets, or statesmen; but when the toast works down to the babies—*we stand on common ground—*

It was the same strategy he would use later in giving platform readings from *Huckleberry Finn*. "Some of you have been boys, some of you have had a good deal to do with boys"—getting his audience on a common ground.

The theme of his speech was that future leaders were now in their cradle as Grant once was with his toe in his mouth. It seemed that Mark Twain was again on the brink of irreverence. He paused, letting the silence spread and then delivered his punch. "And if the child is but the father of the man, there are mighty few *who will doubt that he succeeded!*"

Clemens triumphantly reported to Livy that he had made Grant laugh and that General Sherman, as one of the many who congratulated him for two hours after his speech, exclaimed, "I don't know how you do it!"

As with the Whittier dinner, other accounts did not match Clemens's perceptions of defeat or glory. His bolstered confidence did allow him to agree to another *Atlantic* speech the next month, this time in honor of Oliver Wendell Holmes's birthday. Both Livy and Howells read and approved his address. It did not contain the wit two years previously of his old miner and the literary impostors, but Clemens felt he had redeemed himself. For the Grant and Holmes festivities, Clemens was in control of his audience. That heady moment of power, he often told Livy, was worth any risk.

When Livy returned to Hartford, she resumed her lessons with Susie and Clara. She attributed Clara's quickness in reading English to her German studies. In addition, Susie began studying music and piano. Livy realized the house and new baby would not leave her adequate time to devote to the girls' education. She hired Lilly Foote, cousin of Lilly Warner, as governess, to become responsible for the girls' formal education but always with their mother's supervision.

As the end of the year approached, Clemens neared completion of *The Prince and the Pauper*. The publisher was expecting two tales to go into the book, the other one being *Adventures of Huckleberry Finn*. Livy said no, confirming Huck's role as an outcast and loner.

Clemens wrote his sister, "She says they're going into separate books, and that one of them is going to be elegantly gotten up, even if the elegance of it eats up the publisher's profits and mine too." He didn't know how prophetic Livy was. Her husband agreed with her decision. Clemens was actually relieved she wouldn't allow both stories in one book. One, obviously Huck's story, needed "two or three months' work on it yet."

Elisha Bliss, Clemens's publisher since *The Innocents Abroad*, had died in September. Despite the fact that Bliss gambled on publishing Clemens's first efforts at writing a book, Clemens looked back upon their relationship as "ten years of swindlings," for he was smarting from getting what he called "half profits" from *A Tramp Abroad*. Bliss's son Frank did not have the ambition Clemens desired and also suffered from poor health. Clemens needed a new publisher, so he chose James R. Osgood of Boston. Howells resigned from the *Atlantic* in order to write full-time and joined his friend with Osgood. Clemens's agreement with Osgood was a unique one that pointed toward his desire and ultimate decision to become his own publisher. Clemens would provide the money to publish the books and keep all profits but seven and a half percent which would go to Osgood for selling them.

That fall Clemens made his first investment in a contraption that would change his and Livy's lives forever. As with his agreement with Osgood, he was moving toward controlling the entire writing process, including publishing. A former typesetter himself, he had dreamed of a machine to eliminate the time consumed in setting type by hand. Publishing was ready for the automatic typesetter. Clemens was correct: whoever produced one would be wealthy. He just backed the wrong horse with its proverbial hearty appetite, but this time for money. Once he saw James W. Paige's machine at work in the Colt Arms Factory, he upped his initial investment from two to five thousand dollars. Livy backed her husband's convincing enthusiasm. Clemens, with perfect hindsight, said as he and Livy neared bankruptcy in 1891, "I was always taking little chances like that, and almost always losing by it, too."

As a measure of Clemens's business savy or just bad luck, the one invention he did not take stock in was the telephone. When an agent from Bell came knocking at the door, Clemens said, "I didn't want anything more to do with wildcat speculation." Livy insisted they have a telephone installed to summon the doctor if one of the girls became ill. Clemens agreed to have it if it was installed in a closet in the front hall. On the wall he kept a record of the noise on the line and how many times it rang and disturbed him although his study was on the third floor. Clemens liked to brag that it was the first phone in a private home in the world. That was probably an exaggeration, but just about the only other phone in Hartford was at the doctor's so the ringing of it couldn't have bothered him. He was just angry that he had refused to invest in a device that did make money. It its infancy the telephone could be troublesome. Sue Crane thought she was getting the doctor in Elmira but got the fire department instead, which made a much more colorful entrance than the physician would have. Clemens did have a line installed to the telegraph office for his convenience. "It is like adding a hundred servants to one's staff for a cent apiece for a week."

For the holiday season of 1880, Clemens and Livy could still afford to be generous. Livy fixed a minimum of fifty food baskets for rich and poor alike. Susie and Clara were old enough to participate in their mother's generosities. The girls and Patrick went out the day before Christmas and delivered baskets of food to the poor, each containing a turkey with canned goods of fruit and vegetables. The baskets Livy made up for their friends and neighbors Clemens and the girls delivered on Christmas morning. These were more elaborate, with the basic turkey but also with wine and candy and individual presents for members of each household that Livy had purchased in weeks of shopping. Livy shopped carefully and prided herself on giving gifts that people particularly wanted or needed.

The New Year of 1881 went down in the lore of the Clemens household as "The Three Days." Livy was tending Clara, who was suffering from croup, in her bedroom. Clara's bed was covered with blankets so a steamer could circulate moist air around her.

Livy left the room for a moment. When Rosa entered, she saw the blankets on fire from the alcohol lamp. She snatched Clara from the bed and threw the bedding out the window, suffering only a few burns to her hands. It was Jean's turn the next day. As she slept in her crib in the nursery, a spark from a log set her bed canopy on fire. The wet nurse, Julia, grabbed Jean from the crib. Rosa's calm again prevailed; she again tossed the burning bed-clothes out the window and again burned her hands. Only Susie was left on the third day for her trial by fire. As she intensely practiced her piano lessons in the schoolroom, she was unaware of a burning log that had fallen against the woodwork around the fireplace. This time the fire was extinguished not by Rosa, who had precious little unburned skin on her hands to spare, but by the barber who came to shave Clemens each day.

One of the burdens of success is that others want to be helped to attain it. Many came knocking at the Clemenses' door seeking aid. Livy felt she and her husband, because they had so much, should help others. She was taken with Karl Gerhardt, a young sculptor, and his wife. Hattie Gerhardt came to call one February morning to ask Clemens to see her husband's work and to pass judgment as to whether he had a serious talent. Although Clemens insisted he had no knowledge of art, she persisted, with persuasive talents Livy described as "young & charming & with quick intuitions." Livy and Clemens, along with the Warners and Clara Spaulding, went to view the seminude statue of the young wife and heard her tale of her husband's difficulty in trying to advance his art career while working full-time. The painter, J. Wells Champney, decided it would be a worthy project for Hartford to raise the money to send Gerhardt to study in Paris. Livy convinced her husband that to wait for Hartford would take too long: "Go privately & start the Gerhardts off to Paris, & say nothing about it to anyone else." Livy's attachment to the young couple came from identifying with the excitement of starting anew together with unlimited possibilities, as she and Clemens once had. She was touched by their devotion and happiness while living modestly with yearly expenses of only $350. It made the Gerhardts "seem like story book people." She envied the freshness of "these children" and their unknown future now that her life pattern was cast. "They are just the people to have experiences—" Gerhardt statues would one day stand in the Clemens house—busts of Livy and Clemens, statues of Eve and Mercury—but he never attained the notoriety that all hoped. In further tribute to their benefactress, the Gerhardts named their daughter Olivia.

In March the Clemenses paid twelve thousand dollars for a strip of land adjoining their property. When they saw a man cut down a tree on property separating theirs from another neighbor's, they inquired and found that a house was to be built there. That was too close for Livy and Clemens, so they purchased the lot from Mr. Chamberlain. Livy was "radiant" with the purchase although some suspected that Chamberlain had instigated the wood chopping to get them to pay such a sum for the land. Even Livy called Chamberlain the "most unreliable man in Hartford."

Workmen would enlarge the kitchen and front hall while the Clemenses were absent that summer. The driveway would be changed and ground "lowered" to bring "the house up into view." At last Livy could have her walls and ceilings decorated on the first floor. The Clemenses went to the cooler Connecticut shore and then on to Elmira. From Quarry Farm Livy wrote George Warner to see that her wishes concerning the decoration were being carried out in her absence.

Livy had wanted the prestigious Herbert Lawrence to decorate the house but since he would be out of the country, he suggested Louis Comfort Tiffany, son of the jeweler, who was part of the firm of interior decorators known as Associated Artists. The other members of the organization were Lockwood de Forest, Candace Thurber Wheeler, and Samuel Colman. The firm was known for their use of colored glass and metallic paints and designs inspired by nature with both Asian and American Indian or Oriental influences. Livy left specific instructions even if the decorators disagreed. She wanted the hall window removed; the decorators didn't. She feared the hall would be too dark in the winter without more light, and with good reason. The walls and ceilings were to be painted red and hand stenciled with a dark blue pattern. She chose silver stencils for the paneling. The fireplace had carved wood panels Lockwood de Forest imported from India with an opening above the mantel for a Tiffany stained-glass window called "Autumn." The drawing room contained silver stencils in East Indian designs in panels over the light pink walls. Their huge mirror from their Buffalo home was repainted to match the room. It would shortly have another function when it began to serve as a mirror for the girls to check their posture during dancing lessons.

Whether the decorations were Wheeler's nature patterns, Colman's Oriental motifs, de Forest's East Indian designs, or Tiffany's glass tiles, the house showed Livy's love of ordered finishing reflected in exquisite details. For a woman who took time to strive for perfection in all she did, she expected her house to personify this same quality. By modern standards all of this hand stenciling and ornate design on walls and ceilings compounded with patterned carpeting seems busy, but it is typical of the Victorian period and a reflection of Livy.

By August it was apparent the decoration would not be finished by their return. Livy informed Charley Webster, the husband of Clemens's niece Annie Moffett and a man who was increasingly responsible for their business affairs, to tell the decorators that she would personally see to the lower part of the house. Upon returning home on October 2, they again had to take up residence on the second floor as workmen and decorators occupied the first. While Clemens fumed at the inconvenience, Livy set to overseeing the completion of the decoration, what she called "the settling." She chose an imitation leather wallpaper of red and gold for the dining room. Clemens worried about her preoccupations: "I think my wife would be twice as strong as she is, but for this wearing and wearying slavery of house-keeping." Clemens began to wish the house would burn down so they could flee to the Sandwich Islands and "shut ourselves up in the healing solitudes of the crater of Haleakala and get a good rest; for the mails do not intrude there, nor yet the telephone and the telegraph."

The bill for these improvements, for a house only seven years old, inside and out, with new plumbing, heating and burglar alarms, came to somewhere around eighteen thousand dollars. Samuel and Olivia Clemens spent around one hundred thousand dollars that year of 1881 to improve and maintain their home and lifestyle. One hundred years later, an equivalent value would be about half a million dollars.

CHAPTER 14

"This is my work!"

The *Prince and the Pauper*, with its two hundred pen-and-ink illustrations and impressive binding, matched the plush interior of the newly redecorated Clemens home. In November Clemens traveled to Canada to secure his copyright on the book. On December 1, 1881 it was published in England, Canada, Germany, and the United States in time for the Christmas trade. It was dedicated "To those good-mannered and agreeable children, Susie and Clara Clemens," and Susie declared it her father's best. "The book is full of lovely charming ideas, and oh the language! It is *perfect*." Mrs. Fairbanks called it his masterpiece. Howells stressed "the strain of deep earnestness underlying his humor." This audience of eastern gentility, predominantly women and children, who would sit comfortably in the Clemens drawing room, he wanted and got. At Livy's suggestion, in her continued desire to have her writer-husband taken seriously, Clemens did not publish it anonymously as he once considered. Sales weren't as favorable as the good reviews and although Clemens said it didn't matter, because of the expense of publishing this "beautiful book," it did.

Clemens with this attempt to be a refined author might yet become a refined man at home in the drawing room as well as his billiard room. Livy found it as difficult to keep her husband's temper in check as she did her daughters'. When her daughters were adults, she admitted to them that she admired their ability to release their anger, even if she had punished them for it as children. Livy, too, felt storms rage within, but as the good Victorian wife she largely suppressed them to keep the family waters calm.

Coupled with his anger, Clemens could exhibit traits of monomania. Livy, if anyone, could control his sieges with reason, the same tactic that she used with her daughters. Early in 1882 Clemens became convinced that Whitelaw Reid, editor of the New York *Tribune*, had instigated a campaign against him. The two had not spoken for twelve years because Reid disliked what Clemens wanted—a good book review in advance of publication in order to boost sales. Howells's review of *The Prince and the Pauper* had already been assigned and eventually appeared, even without a byline, in the *Tribune* while Reid was abroad. By the time Clemens heard of Reid's displeasure at this biased journalism, Clemens exaggerated the incident in his own mind to a paranoid belief that the *Tribune* was "in a kind of crusade against me."

Clemens told Howells that since Reid returned from Europe the paper had engaged in "Almost *daily* insults, for two months on a stretch." Clemens relayed to his friend that he was set to make peace or war. With Clemens, preparing for war always came first. He intended to write an exposé, a biography of Reid "which the very devils & angels themselves would delight to read." Clemens, obsessed with his revenge for imagined insults, threw himself into the project by setting people to collect information in England and the United States. He dictated his vindictiveness for three hours to a stenographer. Livy, naturally, was "bitter against the whole thing."

Livy's level head prevailed. She urged her husband to make sure there were any attacks, let alone "almost daily." Clemens asked his already harassed business manager, Charles Webster, to go through newspaper files and send him a copy of every remark made in the *Tribune* about him for the last four months. Webster's search found precious little. One item was an unfavorable review of *The Prince and the Pauper* by an Englishman. Livy had been right. Clemens had gotten himself "into a sweat over so diminutive a provocation" and even admitted that he wasted three weeks.

Clemens magnified small irritants into large temper flares. He never could stand a barking dog, ticking, striking, or cuckooing clocks, shirts lacking a button, or his noisy telephone. On the closet wall beside the telephone he kept descriptions of noise on the line: "Artillery can be heard," "Thunder can be heard," "Artillery and thunder combined can be heard." Mark Twain once declared that swearing had a release to it not even known to prayer. Livy disliked his swearing and yet only had small, temporary successes in getting him to relinquish this form of prayer.

In his birthday letter to Livy from Canada, Clemens named his present for her. "Only three profane expressions have issued from my lips *or existed in my heart* (which is the *great* thing) since the event of the 8th of last August." He qualified this by saying those were waking hours; he still swore in his sleep. The more years Livy spent with her husband, the more she became accustomed to strong language. Her strongest expression was to "disapprove," which carried the power of an edict for Clemens. "In her mouth that word 'disapprove' was as blighting and withering and devastating as another person's damn."

Clemens's effort to conceal his profanity lasted longer than his other reforms. He was accustomed to shaving, dressing and swearing in the bathroom with the door shut, so Livy couldn't hear him. Once when the door was not closed, Livy heard his fine oaths as he threw a number of shirts missing buttons out the window. Katy Leary recalled that at times the lawn looked as if it were covered by snow from his dressing tantrums. When Clemens realized Livy had overheard him, he knew he had to face her. To her surprise she repeated his words. "There, now you know how it sounds." Her recital was so funny they both laughed. Clemens said "Livy, it would pain me to think that when I swear it sounds like that. You got the words right, Livy, but you don't know the tune."

As their daughters grew, Livy made efforts to get Clemens to swear where she thought they could not hear him. They heard and told him so. "We often listen over the balusters when you are in the hall, explaining things to George."

Susie related that her father used strong language to explain but "not nearly so strong as when he first married Mamma." While he prized Livy's request and approval above all, he could not totally give up swearing. If he had, she would have had nothing to admonish him for. After they had been married twenty-six years on his round-the-world lecture tour in 1896, Clemens "swore off" profanity again. When the lurching of the ship broke a glass in their room, Clemens threw the glass out the porthole. He then "released" his voice. Livy requested, "Don't reform any more. It is not an improvement." Livy could be as adamant and relentless as her husband on certain subjects—her hobby horse was his behavior. She insisted he restrain himself in language and deeds, which usually didn't work, when he was away or in polite company, both situations where she couldn't directly correct him. Bret Harte wasn't the only one she warned Clemens to guard his tongue around. There was George Washington Cable, Ulysses S. Grant, Joel Chandler Harris or just about anyone her husband met or knew. On another occasion she chided him, "How I wish that you were less ready to fight, and more ready to see other people's side of things."

Clemens could be like Huck and demand his conscience to "ease up" on him. The southern writer Grace King, who became Livy's friend in the 1880s, relates that Clemens told Livy "for Heaven's sake let up" when she overly protested his remarks to General Fairchild concerning President Cleveland at a dinner party.

In the spring of 1882, Clemens went south for six weeks. His plan was to journey down the Mississippi to New Orleans, then back upriver with Horace Bixby, the captain, who had taught Clemens the river as a cub pilot. He took Osgood and a secretary, Roswell Phelps, with him to expand his "Old Times on the Mississippi" into a book, *Life on the Mississippi*.

Livy missed her husband, but she was glad he was enjoying himself. She stayed busy with the house and children, and she handled his correspondence. "More than ever before I realize what a perfect nuisance your letters are to you" she wrote. She wished she had had him sign autograph cards before he left so he wouldn't be faced with that task when he returned.

Although her husband was experiencing a "whirlpool of hospitality," Clemens's absence meant a curtailment of entertaining. Livy was relieved she was not "whirled around" by the mental and monetary stresses of a house full of company. She found it "a pleasant change after the rush that we have been in—however I should like you to enjoy it with me." She increasingly questioned her role as hostess and felt bad because she did.

> This is my work, and I know that I do very wrong when I feel chafed by it, but how can I be right about it? Sometimes it seems as if the simple sight of people would drive me *mad*. I am all wrong; if I would simply accept the fact that this is my work and let other things go, I know I should not be so fretted; but I want so much to do other things to study and do things with the children and I cannot.

Knowing her husband's generosity, Livy wrote, "Don't be too ready & cordial to invite people to visit you. If we could give them a dinner or luncheon as they do you it would be well enough, but when people come they generally come for twenty-four hours. I have had such a time this winter that I do not feel as if I *could possibly* have such a run of company soon again."

Having never really left her childhood home, Livy could not share her husband's emotions on revisiting Hannibal. She regularly went to Elmira and had childhood friends in Hartford, but Clemens had not been back to the river in twenty-one years. The river town was a world as foreign to her as afternoon tea was to him when he first came to Elmira. His initial response to his journey was enthusiasm that dwindled in disillusionment and homesickness for his wife and daughters. The restless river had cut twenty years' worth of new shorelines, altering the points and landmarks he had memorized as a cub pilot under Bixby. Clemens recognized that time had also worn lines in the faces of Hannibal. He confided to Livy, "That world which I knew in its blooming youth is old and bowed and melancholy now; its soft cheeks are leathery and withered, the fire has gone out of its eyes, the spring from its steps." Time's small but endless modifications are more dramatic when you're not there to witness them. On May 21 he left St. Paul, Minnesota for the East. He wrote in his notebook, "In Hannibal the steamboat man is no longer the god." He returned to Hartford where, like Livy, he was anxious for "the peace and quiet of the farm."

Clara had a birthday party for sixty-seven children to celebrate her eighth birthday on June 8. One of the guests left more than just a present. Livy had everything packed and ready to go for their summer odyssey to Quarry Farm on June 22 when two-year-old Jean's hoarseness and rash was diagnosed as scarlet fever. A few days later Susie was delirious with a high fever. The house was quarantined; only the doctor was allowed to come and go. The family did not get to Quarry Farm until late in July where little Jean continued to suffer, this time with teething. The illnesses cut deeply into Clemens's work on *Life on the Mississippi*.

On returning to Hartford, Clemens labored night and day to finish the last thirty thousand words to complete the book. Another typical Christmas passed with Livy preparing her gift baskets. The tree was decorated, stockings hung, and the girls sent up early to bed on Christmas Eve for a wakeful night after Livy read them " 'Twas the Night Before Christmas." Livy's work had just begun with wrapping presents and putting them in the schoolroom. Wanting to peek, sleeping fitfully, by six in the morning the girls were up ringing for a nurse so they could dress and begin their Christmas. Each had her own table of presents that Livy had laid out. Presents could be much larger, such as when they received a piano. Livy and Clemens rose late, after the girls had gone through all of their gifts. Then callers began to arrive. Clemens often dressed as Santa Claus to greet guests and to hand out more presents.

Once the holiday obligations were out of the way, Clemens was ready to get *Life on the Mississippi* into print. He gave the book to Osgood to set in type in January 1883. Clemens hoped the book would sell a monumental one hundred thousand copies in a year, so he was anxious to get it into the hands of subscription salesmen. Clemens put Osgood in an impossible situation—he wanted the book rushed into print, but he wanted Osgood to abide by any changes Livy might make in the galley sheets.

Although Livy put everything aside in order to proof the typeset copy, her task was delayed by illness. The quarters of Patrick the coachman over the stable were quarantined as each of his seven children came down with scarlet fever. Livy herself took ill and was bedridden for several months with what Clemens called "a procession of diseases passing through her: first diphtheria, then a couple of days of peculiarly vindictive fever, then a week of quinsy; then several minor things, representing citizens on foot and in carriages whose technical names I have forgotten." As quinsy was a severe inflammation of the throat, Livy had no appetite and lost so much weight that Clemens told Howells she was "proportioned like the tongs." She also had difficulty sleeping and speaking. Clemens wanted to take her to Elmira to be nursed by Mrs. Langdon, but she refused to leave. She wrote her mother, "There is so much scarlet fever about that it makes me anxious about the children."

Osgood hurried and waited. By May he had forty thousand copies of *Life on the Mississippi* bound when he learned that Livy wanted two illustrations cut from the book. Both illustrations dealt with death—one was of Clemens being cremated beside an urn with the initials "M. T." The other illustration was of a corpse. Livy's judgment in taste was sound, but any changes meant delays and added expense.

While Clemens traveled to Canada in May to again secure his copyright, Livy stayed behind. Now Jean was old enough to disobey. Livy wrote her husband that Jean needed a "whipping, but I was too cowardly to give it to her." Clemens recalled later of Livy and her correcting the children: "They . . . knew that she never punished in revenge, but in love; and that the infliction wrung her mother-heart, and was a sore task for her. Let them bless her more for those punishments, whilst they live, than for her gifts; for she was born to give, and it cost her no pang; but to deal out penalties was against her nature; but she *did* deal them out, firmly and unflinchingly, for the great love she bore her children." Livy could report in her husband's absence that she and Susie were getting on well. While taking an afternoon ride, Susie said, "Mamma we can never disagree we think just alike about things, why Mamma we seem like *one* person." The ten-year-old recognized what most girls don't want to acknowledge at any age—similarities she held with her mother.

At Quarry Farm that summer Livy described her main occupations as reading to the children and making paper dolls. Clemens felt equally good about his occupations that summer as he worked on the story that had been ejected from his book on Tom Canty and Edward VI. "I am piling up manuscript in a really astonishing way. I believe I shall complete, in two months, a book which I have been fooling over for 7 years." The book was *Huckleberry Finn*, a true pauper destined to become the prince of American literature.

CHAPTER 15

"I love you, I idolize you and I miss you."

George Washington Cable arrived in February 1884 for reciprocal hospitality after he had hosted Clemens in New Orleans. Those who came to visit at 351 Farmington Avenue were so generously treated that they were sometimes reluctant to leave. This might have been the case with Cable when he became ill. Livy pampered his lingering sore throat until the Clemenses engaged a nurse for him. Thinking of how she would feel if it were her Youth, Livy wrote Cable's wife and mother every few days with an update on his condition. Too late they discovered he had mumps that were passed on to the three Clemens girls and even the nurse. Susie was very sick but by far a better patient in her father's opinion. She might have been thirteen times more ill but she didn't "make as much fuss in the 4 days as he used to make in 15 minutes; though she had shed barrels of noiseless tears." Clemens reported to Howells that Livy sat up with the little girl all night praying. Livy most certainly was praying for Susie's recovery, but perhaps also for strength to help her husband suppress his desire to laugh at or swear at his guest's aches and pains.

As angry as Clemens was with Cable's unwanted illness, their conversations had planted an idea. Cable had been passing through Hartford on a reading tour when he came to visit and to be sick. As much as Clemens hated the lecture circuit, perhaps journeying with another author would make it more palatable, and Clemens was in need of money.

He was disappointed with the sales of *Life on the Mississippi*. It had cost him fifty-six thousand dollars to get the book into print. By December 1883 he blamed Osgood when he discovered that the American Publishing Company had sold as many old books as Osgood had new ones. These losses pushed him in a direction he had been heading for years—to be his own publisher. In the spring of 1884 Clemens created Charles L. Webster and Company.

The thirty-one-year-old Webster was married to Annie, the daughter of Clemens's sister Pamela. He had already been Clemens's business manager for three years. Perhaps because Webster was a relative, Clemens and Livy put so many tasks onto him. Before there was such a thing, Webster had a stress-related job that led to his breakdown in 1887. His duties could range from engaging a plumber to the publishing of a book or measuring a drawer in New York to see if it would fit in Aunt Livy's dresser or buying her birthday and anniversary presents from Uncle Sam. Details that could obsess Livy and did possess her husband, they asked Charley Webster to manage. Even Livy, who always considered others before herself, didn't seem to realize that Charley did not need yet another task to perform. Letters to Webster from Uncle Sam and Aunt Livy are all in the imperative—Send, Write, Do, Accept, Look, Bring, Show, Find, Buy, Sell, Order, with "Thank you" the rarest word of all. Livy did have Clemens, at one point, tell Webster to relax because overwork had killed her father.

What Clemens needed was a clone of himself who could manage all his enterprises exactly as he would. He gave Webster the responsibility of being Mark Twain's publisher and negotiating his works away from Osgood in addition to preparing to get *Huck Finn*, the first book of the Webster Publishing Company, into type. Again, Clemens hoped it would make up for some of the losses of his previous books. "Keep it diligently in mind that we don't issue till we have made a *big sale*," he instructed Webster. He hoped to have the book ready for the Christmas trade, "but if we haven't forty thousand orders then, we simply postpone publishing till we've *got* them."

That summer at Quarry Farm as Clemens prepared for his reading tour with Cable, Livy began editing *Huckleberry Finn*. In Susie's biography of her father that she began when she was thirteen years old, she recorded her mother's contribution.

> Papa read *Huckleberry Finn* to us in manuscript, just before it came out, and then he would leave part of it with Mama to expergate [sic], while he went off to the study to work, and sometimes Clara and I would be sitting with Mama while she was looking the manuscript over, and I remember so well, with what pangs of regret we used to see her turn down the leaves of the pages, which meant that some delightfully terrible part must be scratched out. And I remember one part perticularly [sic] which was perfectly fascinating it was so terrible, that Clara and I used to delight in and oh with what despair we saw Mama turn down the leaf on which it was written, we thought the book would almost be ruined without it. But we gradually came to think as Mama did.

Twain recalled the same incident.

> . . . it is possible that especially dreadful one which gave those little people so much delight was cunningly devised and put into the book for just that function, and not with any hope of expectation that it would get by the expurgator alive. It is possible, for I had that custom.

He further admitted in his *Autobiography*:

> For my own entertainment and to enjoy the protests of the children, I often abused my editor's innocent confidence. I often interlarded remarks of a studied and felicitously atrocious character purposely to achieve the children's brief delight, and then see the remorseless pencil do its fatal work. I often joined my supplications to the children's for mercy and strung the argument out and pretended to be in earnest. They were deceived and so was their mother. It was three against one and most unfair. But it was very delightful and I could not resist the temptation. Now and then we gained victory and there was much

rejoicing. Then I privately struck out the passage myself. It had served its purpose. It had furnished three of us with good entertainment, and in being removed from the book by me it was only suffering the fate originally intended for it.

Livy knew her husband well enough to participate in this fun. His writing to shock was part of the game he played with the family, and all seemed to enjoy it. Although these passages refer to *Huckleberry Finn*, we can assume that other manuscripts served the same purposes and experienced the same fate. Clemens liked to present Livy as shocked at what he wrote, as well as shocked at his behavior. If his smoking, drinking, swearing ceased to astonish her, why should his writing? Livy allowed herself to be surprised because her husband desired it, but she conscientiously read his manuscripts with suggestions for improvement. Only a woman of great perception and intelligence could sustain both these editorial positions out of love for her husband. Clara recognized, as an adult, her mother's valuable role in Mark Twain's creative processes. "The healthy guide of constructive criticism is as necessary to an artist, however great he may be, as the nourishing administration of applause. And Mother was able to fill both capacities."

But Mark Twain was his own man. He followed his wife's advice but he never changed anything in his writing, not even a comma, if he didn't want to. Conversely, he could even be more conservative in print than his wife. Livy had read the manuscript of Huck's buddy, Tom Sawyer. Even after Livy's reading, Twain wanted further editing and submitted it to Howells. Howells objected to two scenes that Livy had passed. Howells felt the description of the dog running down the aisle "with his tail shut down like a hasp" to be somewhat "dirty." He also disliked the scene in which Becky looks at the forbidden medical book, so Twain altered it. But after two editors, Clemens was bothered about a section. He wrote Howells:

When Huck is complaining to Tom of the rigorous system in vogue at the widow's, he says the servants harass him with all manner of compulsory decencies, & he winds up by saying, "and they comb me all to hell."

He further told Howells that not only did Livy let "hell" pass, but also Livy's aunt and mother who were "both sensitive & loyal subjects of the kingdom of heaven, so to speak." Howells missed it too. Clemens knew it was there and eventually wrote the passage to read "they comb me all to thunder." Although it passed four approvals, Twain changed it because "that dern word bothers me some nights."

As her husband's editor, Livy protected his credibility as a writer by acting as a judge of the material his audience would prefer. She kept him from publishing certain things that she felt might harm his reputation. Clemens described her editorial capacity:

> Ever since we have been married, I have been dependent on my wife to go over and revise my manuscript. . . . Not but that I can do the spelling and grammar alone—if I have a spelling-book and a grammar with me—but I don't always know just where to draw the line in matters of taste. Mrs. Clemens has kept a lot of things from getting into print that might have given me a reputation I wouldn't care to have, and that I wouldn't have known any better than to have published.

Livy kept out of print much of his black humor concerned with death and offensive smells. She was a careful observer of the taste of her times, and she knew what the reading audience would and wouldn't accept.

If Livy were a prude and would object to any of her husband's books, it would be *Huck Finn*. It is far from *The Prince and the Pauper*. Huck is not refined, but uncouth in manners and language. The villains are worse, and the book is violent. As a wife and editor, she recognized her husband's talent and this book's value. Livy was in fact, in her husband's words, fond of "dear old Huck," for she saw beneath Huck's rough exterior to his "sound heart."

Her editorial changes were not so much concerned with decorum as with word usage or accurate details. As always, the author made the ultimate decision. In the margin of Twain's chapter on "The Royal Nonesuch," Livy wrote the word "scandalous." The

word "stark" preceding "naked" was eliminated. Huck's description ultimately read: "The king came a-prancing out on all fours,
naked; and he was painted all over, ring-streaked-and-striped . . .
but never mind the rest of his outfit, it was just wild, but it was
awful funny." Livy knew what was going on; if she disliked the
scene, Twain obviously wanted it to appear as it did.

Livy considered editing her husband's manuscripts, making
suggestions for stories and his platform presentations, to be part
of her "work." If Clemens did not want her advice, he told her
so. When he spoke of writing his autobiography in the home of
Mr. and Mrs. James T. Fields, Mrs. Fields recalled that Livy "laugh-
ingly said she should look it over and leave out any objectionable
passages." Clemens responded as Mrs. Fields remembered,
" 'No,' he said, very earnestly, almost sternly, 'you are not to edit
it—it is to appear as it is written, with the whole tale told as truly
as I can tell it.' "

In addition to her household tasks, what Livy did not finish
editing in the day, she did in the evening. Katy Leary's recollection
was that Clemens would often leave pages by his wife's bedside
for her to read. "I think she read everything as fast as he wrote
it—"

Livy also influenced Mark Twain's writing by serving as a model
and providing incidents for him to narrate. His stories on the
McWilliamses and their difficulties with burglar alarms, membra-
nous croup, and lightning come from their own experiences in
their Hartford home. His unfinished manuscript about David and
Susan Gridley, written after Livy's death, is a thinly disguised
portrait of their relationship. He described Susan Gridley (Livy):

> In Susan Gridley's make and character there were no flaws. She
> was educated, utterly refined, scrupulously high principled,
> deeply genuine to the marrow, deeply religious; she had none
> but high ideals, it was not within the possibilities of her nature
> to entertain a low one. She was firm and strong, she was as
> steadfast, as faithful, as trustworthy as the sun and the atmo-
> sphere and the fixed stars; she was fastidiously truthful, she was
> cautious and deliberate about making promises, but a promise

once made, she would go to the stake rather than break it even the outside edge of it; she was delicate in her feelings, modestly shrinking, but when courage was required to back principle, she had it. She was just and fair in her judgments, leaning—if at all—to the generous side always; she was loving and lovable, and although she did not open her heart to everyone, or indeed to very many, whosoever entered it was its guest forever, and content to stay.

When Clemens was on his reading tour, Livy wrote him, "I have been reading a good deal in your books . . . and I have found three or four things which might be good to read, at any rate if you have not enough you can try them if they appeal to you." After being in his audience, she recommended parts from *The Prince and the Pauper*, the lost sock chapter from *A Tramp Abroad*, and also from it, "The Blue Jay Yarn," and selections of his difficulty with German. Clemens's reading tour with Cable began on November 5 in New Haven and was to continue on into February 1885.

On the surface, a reading tour, as opposed to a lecture, seemed easier to Clemens. He soon realized he had to memorize his material as he had with the lecture, but yet appear to be just telling a story. With much rehearsal, study, and given his natural storytelling abilities, he chose humorous selections but also those with literary value. He included portions from *Huckleberrry Finn* to encourage sales. Livy approved: "I am delighted the new selections of *Huckleberry Finn* went well." Money was not the main reason his creator brought Huck onstage with him. In Mark Twain's great affinity for this work and this character, he would always include Huck in his platform recitations.

Livy's "tour" was in Hartford with her usual audience of children, servants, and friends. She placed Susie in West Middle School despite her husband's protests. Clemens felt because he could afford it, he wanted his daughters educated at home with tutors. His own limited education could be called "private" in the sense that he described it as "twenty-five cents per week per pupil and collect it if you can." Livy preferred for all three daughters to attend a public high school. As a young girl before her paralyzing back injury, Livy had only a few years of public education in the Elmira Seminary. She wanted to give them the opportunity that she had missed of making friends their own age and being with others besides their own family. Ultimately Livy and her husband would compromise by deciding that the girls could have lessons at home and at public school until business problems changed all their plans.

Livy wrote her husband, "Life is not so interesting with you away—" After fifteen years of marriage, they still missed each other acutely when separated. "You & the children have been in my mind all the day, & I have been very homesick & still am," he responded. Livy's letters to the absent Clemens were the same tenor as when she was a young engaged woman missing her fiancé away on his speaking engagements. "You cannot be gone one day after the time your contract calls for, so remember that," she wrote and underlined while also reminding him to eat sensibly and curb his temper toward Cable.

Clemens missed Livy's birthday, but he sent her a diamond solitaire ring from Tiffany's purchased by Webster amid his other duties. Livy lovingly declared, "It is certainly a beauty and I shall wear it constantly with my wedding ring."

Occupied with the house, children, paying the bills, taking care of her husband's business correspondence, she wrote him, "I love you but I can only send you this line today there are so many things waiting to be done." German lessons continued as part of the daily routine of the Clemens household. Susie was memorizing and reciting Tennyson, as Clara was doing with Aesop's fables. With Livy's further encouragement, Clara began violin lessons in addition to the piano.

Livy's main project that fall of 1884 was one that eluded Clemens—a successful dramatization of *The Prince and the Pauper*. Clemens long lusted after a worldly stage adaptation of one of his works that would make money. Livy was only interested in surprising her husband when he was home for the Christmas holidays. The Gerhardts had returned from Paris and participated in the painting of scenery and the making of costumes. Susie wrote that even little Jean was involved by keeping their father busy as they packed costumes for a dress rehearsal at the Warners, but Jean couldn't help dropping hints and saying, "It's a secret papa." The next evening at the Warners, Clemens sat in the front row where he saw Margaret "Daisy" Warner as Tom Canty and Clara as Lady Jane Grey. The scene stealer of the show was Susie as the Prince with her immortal lines: "Fathers be alike mayhap; mine hath not a doll's temper." It brought down the house.

Clemens recalled, "It was a charming surprise, and to me, a moving one. . . . This lovely surprise was my wife's work." Clemens liked it so much that the play was repeated again after Christmas. When Frank Warner had to leave his role, Clemens immediately took over as Miles Hendon. The play was presented for the entire neighborhood in the Clemens library with the conservatory playing the role of Palace Garden and English countryside. Susie recorded the historical event.

> Papa acted his part beautifully. . . . He was inexpressibly funny, with his great slouch hat and gait—oh, such a gait! Papa made the Miles Hendon scene a splendid success and every one was delighted with the scene and papa too. We had great fun with our "Prince and Pauper," and I think we none of us shall forget how immensely funny papa was in it. He certainly could have been an actor as well as an author.

Jean was only three and too young for a part, but as her father described it, "She produced the whole piece every day independently and played all the parts herself." Susie, who like her mother could be easily frightened, was a trooper of an actress. When her coronation throne tipped backward into the conservatory, she went on, not missing a line while the audience jumped at the crash. The play was produced a number of times in the Clemens home for guests and even the author remarked, "As *we* played the piece it had several superiorities over the play as presented on the public stage in England and America, for we always had both the prince and the pauper on deck, whereas these parts were always doubled on the public stage."

Again the Prince and the Pauper were fair-haired boys while Huck remained a problem child. Clemens had hoped to have the book ready for the Christmas trade. He had chosen E. W. Kemble as the illustrator and vetoed Kemble's earliest impressions of Huck as "ugly." Other illustrations that passed Livy's eye, Clemens turned down as "too violent," but he couldn't control everything.

Sam Clemens as an apprentice typesetter in Hannibal was not above a practical joke. In his autobiography he relates how as a young man, he and another typesetter were chastised for putting "J. C." rather than Jesus Christ in setting up the text of a sermon. They were told by the editor, " 'So long as you live, don't you ever diminish the Savior's name again. Put it *all* in.' " Mark Twain related that his fellow typesetter then promptly changed the abbreviation to "Jesus H. Christ." Knowing both Clemens and his nemesis Twain, he certainly had a larger part in this incident than that of observing bystander.

Now it seemed that this lighthearted gesture and many others had caught up with him. An engraver, who still remains anonymous, working on the Kemble illustrations, added an erect penis to an illustration of Silas Phelps. Aunt Sally's words in the caption "Who do you reckon it is?" sent Clemens into shock. It made Livy "sick." It postponed publication of *Huckleberry Finn* until February, missing the Christmas trade that Clemens so coveted. Silas's conspicuous manhood was discovered only after the canvassers' copies had been published. Had it gone unnoticed, Mark Twain would have been ruined morally and Samuel Clemens financially.

To vindicate Huck and Twain, the book did well despite attacks of coarseness against it and being banned from the Concord, Massachusetts Library. Livy and Howells stopped Clemens from attacking the Concord Library in the novel's defense. By March of 1885 the novel, out for one month, had sold forty-two thousand copies, reaching Clemens's goal of forty thousand before its release. Huck, the self-reliant American of the Mississippi Valley, has taken care of himself ever since. It is estimated that worldwide the novel has probably sold twenty million copies, with as many as sixty foreign editions.

Following the Christmas holidays, Clemens went back out on the road to finish his tour with Cable. By January he felt oppressed with the tour and outraged with Cable. By mid-February, Clemens called him "the pitifullest human louse I have ever known" to Livy, even when he knew she would scold him for saying so. Tight and cheap when it came to his own money, but extravagant with others' funds, Cable even mooched paper from Clemens when there was none in their lodgings. Cable ate heartily when he didn't have to pay for it, but ate nothing and complained when he was forced to pick up the tab. It further aggravated Clemens that Cable observed the Sabbath so resolutely that he left receptions at midnight Saturday night. Cable refused to do the simplest tasks on Sunday, reserving his time to visit church after church and trying to read the Bible aloud to his fellow platform performer. Clemens wrote Howells, "He has taught me to abhor & detest the Sabbath-day & to hunt up new & troublesome ways to dishonor it." Livy, a product of regular church and Sunday school attendance, reminded her husband, "Sunday is good in spite of his bad use of it."

All bad things come to an end too. Clemens returned home to concentrate on another publishing venture—the memoirs of General Ulysses S. Grant, although Clemens stated in his autobiography, "It had never been my intention to publish anybody's books but my own." Clemens had proposed to Grant in 1881 that he write of his experiences. "He had declined at the time, and most decidedly, saying he was not in need of money and that he was not a literary person and could not write the memoirs."

By chance Clemens and Livy overheard someone say that Grant intended to publish his autobiography. It was now 1884 and Grant needed the money. Clemens, whose admiration had not dimmed for the former president, approached the general again. He wanted the book so badly he offered Grant his choice of 20 percent gross royalty or 70 percent net profits despite Livy's trying to discourage her husband, because she thought the project too risky. Grant was considering another publisher when Clemens convinced him that since he had first proposed the idea to him, it was only fair he be allowed to publish the book. Mortally ill, Grant struggled to finish his memoirs before he died of throat cancer on July 23, 1885. For Clemens, it always remained a great matter of pride that he published the Grant book. The two-volume set would sell three hundred thousand copies. Clemens presented Grant's widow with the largest royalty check ever paid for that time—two hundred thousand dollars. She eventually made much more, as Clemens related: "It is no great marvel to me that Mrs. Grant got a matter of half a million dollars out of that book."

Clemens was euphoric with his two publishing triumphs. Livy feared he was so involved with the publishing company that he would give up what got him into the business—his writing. He postponed a reading trip to England and Australia, saying he wouldn't go without his family, and Livy wouldn't take the girls out of school. In reality, he had no desire to go with such success at home.

The writing he did at Quarry Farm the summer of 1885 was about his wife.

> In all my life I have never made a single reference to my wife in print before, as far as I can remember, except once in the dedication of a book; and so, after these fifteen years of silence, perhaps I may unseal my lips this one time without impropriety or indelicacy. I will institute one other novelty: I will send this manuscript to the press without her knowledge and without asking her to edit it. This will save it from getting edited into the stove.

Susy[1] called it "a beautiful tribute to mamma and every word in it true." When the *Christian Union* arrived at Quarry Farm, the girls, who had served as their father's editor for this piece, could hardly contain their excitement. Finally, Clemens "told Clara and I we could take it to her, which we did with tardiness, and we all

[1]In an expression of adolescent independence, Susy had changed the spelling of her name.

stood around mama while she read it, all wondering what she would say and think about it." Clemens's article was on a topic that Livy took most seriously and sensitively, her relationship with her children and disciplining them. Intensely protective of her privacy, she was not happy, as Clemens suspected she might not be. Her husband's glowing testimonial calling her "the best and dearest mother that lives" with children who "worship" her was not something Livy wanted strangers to know. Susy described it: "When she remembered that this article was to be read by every-one . . . she was rather shocked and a little displeased." Her displeasure grew when they began to receive letters on the article, and soon Clemens wished he had never written it.

Even if Clemens was not doing a lot of writing, Susy was not the only member of the family putting her thoughts on paper. Livy began a journal in June 1885, her first since her commonplace book as a girl. In a visitor's book that she usually forgot to ask people to sign, she wrote that she would "try to make some use of it." She recorded Clara's eleventh birthday celebration on the Ombra after the little girl was allowed to leave her lessons half an hour early. She called her daughters "blessed children and tremendous comforts" and wondered, as fortunate parents do, how they had turned out so well. "There is much satisfaction in doing anything for Susy and Clara they are so grateful for every thing that is done for them, and express it so earnestly. It seems almost strange when they have always had so much done for them."

School examinations took place in the schoolroom under the supervision of Miss Foote with Mrs. George Warner, Daisy, Miss Price, and Miss Corey in attendance. Susy and Clara were examined in arithmetic and United States and world history. Susy, as the older, also had questions to answer on geography and Latin. Livy felt Susy gave a "brilliant recitation in Ancient History." For nearly an hour Susy spoke on ancient civilizations. What pleased Livy most were Susy's personal interpretations that sometimes deviated from the text but showed Susy's original thought. Livy wrote of Susy's recitation, "Occasionally she would say, well Miss Foote, the book says so and so, but it seems to me in this way, stating something quite different." Livy was "well satisfied" with what her daughters had accomplished in their school year.

The school year completed, all could begin the laborious tasks of putting the Hartford house in storage and packing for Quarry Farm. On their last night in Hartford, the Clemenses attended one of Mrs. Colt's smaller dinner parties—only two hundred guests.

Livy maintained a schedule at Quarry Farm even if it was the summer holiday. Lessons continued. Livy spent one hour each with Jean and Susy every morning reading German. She passed another hour reading English history with Clara and Susy because, as Susy said, "We hope to go to England next summer." After lunch, mother and daughters spent another hour reading in the afternoon. That summer Livy started to teach Jean about insects with the dilemma of showing them to the child without killing them. A grasshopper jumped around when captured in a glass and made it difficult for the youngest Clemens to see all of its parts. Livy wrote, "I did not want her to kill it, because I cannot get away from the feeling that it must greatly blunt a child's sensibility to allow it to kill the little creatures." They had to be content with ladybugs, which were not very mobile, and some dead flies that Jean found in her room. Jean in her enthusiasm collected a plateful of dead flies to show her mother at supper.

It was not all hard work—the children played with a new resident at the farm, a donkey. Livy described the new pet: "She seems a docile beast, the children have caught her in the field, bridled her and mounted her alone, but when they would ride their father went with them. We hope the donkey has no bad tricks that will in any way frighten or inconvenience the children. They have named her Patience Cadichon, pronouncing it Kaditchin." Riding the donkey was such a treat that Clara had to write herself a note and place it in her Bible not to be selfish about it because "Jean enjoys it just about as much."

There was a picnic and fireworks on the Fourth. The Cranes and Clemenses all celebrated with the usual decorated table of presents for Jean's fifth birthday in July and Mrs. Langdon's seventy-fifth birthday in August. Clemens, who was in New York seeing to the publication of the Grant book, telegraphed his daughter sixty-five happy returns. The gesture made Livy ponder, "Where shall we all be at that time in 1950?"

The generous Mrs. Langdon always gave more birthday gifts than she received. Livy recounted her frustration at trying to surprise her mother, "It seemed almost useless to prepare anything for Mother, for she does so much for us, it seems wrong for her to give us gifts on her birthday besides doing so on ours—but it is her pleasure so I suppose we must all be content." Mrs. Langdon gave each of her children a check for one hundred dollars, plus fifty dollars for each grandchild along with a teapot, sugar, and creamer for Livy. For Jean's birthday, Grandma Langdon gave her "a heavy silver spoon" to add to her collection. It was always Mrs. Langdon's gift-giving practice to help her granddaughters build their silver and china sets, looking forward to the day they would marry.

"It is terrible!" Livy wrote when she heard of the death of an old friend of her parents', Mrs. Henry Sage. "She was such a lovely woman, and seemed like a woman that ought to have a long life." Mrs. Sage was killed when a runaway carriage tipped over. Livy sadly closed her account for July 12 with the words, "I cannot help wondering if she will see father and tell him about us."

The idyllic summer of Quarry Farm always came to an end too quickly. But when the sound of cicadas hummed through the hills, Livy knew it was time to return to Hartford. "This afternoon as I lay on the bed feeling rather depressed at the thought of leaving Mother and Sue and the friends here and a little tired from the packing &c Susy came to my bed side bringing a little bag that she had filled with articles to amuse Jean on the journey." Livy chided herself, "While I lay on the bed mourning she was doing something for the pleasure of someone else."

They returned to Hartford on September 18. The girls were soon back at their lessons, and the social whirl began accelerating. Livy wrote her last entry in her journal that she did not take up again until 1892. It began as midlife does—no remorse or reprimands, a few regrets, but primarily just a response: "My birthday, forty years old today."

CHAPTER 16

*"I wish there was no one in this world troubled for
money."*

"I am frightened at the proportions of my prosperity. It seems
to me that whatever I touch turns to gold," Clemens gloated
at the opening of 1886 over the success of the Grant book.
Livy and Susy feared not prosperity, but that Clemens would give
up writing entirely in favor of his business ventures.

Clemens had already proclaimed that he would write only one
more book, having, as he told Susy, "written more than he had
ever expected to." *A Connecticut Yankee in King Arthur's Court* owed
its initial conception to George Washington Cable, who had introduced Clemens to Malory's *Morte d'Arthur*, but it owed its continuing inspiration to Clemens's longstanding fascination and
eventual irritation with gadgetry. Hank Morgan, the nineteenth-
century "Boss" from the Colt arms factory, finds himself back in
sixth-century Arthurian England and proceeds to improve the society with all the contraptions that Clemens admonished yet
adored: lightning rods, telephones and telegraphs, typewriters,
printing presses, bicycles, railroads, photographs, steamships,
and sewing machines.

Clemens worked on the story in February when "Clara's case
keeps us all shut up in the house, these days." Her illness, croup
again, meant the house and his time were not preoccupied by

guests and social functions, but he was easily distracted by his publishing firm. By November the same year he told Mrs. Fairbanks,

> Only two or three chapters of the book have been written, thus far. I expect to write three chapters a year for thirty years; then the book will be done. I am writing for posterity only; my posterity: my great grandchildren. It is to be my holiday amusement for six days every summer the rest of my life. Of course I do not expect to publish it; nor indeed any other book—though I fully expect to write one other book besides this one; two others, in fact if one's autobiography may be called a book—in fact mine will be nearer a library.

At fifty years old, Clemens had learned that writing was a lonely profession and never as lucrative as he would have liked. Society might honor words and books, but it always glorified business success. With the confidence of his Midas touch, Clemens reached toward two projects that he thought would free him from writing— the Paige typesetter and the biography of Pope Leo XIII.

On the third floor of the Hartford house in the billiard room where he worked sporadically on Hank Morgan's designs of progress, Clemens met again with James W. Paige and the lawyer William Hammersly in January 1886. Clemens had already invested thirteen thousand dollars since 1881 in Paige's invention and was now prepared to start investing more in order to not only manufacture but sell the typesetters. Clemens was as enchanted with Paige as he was his machine: "He is a poet; a most great and genuine poet, whose sublime creations are written in steel." In 1881 Clemens had described the machine as "almost a complete compositor; it lacked but one feature that a human being was still required to do—it did not 'justify' the lines." That January, Paige asked for more money to "perfect" his contraption, so it would be a complete compositor—justify as well as set type. Clemens agreed to no more than thirty thousand dollars.

It was a scenario that evolved into a tragedy over the years. It went like this: The perfectionist Paige wanted more money to make the typesetter work even better. The earnest Clemens, convinced it would be the last monetary infusion, would sign another check, certain the machine would soon repay with vast wealth. The machine was in pieces more than it set type over the years as Paige labored, and Clemens paid for yet another adjustment. When it did operate, it was amazing. It took the place of six men setting and justifying type. Clemens called it a "cunning devil, knowing more than any man that ever lived." But it didn't know how to stop its inventor tinkering with it. The Mergenthaler Company's machines might not have run as well as the never-perfected Paige machines, but they did run reliably.

For Clemens and Livy to give up on Paige and his machine at any point would have been an admission that they had squandered their monetary and spiritual investments. They poured nearly three to four thousand dollars a month into what Clemens aptly named "the eternal machine." What the Clemenses needed was not a typesetter but a press to print money, as Paige's contraption eventually gulped down over one hundred thousand dollars until they declared bankruptcy in 1894.

Friend and business advisor F. G. Whitmore warned Clemens that the project would bankrupt him when Paige asked for money to start over from scratch and build a typesetter with a justifier in 1886. Livy, who had initially been against the successful Grant project, now supported her husband's judgment and enthusiasm. If she had protested, it wouldn't have mattered. Clemens was flush with the success of his publishing company and was ready to use the money he had made to make more.

Livy wished to buy some new furniture. She desired a particular sofa, but deemed it too expensive because "there is so much need of money in all our business both in New York and in Elmira." Since December, Clemens had worked to secure the publication rights of the authorized biography of Pope Leo XIII by Father Bernard O'Reilly. In April, Livy asked Charles Webster, "I want to bother you a little about some of my affairs." She asked him to go to Burghart's, the furniture purveyors in New York, to look at the sofa with the instructions to ask Burghart to hold it for her. If the contract for the pope's book was signed, then order it, if not, write her and she would use her birthday money from her mother to buy it. By May 1886 Clemens confidentially told his wife, "You can order 1000 such sofas now, if you want to—the future bank account will foot the bill & never miss it. The Pope's book is ours, & We'll sell a fleet load of copies."

Her husband's words gave Livy the confidence to later send Charley back to look at a bureau with drawers longer than nineteen inches and less than forty dollars. It took several letters to the harassed Webster and several visits with his measuring stick to get the bureau shipped by Christmas. Just as with his Uncle Sam, he had to negotiate for his Aunt Livy. She wrote, "I bought a few weeks ago a pair of shovels and tongs of Mr. Burghart, and they proved to be entirely *worthless*. I can't pick up a piece of wood with them without their bending. Perhaps he would take these back or let you have the bureau somewhat cheaper on account of them."

Clemens was buoyant that the pope's biography would be more successful than Grant's *Memoirs*. In Clemens's words, the pope was "head of two or three hundred millions of subjects, whose empire girdles the globe, & whose commands find obedience somewhere in all the lands & among all the peoples of the earth." His grandiose estimates of book profits came from his assumption that these Catholic subjects would feel obligated to buy the biography from Webster and Company. Clemens sent Webster with a leather-bound, gold-lettered presentation copy of Grant's *Memoirs* as a gift to a private audience with the pope in July. The grandeur of the audience with Webster arriving in a carriage with uniformed footmen made Livy exclaim, "Ah, why didn't we go, too!"

That summer she and the family had to make do with a trip, not to the Vatican, but to visit with Jane Clemens living with Orion and Mollie in Keokuk, Iowa. Grandma Clemens, a woman who had been physically and spiritually strong all her life, was increasingly frail at eighty-three. Jervis Langdon's death had left several scars on Livy. Because she was at her father's deathbed, she feared that she or others in her family might not be near their loved ones at death and that a family member would die without seeing those close to him or her. Livy pressed for the trip so that the woman could see, possibly for the last time, her son and granddaughters, especially her namesake, little Jean. The whole family traveled by steamer from Buffalo through the Great Lakes as Clemens believed it would be a cooler route. At St. Paul they took a steamboat down the Mississippi to Keokuk where they heard the leadsman call out "Mark Twain!" Clara reacted by telling her father, "Papa, I have hunted all over the boat for you. Don't you know they are calling for you?"

The Clemenses may have tried to take a cooler voyage, but no one can bypass the sauna that is the Midwest in the summer. The baking sun and steaming humidity from the river saturated the flat flood plain and made daily activities unbearable. Livy was prostrate from the oppressive heat, and Clemens was left to entertain his daughters. "Did you ever try to amuse three little girls at the same time? It requires real genius."

After all Livy's and Susy's worries about Clemens not writing, Keokuk did become the site of a literary loss. Sadly it was there Susy stopped writing her biography of her father.

Quarry Farm proved a cool relief after what Clemens called the "hell-sweltering weather in Keokuk." As Livy once remarked, "The summer time goes so quickly" at Quarry Farm, and they were all soon back in Hartford. With fall, the girls resumed their school and music lessons. Susy, now fifteen, was moving close to her entrance into society, so she added dancing lessons to her regimen. Lessons at Riley's Dancing Academy included etiquette on how proper young ladies dance with proper young gentlemen. Susy and Clara continued other disciplines that were part of living in a polite society. They belonged to an embroidery club.

Fall and winter activities occupied the adults in the house on Farmington Avenue. Clemens became a reader to the Browning class started by Livy, Susan, and Lilly Warner, plus "a New Haven lady & a Farmington lady." The society met on Wednesday mornings in his billiard room. Clemens spent several days in preparation for each meeting, memorizing poetry and preparing for the literary discussion. The reading was the only topic on the agenda, as conversation on lesser topics was forbidden. Browning had long been a favorite of Livy's, and talking about her reading remained her favorite pastime. Livy wrote her mother, "We do have such good times." Clemens felt the society to be a challenge and privilege. Proudly he told Mrs. Fairbanks, "Folks ask permission to come,—as if it were a privilege. When you consider that these folk, & the class, are women who are away above the intellectual average, it is no nickel-plated compliment for the poet."

As with Jane Clemens, age was taking its toll on Olivia Lewis Langdon. At seventy-six, her health was precarious and during her holiday visit, she needed care nearly round the clock. Cherished even more for her fragility by her daughter, son-in-law, and granddaughters, Mrs. Langdon returned to Elmira, leaving Susy to symbolically remark, "The fire has gone out in Grandmama's room." Livy echoed her thoughts: "We all feel how lonely the room is."

With illness playing such a prominent part in the Clemens family, it was natural that they should try a variety of cures. The late nineteenth century flourished with ideas on mental health that passed through Nook Farm and were tried by the residents and abandoned for yet another cure. The Clemenses flirted with "mind cure" theory at the suggestion of Miss Foote, the girls' governess. (Mind cure, or mental science, was the belief that people could will away their aches and pains. The theory would become part of Mary Baker Eddy's Christian Science movement.) It gained credibility when Clemens became convinced that not starving his cold but trust in starving it cured him. Miss Holden, who was the mind cure advocate in Hartford, told Livy that even nearsightedness could be corrected. Susy had inherited her nearsightedness from her mother, so both began the treatments. At first they felt it worked, and even Clemens stopped using his glasses. Livy's and Susy's nearsightedness remained, but they still used mind cure for minor stomach and headaches where they believed it most effective.

If only mind over matter could solve all problems. Near Christmas, Clemens was hit with a crippling blow from his daughters whom he so adored and thought his adoration completely reciprocal. Painfully, he wrote Howells in a letter dated December 12:

> Yesterday a thunder-stroke fell upon me out of the most unsuspected of skies. . . . I found that all their lives my children have been afraid of me! have stood all their days in uneasy dread of my sharp tongue & uncertain temper. The accusing instances stretch back to their babyhood, & are burnt into their memories: & I never suspected, & the fact was very guessed by *anybody* until yesterday.

Susy was nearly fifteen and Clara almost thirteen, with little Jean only six. Clemens's two oldest daughters were growing into young adults and away from their father. This probably disturbed him more than what he believed was their fear of his anger, for the family knew about his capricious moods and always joked about his temper. Susy recorded in her biography of him, "He *has* got a temper, but we all of us have in this family." As an adult Clara recalled, "He was a constant surprise in his varied moods, which dropped unheralded upon him, creating day or night for those about him by his twinkling eyes or his clouded brows." Following their mother's advice and practice, the girls simply left their father alone when he was in one of these rages. Once he had vented his anger, Livy then approached him rationally. For Clemens, this discovery was a sad portent for the coming year.

Clemens's Midas touch tarnished in 1887. As a publisher, he advanced five thousand dollars to Henry Ward Beecher to write his autobiography. It could have been a successful book, for scandal and sensation die hard. The public might still have wanted to read this minister's side of the adultery accusations and trial that had been the headlines of 1874–75. Clemens estimated a "three quarters of a million dollars' profit," when Beecher, at seventy-three, died only three weeks after agreeing to the project and accepting the check. Clemens lost more than the five-thousand-dollar advance. He estimated the firm's loss to near one hundred thousand dollars, as they had begun to purchase paper and other materials to print the autobiography.

The once-powerful New England Beecher dynasty was crumbling. Livy and Clemens's neighbor Harriet Beecher Stowe progressively descended into senility until her death in 1896. On her daily walks in her house slippers, she stopped conversing with herself long enough to accost people and ask them if they had read her book *Uncle Tom's Cabin*. If they hadn't, she wanted their name and address to send them a copy. If they had, she wanted their opinion of it. Either way, like Coleridge's Wedding Guest, no one could escape.

The residents of Nook Farm knew her idiosyncracies as she meandered freely in and out of their unlocked homes. She wandered into the Clemenses' conservatory and greenhouse to pick the roses despite the gardener's protests. Livy had the gardener hang up scissors in convenient locations in the hope Mrs. Stowe would use them rather than break off the stems. Mrs. Stowe often gave Livy her own flowers, and Livy accepted them as graciously as if they had come from the Stowes' garden and not her own. When not gathering flowers, Harriet liked to play the piano and softly sing in the Clemens drawing room. The kindhearted Livy informed the servants to let Mrs. Stowe "do as she liked" even if it could be quite frightening.

If you didn't know Mrs. Stowe was in your house, she could, as Clemens said, "slip up behind a person who was deep in dreams and musings and fetch a war whoop that would jump that person out of his clothes." Her mind had deteriorated considerably with the death of her husband Calvin Stowe in 1886. He also had been a colorful individual. As a little girl, Susy had declared, "Santa Claus has got loose!" when she first saw him with his long white beard and ruddy cheeks.

Henry Ward Beecher's death was followed by another business calamity. In March, Clemens discovered that F. M. Scott, the bookkeeper for Webster and Company, had embezzled twenty-five thousand dollars. Eventually, Scott repaid approximately eight thousand of the amount and served five years for his crime. It was not enough for Clemens. He also wanted to sell Scott's house and keep the money, although the man had a wife and three children. With these various business setbacks, Clemens began using money from the publishing house to support the Paige typesetter. Webster and Company then found it necessary to borrow in order to get to press the books Clemens hoped would turn his fortune around: the *Library of Humor*, General Sheridan's memoirs, and a ten-volume *Library of American Literature*. The pope's biography did not even approach the minimum one hundred thousand copies that Webster had told His Holiness would only be a beginning. The world's Catholics did not feel commanded to buy it, and it did not appeal to American Protestants.

That summer at Quarry Farm, Clemens worked on *Connecticut Yankee*, venting in words his disappointment over barely being able to afford one sofa, let alone one thousand. He described Hank's fear of the Catholic Church and its oppression of the people. "There you see the hand of that awful power, the Roman Catholic Church. In two or three little centuries it had converted a nation of men to a nation of worms. Before the day of the Church's supremacy in the world, men were men, and held their heads up, and had a man's pride and spirit and independence; and what of greatness and position a person got, he got mainly by achievement, not by birth."

While Clemens fretted about the machine and his book, Livy still handled the family crises. Little Jean's nurse left. Again, Livy felt she hired as a replacement a better-educated young lady— German, of course, who had only been in America six weeks. Still a mother worries, "Jean does not know it yet, I expect she will be broken hearted when she does. It is well that there are dogs and cows and horses to amuse her in that emergency." Jean's love for animals even surpassed that of her two sisters. Clemens wrote his sister Pamela, "Jean thinks she is studying, too, but I don't know what it is unless it is the horses. She spends the day under their heels in the stalls—& that is but a continuation of her Hartford system of culture." Indeed, there was a new dog to help Jean over her sadness. It was a collie that Clara described as "the most excitable dog that I have really ever seen he races around everywhere chases the cats, and drives the cows up from the pasture."

Charley Webster had raced around too long trying to meet his haranguing Uncle Sam's constant demands. "I blame myself for not looking in on you oftener in the past—that would have prevented all trouble," Clemens wrote concerning Scott's fingers in the till. What Webster did not need was more of his uncle's "looking in." Webster's neuralgia increased with the pressures. Mentally and physically he was bankrupt long before Webster and Company. By the summer of 1887, he was only thirty-six but often too ill to go to the office. By the end of 1888 he sold his shares to Fred Hall, who took Webster's place at the publishing company, but even then Webster was not free. Clemens blamed him for all of his subsequent disappointments and failures far beyond the man's death in 1891. To Pamela, Clemens referred to Webster as "not a man, but a hog." Clemens's venom for Webster ceased only with his own last breath in 1910.

Livy did not actively participate in her husband's business except to supply moral and monetary support. Her primary concern remained raising her daughters to be proper ladies. The Clemens girls were old enough to help smooth out their father's rough western exterior, with his collusion, although he had lived in eastern society for nearly thirty years. Susy once stated, "Pa . . . was an awful man before Mamma took him in hand and married him," and Clemens liked to maintain this guise. His daughters played a game called "dusting off papa" with rules established by Clemens. They made sure their mother corrected their father whenever he breeched some rule of host etiquette as they entertained in Hartford. Clemens improved on the game by suggesting a series of signals which could be given by the girls if they caught him in some social infraction. Then he could supposedly correct himself.

> The children got a screen arranged so that they could be behind it during the dinner and listen for the signals and entertain themselves with them. The system of signals was very simple, but it was very effective. If Mrs. Clemens happened to be so busy, at any time, talking with her elbow neighbor that she

overlooked something that I was doing, she was sure to get a low-voiced hint from behind that screen in these words:

"Blue card, mamma"; or, "Red card, mamma—Green card, mamma"—so that I was under double and triple guard. What the mother didn't notice the children detected for her.

The color of the card might mean Clemens was speaking too little or too much or to the wrong person. Livy hinted to him by making such a remark as "What did you do with the blue card that was on the dressing table?" As with all Clemens's reforms, it could safely be said he followed these corrections only as much as he wanted and as long as it was fun for his daughters and himself.

As 1888 approached, any diversion from the machine was welcome, for it had already consumed fifty thousand dollars. At only eight, Jean scolded a maid who wanted shoe polish, "Why, Marie, you musn't *ask* for things now. The machine isn't done!" Livy cut back on the number of Christmas baskets and their contents she made that season. Clemens apologized to Orion and Mollie that he could only send them fifteen dollars because the typesetter's appetite for money "goes on forever," but he was hopeful. "We'll be through now in 3 or 4 months, I reckon, and then the strain will let up and we can breathe freely once more whether success ensues or failure."

Worry from the machine took its toll on Livy. She became ill during the early winter months of 1888. She suffered from quinsy, a severe sore throat associated with tonsillitis. Weak, she stayed in bed until by April she was allowed to sit up and follow the doctor's orders to eat every few hours to regain her strength.

Both she and Clemens found difficulty eating, sleeping, and concentrating as their mental and physical health hinged on an inanimate machine supposed to be as intelligent as a human being but that showed no compassion for its investors. Livy didn't want to add to her Youth's worries by telling him of her own, so she began to confide in a female friend who did not live in the open atmosphere of Nook Farm or Elmira and so could not relate to neighbors the Clemenses' investment disappointments.

Livy had not found a close girlfriend since her school days. Clara Spaulding had married in the fall of 1886 and was occupied with her own new life. Elinor Howells was often too ill for any activity, and Livy only knew her because of their husbands' friendship. Livy was friendly with all her neighbors but not close to them. As Clemens became more embroiled with Paige and his machine, Livy relied on writing her feelings to Grace King, the southern writer. Livy had met Grace when she was a houseguest of the Warners the summer of 1887. Charles Dudley Warner liked to promote young women writers, and he helped King publish her first novel. Although six years younger than Livy, Grace shared with her common interests in reading and writing. Livy enjoyed discussing these topics with Grace, who had already published stories of Creole people and blacks of the Reconstruction period. In her career, King would publish three novels, two collections of short stories, and biographical and historical studies of the Louisiana Territory.

King and Clemens got on well because they had a common dislike—George Washington Cable. King, a native of New Orleans, disliked Cable's portrayal of the South, feeling he favored the blacks over the Creole people. Clemens could always entertain King by telling her stories of Cable's observance of Sunday, and for this Grace called Clemens, "the greatest circus I was ever at." Although Livy described herself as "commonplace," Grace King found her intelligent and articulate. Because she had grown up in the Reconstruction South and an occupied New Orleans, Grace was impressed with Livy's fine clothes and generous entertaining. She called Livy "a prim and precise but an unaffected little woman, the very essence of refinement."

King visited the Clemenses in October 1888 because Livy pleaded with her, "There are so many things that I should like to talk with you about. I never read a book that I don't feel that I should like to know your opinion regarding it." King worked part of the day as did Clemens. She worked on a dramatization of her novel *Monsieur Motte,* and Clemens on *Connecticut Yankee.*

Clemens had begun to associate finishing the book and machine at the same time. Both, he hoped, would provide him with enough money to free him from writing and from business. When he didn't complete it the summer of 1888, he wrote Howells, "I want to finish the day the machine finishes, and a week ago the closest calculations for that indicated Oct. 22—but experience teaches me that the calculations will miss fire as usual!"

Sue and Theodore Crane came to winter in Hartford, making everyone "hermits" in Clemens's words. Crane had suffered a stroke in September and Sue and Livy exhausted themselves caring for him. The somber mood on Farmington Avenue drove Clemens to take his work to Twichell's home. Despite his illness, Livy could report that her brother-in-law "had an unusually good and gay Thanksgiving." Livy struggled to celebrate another economical Christmas as Clemens described, "She is scouring around all the time, after economical Christmas presents—presents unobtrusively capable & clever in the expression of love & a low financial condition—"

Family illness, financial worries—Livy longed to have someone she could talk with about her troubles. She wrote Grace King, "When you do write you may be sure that your letter will have a most hearty welcome at this end. There is no hand writing that I more rejoice to see than yours." Despite all her difficulties, Livy felt having a close friendship with Grace made her "richer than I was last Thanksgiving."

The "misfired calculations" continued into the new year. Clemens sent Livy a New Year's greeting printed by the machine. The machine was finished again on January 5 and on January 7. Livy felt relieved enough to say, "How strange it will seem to have unlimited means to be able to do whatever you want to do, to give whatever you want to give without counting the cost." Once again, her optimism and her husband's was too early.

Clemens completed *Connecticut Yankee* in May 1889 after three years. The machine was again declared prematurely finished on July 2. Sadly, human beings do not get the resurrections of machinery, for Theodore Crane finished his life the next day after what Clemens called "ten months of longing to go." Crane had never understood, and sometimes resented, the closeness of the Langdon family who had taken so readily to Clemens. Clemens described the effect of her uncle's death on Jean. "Jean's grief was good to see. The earned heartbreak of a little child must be high and honorable testimony for a parting spirit to carry before the Throne."

Livy, once more, was transported back to the emotions of her father's death. While her sister would dress in mourning the rest of her life, Livy wore her "suit of woe" within for the rest of *her* life. The gnawing feeling that she had entered a new, sadder phase had begun with the trip to Keokuk on what she correctly felt would be the last time she would see Jane Clemens alive. Her apprehensions were heightened with Crane's death and with their financial problems and would increase with the coming years until the cynicism that scarred her husband's life would also mark her. "If you speak of next year, the Devil laughs," she would note to herself.

CHAPTER 17

"Such is life."

Pinkeye became Livy's chief physical tormentor during 1889. It started as a mild eye irritation accompanying her quinsy or throat infection in February, and it raged during Theodore Crane's final days.

She consulted a New York occulist in March. On the same trip, her brother, concerned about another infection in her life, gave her some advice. Charles was shocked at the rate the Paige typesetter, her chief spiritual tormentor, was devouring her personal fortune. It seemed that her family's first fear—that she would marry a man who would squander her money—had finally come to pass after twenty years. Charles was planning a year abroad. He could do little more than express his alarm at his sister's shrinking inheritance except to refuse to buy stock or loan his brother-in-law any money for the contraption that was again in pieces on the workshop floor.

Being deprived of her great diversion of reading was bad enough, but eye problems also meant Livy could not act in her usual capacity as her husband's editor. When she tried to read proof of *A Connecticut Yankee*, Clemens reported, it sent her to bed with a severe headache, rendered partially blind simply "by reading half a dozen lines of print." Livy insisted that Howells read the manuscript to search for, in Clemens's words, "coarseness which ought to be rooted out, & blasts of opinion which are so strongly worded as to repel instead of persuade."

It was an additional burden to place upon Howells, also in mourning. Winifred, his twenty-five-year-old daughter, had died in March, her delicate body worn out by Dr. S. Weir Mitchell's "rest cure" for nervous exhaustion. Mitchell's regimen—total bed rest and sense deprivation or being kept in a darkened room with no activities, plus forced feedings of oatmeal—took its toll on a body that was suffering organically, not hysterically. Howells scourged himself for this misdiagnosis. Still, he graciously agreed to edit the manuscript for Livy's sake. "Give her all our loves, and next time try to ask something of me that I don't want to do."

Livy's swollen red eyes only added to her loneliness. It was all too easy for an active mind that didn't have the outlet of reading to turn its energy to worry. Her daughters' education troubled her again. She wrote her mother, "I feel very unsettled about what I shall do with them, nothing in the way of a school seems to be exactly what I want."

She again begged Grace King to come for a visit. Each letter echoed, "How I wish you were here so that we might sit down by the fire and talk, talk together." "Tell me, Grace dear, everything that you are doing particularly the books that you are reading." Grace had told her friend to call upon her if needed. Livy reminded her, "You will have to come you know, because I have not forgotten that lovely promise that you made me." Her incapacitated eyes darkened the world around her and depressed her. "I am unable to use them for reading, that is a terrible trial. So do tell me just what you are reading so I may make the more plans of what I will read when I can use my eyes."

But at Christmas, Livy was not yet reading, and Clemens and Susy were writing her letters. Clemens even tried carrying out some social obligations for her, for Livy made few trips out of the house and then only to occasionally attend church or visit a neighbor. He called on a new bride, stayed for lunch, and suffered Livy's chastisement later when he learned that the reception hour was three and at another home. "However, as I meant well, none of these disasters distressed me," he commented to Howells.

Despite her eye problems Livy tried to carry on her usual Christmas preparations. Clemens disgruntedly described her activities "for she has had otherwise little or nothing to do that fourteen people and a horse couldn't do." "And now at last just as she has got everything cleared away and nothing in the world to do but sit around and buy Christmas gifts for 4,000 people and lie awake nights wondering if they'll be 'satisfied with theirs.' "

Although *A Connecticut Yankee in King Arthur's Court* was published in December, everyone still looked with hope upon the Paige typesetter that by January 1890 gave its usual brief New Year's performance.

Livy's eyes remained in as poor working order as the machine. In February she wrote Grace sadly "I have had no eyes." Another trip to her New York doctor brought a recurrence of her sore throat, and she stayed in bed for a week in New York with Clemens as her nurse.

The continued financial strain of the typesetter compounded their physical problems. Livy's eyes, Clemens's and her own rheumatism, and their bruised bank account set them to thinking about traveling to Europe. She cautiously wrote her mother:

> Mother, Sweet I have something to say to you which I fear you will not approve and so I dread to say it. We have a great hope that we may be able to go to Europe the first of June for the Summer months. We are not entirely certain yet whether we can go or not, it will depend somewhat upon Mr. Clemens' business. It may be that it will be necessary for him to go to England on account of the machine, and then of course we should be with him. Then we want to have the children settle in France for a little while on account of their French. If Susy enters Bryn Mawr next year she must get more French during the Summer & this seems the best way to do it.

In his autobiography Mark Twain wrote that one of the most endearing qualities of his wife was her continued optimism in the face of adversity, her ability to hold him up. "She was always cheerful; and she was always able to communicate her cheerfulness to others. During the nine years that we spent in poverty and debt she was always able to reason me out of my despairs and find a bright side to the clouds and make me see it." In May, Livy had to put aside her own discomforts to lift her husband's spirits. They could not afford to stay in the United States, neither could they afford to leave the Paige typesetter. Clemens began making business trips to New York looking for investors. Livy wrote her absent husband in an attempt to cheer him. "Youth don't let the thought of Europe worry you *one bit* because we will give that all up. I want to see you happy *much* more than I want anything else even the children's lessons. Oh darling it goes to my very heart to see you worried. I don't believe you ought to feel quite as you do, things are not yet quite as desperate as they appear to you."

They did not summer in Europe, but in the Catskill Mountains. Livy employed a tutor to work with Susy. Susy had already passed Bryn Mawr's entrance examinations in mathematics, geography, German, and English grammar and composition. Her summer study prepared her to be tested in French and geometry. Although the dream still remained that Clemens might take them to Europe and return to take care of the machine and join them later, it soon faded through necessity. Susy began college classes that fall.

At eighteen Susy was her parents' daughter—intelligent, creative, delicate, high-strung. In words that echoed those her mother had written in being old at twenty-two, Livy's daughter was equally hard on herself.

> I dread to have to say I am so old! And nothing done and such unsettled notions of things. Why, I should be a well-poised woman instead of a rattle-brained girl. I should have been entirely settled and in mechanical running order for two years! I am ashamed I am not a more reliable, serene character, one to be depended upon. I know so well what a girl of eighteen should be!

To their mutual duress and stress, Susy and her father adored each other, but adoration needs distance, physical and emotional. Despite that she "dreaded" it, Livy wanted Susy to go away to school, fearing that Susy's life, as her own, had been too sheltered. Livy confided to Grace King that her "mother's pride" had been wounded by a remark from someone to whom it was obvious the Clemens daughters had been overprotected. To this unidentified woman, it showed "in the way in which they estimate people." It tore at a father's heart to leave Susy at college, although both Livy and Clemens had stayed with her the first few weeks of classes until rooms could be found for her. He wrote Pamela: "The last time I saw her was a week ago on the platform at Bryn Mawr. Our train was moving away, & she was drifting collegeward afoot, her figure blurred & dim in the rain & fog & she was crying."

Livy was sleepless worrying about her homesick daughter. In another week, Clemens, not as disciplined as his wife, took Clara to visit Susy. After that, Livy went to see Susy so Clemens wouldn't, although he searched for excuses to go. Livy told Evangeline Walker, one of Susy's classmates, that he would have brought Susy's laundry from home if Livy had let him. Livy wrote Grace King, "I shall keep her there this year, but if she is not more contented I shall not send her back next year but make other plans." Livy felt it was a good idea for father and daughter to be separated, and she clearly made the decisions about her daughters' education. Evangeline Walker recalled her impressions of the situation.

> At the time, it seemed to us very natural that Olivia [as Susy was called at school] like ourselves should be coming to college, but later I realized how strong was the tie between her and her father, how much they minded being separated, and also how eager Mrs. Clemens was that Olivia should be happy in a new environment, leading an independent life of her own as a college student among girls her own age, free from the limiting influences of home.

Livy was no different from every other mother, before or since. She simply thought her daughter would desire what she herself had missed in growing up.

Clara at sixteen was leaning toward a career in music. She had already begun piano lessons with a former student of Liszt. Jean

at ten, according to her father, "is going to be a horse jockey &
live in the stable."

The failing health of both Jane Clemens and Olivia Lewis Langdon was another factor in postponing a European trip. Clemens
wrote his sister Pamela in October, "A letter today from Orion
indicates that there is little hope left for Ma—save the hope that
her release is near." Clemens had traveled to Keokuk in August
thinking his mother was dying. With frontier tenacity, Jane
Clemens rallied one last time to be finally "released" on October
27 in her eighty-eighth year.

Exactly one month later, Olivia Lewis Langdon died at eighty
in Elmira with Livy and Sue by her side. Livy had written her
husband earlier in the day, "It is a terrible time. I wish she might
be released in her sleep."

Clemens had stayed behind in Hartford with Jean who was ill
with a puzzling malady whose chief symptom was "a sudden and
unaccountable change" in her personality. It was the first stirring
of epilepsy in her body. Livy telegrammed daily for her husband
to join her, but neither the doctor nor Susy nor Clara would let
him go. When Grandma Langdon died, Susy and Clara went to
their mother.

Livy bore the grief of her mother's death as all must grieve—
alone. She poured out her feelings on paper to Grace King, whom
she lamented she had not seen in two years or who had even
known her mother.

> I feel so much older since mother was taken away. When you
> are no one's child when no one will pet you as your mother has
> always done, when you are the oldest generation of your family,
> then you begin to feel that you are growing old.

It was a few days after that Livy realized her mother had died on
her own forty-fifth birthday.

Ironically, one of Mrs. Langdon's last generous gestures was to
give her son-in-law ten thousand dollars toward the Paige typesetter. As was the yearly pattern of the beast, the typesetter
seemed to be working in January 1891. Livy, desiring some di-

version, went to visit Susy, who had a singing role in the opera
Iolanthe. As a backstage mother, Livy helped with costumes. Her
generous, sweet nature captivated the girls. Clemens, who did
not attend, as no men were invited to student productions, proclaimed of her favored status, "You are so loved!" He had experienced her popularity when he and Clara had gone to visit Susy.
"Everybody asked after you and was disappointed when I said
you hadn't come."

Livy returned from Bryn Mawr and to her bed for two weeks
having exhausted herself from the trip and worry.

Clemens wrote Howells about how Susy "to my private regret
is beginning to love Bryn Mawr." Clemens eagerly accepted an
invitation to speak at the college in March 1891. Susy, a rather
nervous girl, made her father promise not to tell the story of "The
Golden Arm." It was an old slave ghost story he had learned as
a boy in Missouri. In the story a man digs up his buried wife to
steal her golden arm. He is then haunted by her ghost demanding
the arm. As with all good ghost stories, the suspense builds
through the repetitive question, "Where's my golden arm?
Where's my golden arm?" until the climax when the audience
jumps at the husband saying "Here! Take it!" (In other versions,
the ghost says "You've got it!") Susy, who had just lost both
grandmothers and who had a mother who was often ill and a
father who was dependent on his wife's "golden arm" and increasingly dependent on his golden writing arm for their income,
begged her father not to tell the story because it scared her. The
sensitive young woman didn't want to be frightened in front of
her peers.

Livy had vetoed the idea of Clemens speaking at the college,
knowing it would be a strain on Susy. From the moment Susy
knew her father was to lecture she wrote asking him not to tell
the ghost story. It was not right for "the sophisticated group at
Bryn Mawr College." The moment Susy met him at the train station on the day of his presentation and repeatedly through the
day up to the moment of his lecture in late afternoon she implored
him, "Father, *promise* me that you will not tell the 'Ghost Story!' "

With equal conviction, he tried to ease her mind by promising again and again he wouldn't. Evangeline Walker remembered:

> I was sitting with Olivia on the main aisle about the middle of the room holding her damp hand in mine, while she was shaking like a leaf.
> Olivia was whispering in my ear: "He's going to tell the 'Ghost Story'—I *know* he's going to tell the 'Ghost Story.' And he's going to say 'Boo' at the end and make them all jump."

When he started the story, Susy quietly ran up the darkened aisle to a classroom where she put her head down and sobbed. What drove Clemens to do the very thing he knew would break his daughter's heart? The nerves of this tense family were drawn as taut as the wires on the typesetter with the ever-compounding stresses and strains of financial worries, family losses. Clemens, the eternal little boy, erred to be pardoned. Livy knew her husband and almost expected him to do the opposite of what was asked of him. She could then say, "Oh, Youth," and scold him. He, in turn, could then ask to be forgiven. Susy also knew her father, but she could not handle him as her mother could.

Evangeline Walker further related how Clemens tried to comfort Susy.

> While she cried he said, "I tried to think of something else and my mind refused to focus. All I could hear was your voice saying 'Please don't tell the *Ghost Story*, Father—*Promise not* to tell the 'Ghost Story'—and I could think of *nothing* else. Oh, my Dear, my Dear, how could I!"

Clemens continued with his daughters the pattern he had shown with his mother and wife—the larger the transgression, the deeper the wound inflicted, the greater the forgiveness required.

By April of 1891 it was no longer a question of going to Europe but a necessity. Susy pined away her health until Livy went to Bryn Mawr, packed up her belongings, and withdrew her from school. Rheumatism crippled both Livy and Clemens. Dependent on his writing to support the typesetter, his publishing house, and his family, Clemens's "golden arm" sometimes hurt so that he couldn't hold a pen. He had even tried, at Howells's suggestion, dictating into a phonograph.

Livy had begun to feel heart palpitations that the doctors felt were aggravated by her depression. A fourth death in two years, that of Charles Webster, increased Livy's melancholy despite Clemens's endless blaming the man for all their publishing and financial problems.

Livy searched for ways to cut expenses, knowing that it was nearly impossible "unless we sell our house," she had confided to her mother just a month prior to Mrs. Langdon's death. "Such is life" is all she could say of their financial difficulties. It was not yet a serious proposition, but leaving her home after seventeen years to live abroad was nearly as traumatic. Livy had Sue Crane, who would travel with them, help her break the news to the servants. She had long worried that their financial situation would force them, in Katy Leary's words, "to send them all away." For the servants' sake, Livy tried to be optimistic and to say they would soon return, but she could not convince them of what she didn't believe. Livy wrote Grace King of the heavy-hearted, but frenzied preparations, "It seems as if everything must be done and *at once.*" They would sail June 6, 1891 on the *Gascogne*.

Livy and Clemens found positions for Patrick, their coachman of twenty-one years, and George, the butler. John and Ellen O'Neill stayed behind to care for the house. Katy Leary would accompany them to help with the girls and the packing and moving of twenty-five trunks.

Oddly, Clemens did not tell Howells of his travel plans until Howells read of them in the newspaper. Clemens, ignoring his money problems, explained Livy's health "has determined us to go to Europe." He admitted his lack of desire. "Travel has no longer any charm for me. I have seen all the foreign countries I want to see except heaven & hell, & I have only a vague curiosity as concerns one of those." To Mrs. Fairbanks he related that they would stay until they were tired—"a point which I shall reach in thirty-days, Jean in sixty, Clara in ninety, Susy in a hundred, and Livy in six months." Livy knew the stay would be at least one year and probably two. Perhaps, she sensed, even longer.

RESA WILLIS

When her house was being built, Livy had with joy and pride walked through it each evening surveying the day's progress. Now as the carriage waited to take her to the station, she moved slowly from room to room, savoring the sights and sounds of her seventeen years on Farmington Avenue. When Livy closed the front door behind her, crossed the Ombra, and stepped into the carriage, she looked back on a house that she loved but would never enter again.

CHAPTER 18

"I cannot afford it."

Following a week in Paris, Livy placed Susy and Clara in a French family's boarding school in Geneva. She and the others moved on to take the cure at Aix-les-Bains; the "paradise for rheumatics," Clemens called it. Then all reunited for the Wagner festival in Bayreuth. This music-loving family, especially Clara, delighted in ten days of opera, for which they had purchased their tickets a year in advance, performed against a mountain backdrop. As this was the social event of the year, accommodations were scarce and restaurants crowded. When only frankfurters could be found, Clemens contented himself with eating corned beef and cabbage which Katy Leary described, "the rest of the family wouldn't look at." Clemens reasoned if he could eat that he could stand anything, "even Wagner operas." His taste in music was not as refined as that of the women in his family. "Whenever I enjoy anything in art it means that it is mighty poor." So at the six-o'clock intermission, Clemens didn't mind leaving early from six hours of *Parsifal* to find the family a place to eat before returning for the conclusion of the opera.

Filled with culture, Livy and Clemens traveled to Marienbad, best-known for its mud baths, to fill and surround themselves with more curative waters. After eating a healthy biscuit washed down with mineral waters, health seekers jumped into mud baths with band accompaniment in the background. They passed through three pools of progressively thinner mud until they were in pure water. Even Katy Leary recognized that all said they felt better after this ordeal even if they weren't. "I guess their thinking so helped them as much as the mud!"

With all this curative soaking and drinking, Livy thought at least her husband was making some progress. Although he had already begun trying to train himself to write with his left hand, Livy reported to Grace King that his right shoulder was better and he was doing some work. (He had contracted to write some travel letters for the New York *Sun.*) Livy found the places they stayed "interesting and charming, yet I must confess to homesickness, when I should like to see my friends and sit down in our library beside an open wood fire instead of a stove, for a visit with them."

They stayed a few days in Heidelberg for Livy to show Katy the town she had long admired as a picture hanging on Livy's wall. Years ago in Hartford, Livy had told Katy, "I hope before I die, that I shall be able to take you right up there on that mountain so you'll see it too, just as I have."

Leaving the women in Ouchy near Lausanne, Switzerland, Clemens returned to the river for inspiration; this time he floated down the Rhône. Livy, who tried to not show her worry around her husband, let it slip out in his absence. She wrote her friend Mrs. Whitmore, musing about the typesetter, "How I wish we might here [sic] something good about it." Franklin Whitmore, who had warned Clemens of further investing in Paige, was handling their business affairs back in Hartford. He had not sent any news, good or bad. In Europe, Livy did not want to feel cut off from what had sent them abroad. For their own peace of mind, they needed news of their money.

Charlie informed her she had ten thousand dollars. This sum she wanted to cover their living expenses for a year. She wrote Fred Hall, running the Webster Publishing Company, that she thought it a poor idea to invest the sixteen thousand Clemens earned from writing back into the publishing company. "It surely is very bad to have all one's eggs in one basket so I think it will be well for him now to make small investments when he can outside Webster & Company."[1] By this point, Livy recognized that money into Webster went into Paige and into oblivion. She asked Hall that he write her husband "a line or two every week. I know that you will not have much to write and I am afraid it may tax you to write it, still I think it would be enough of a comfort to Mr. Clemens to repay you."

Autumn, even in Europe, made Livy think of home, for while they went away for the summer they always returned to Hartford in the fall. Susy, too, missed the New England fall: "I still keep thinking of American trees. . . . How blood red they are by this time!"

Despite homesickness, Livy hoped her family was content. Clara practiced the piano in preparation for more lessons in Berlin where they would live in what Clara called "a cheap apartment in a disagreeable quarter of the city." Livy called it "the most economical way" to spend the winter. To further economize, Katy Leary went back to Elmira to care for her sick mother—"the first time I ever left them." The Clemens ladies would have to pack their own luggage. Livy, uncertain of their future economic condition, knew it was time the girls learned to do these tasks for themselves.

While their parents pursued health and wealth, Clara and Susy, approaching eighteen and twenty, couldn't help but notice the handsome young military men. "What a world of romance lay in those braided coats and plumed helmets!" declared Clara. While Katy had been horrified at the dueling scars the young men proudly displayed on their faces in Heidelberg, she noted, "The girls seemed to think it was wonderful."

Susy remained restless. Clara had her music to occupy her, but Susy gave up her piano lessons only to decide later to take voice lessons. Livy blamed herself that Susy gave up an instrument she

---

[1]Clemens quoted the same maxim to Andrew Carnegie in trying to get him to invest in the Paige typesetter. Carnegie replied, "That's a mistake; put all your eggs into one basket—and watch that basket."

seemed to love and her years of study: "It is too bad, too bad, yet I was too ignorant to prevent it."

The letters Susy wrote to her friend and college roommate Louise Brownell are as poignant as her mother's to Grace King. The recurring theme for both was loneliness, the desire to speak with a friend, to share readings and thoughts. Susy, like her mother, felt responsible. "We are still living a perfectly quiet eventless life. We have not met a soul. I blame myself for being lonely and uninterested, for I fear it is an indication of a lack of resources within myself."

After two months, the Clemenses left Kornerstrasse for a modest hotel. The flat had amused Clemens but embarrassed Livy after they learned of the area's bad reputation. Livy and Sue had originally settled on the apartment because it was on the ground floor and Livy couldn't climb stairs.

Her Hartford home never left her mind. The roses Livy saw in Switzerland prompted her to write John and Ellen O'Neill stating she knew from Mrs. Whitmore's letters that John was making money by selling her roses. Livy, who always administered praise and blame in equal amounts, stated, "It is a great comfort to me to have you there." She ordered coal, for "I do not want the living in our house to be any extra expense to you." Then she requested that he occasionally take roses to their friends, for free, just as she had done.

Clemens returned to the States in June 1892 to check on the typesetter and the publishing company. It was the first of fourteen transatlantic crossings he would make in the next three and a half years. Clemens knew the machine would never make any return on his investment until someone was willing to manufacture it, and Paige had hinted at backers willing to build it in Chicago. Trying to keep her husband's and her own spirits up, Livy wrote, "Wouldn't it be glorious if you arranged things in such a way that you could come back feeling at rest about it all."

Wintering in Berlin provided an active social life, as Livy and Clemens knew the ambassador, William Walter Phelps. In addition, other party doors were opened by a distant Clemens relation from St. Louis who had married a German, General Von Versen. Livy confided in her old friend Alice Hooker Day, "It seems particularly hard that just as we mothers are particularly needed to help our daughters into society is the time when we seem unable to meet the social duties." Despite their mother's illness, Clara and Susy along with the rest of the family had been received by the German emperor William II and attended court balls.

Clemens's books were on sale everywhere in Berlin, and he was recognized when he went out, a nicety for a writer who as businessman had resolved nothing on his trip back to the U.S. Sometimes Clara and Susy enjoyed being noticed when they entered a room. Sometimes, as capricious as their maturing emotions, they resented the adulation. People would watch them at dinner, until one of the girls exclaimed, "Look at those people, Father! They are getting a fine view of your appetite!" Clemens was usually oblivious to the attention, much to his daughters' further chagrin.

Having a famous father was not easy for a young woman searching for her own identity. Susy told Grace King that she despised only being known as Mark Twain's daughter. "How I hate that name! I should like never to hear it again! My father should not be satisfied with it! He should not be known by it. He should show himself the great writer that he is, not merely a funny man."

Livy and Clemens spent their first European winter of self-exile as they had others in the past, both ill with aches and colds. One month in bed with rheumatism kept Clemens from writing and Livy from sightseeing. Finally, seeking relief, they left the girls to their lessons in Berlin and went to Mentone in southern France looking for "healing weather." The girls, chaperoned by the family courier Joseph Verey, would meet them in Pisa in the spring, so all "the tribe" would tour Rome, Venice, and Florence together. They were looking for a warm place to winter for Livy's health, and they found it in the Villa Viviani outside Florence.

Before settling down for the winter, Livy went back to Germany, this time to Bad Nauheim (Bath No-Harm to Clemens) in August 1892 for more treatments. She was "trying to make myself a very strong woman for next winter." The doctors advised that Livy's heart muscles were not ravaged by heart disease, but only weak and could be strengthened with rest. Clemens happily declared, "That was worth going to Europe to find out." But he spoke too quickly.

When Sue Crane returned home, Livy grieved over her sister's absence, and her condition worsened. She was bedridden with headaches and a swollen face and neck. "It has set her back weeks," Clemens declared. The doctors who had been so optimistic now saw Livy had erysipelas, a skin infection of large red swellings and, much worse, a hyperthyroid condition. The least serious result of excessive thyroid secretions was goiter. Increased thyroid in Livy's system caused her heart to work harder, leading to high blood pressure, rapid heartbeat, difficulty in breathing, increased fatigue, and irritability. Hyperthyroidism, or Graves' disease, could be aggravated through stress and would also explain her recurring throat maladies and eye problems. The best-known treatment was the iodine-rich mineral waters of the German spas. Shortness of breath now plagued her the rest of her life and instilled in her a terror of choking to death. To Grace King she recognized the seriousness of the condition that would one day lead to her death. "One feels at this time that one holds life and health by a very slender thread."

The Clemenses left Nauheim on the tenth of September but had to stop at Frankfurt and Lucerne because Livy's headaches were too severe to travel. They didn't wish to expose anyone to disease. In Susy's words, "The Cholera still rages. We can't venture to go to Italy till it is decidedly on the wane."

Once at the villa on September 26, Livy could little appreciate its twenty-eight rooms which she found ugly and scantily furnished. The diarrhea that accompanied her hyperthyroid condition had developed into dysentery, and she also had dental problems. Only the view of Florence in the distance with its vineyards and olive groves made this journey worthwhile for her. To Livy's relief, they were three miles from the city, which prevented people from just dropping in on them as they had done in Berlin. Clemens wrote of his wife's suffering, "It is just heart-breaking to see her.

She is patient & uncomplaining—just as always—but she is very weak & all wasted away."

Clemens, who had a scalp irritation, shaved his head, to Clara and Susy's mortification. Clara described her father's head as "clipped like a billiard ball" and guessed he had done it as a perverse joke. "He must have consented to all this shorn beauty for the fun of seeing horror expressed not only in our faces, but also in the face of the artist who was painting his portrait at the time." In Susy's words, "You cannot imagine what a sight he is! His poor afflicted family wishes he would decline all invitations and withdraw to live the life of a hermit till it grows out again."

Clemens agreed. "There is going to be absolute seclusion here— a hermit life." Quiet allowed him time to write. In May 1892 he had published *The American Claimant*—the further adventures of Colonel Sellers—this time an inventor desirous to be an earl. Despite disappointing sales, Clemens, ever enchanted with his own schemes, felt a great affinity with his creation Sellers. Now nestled into the Villa Viviani, he "boomed" (Clemens's word for when his work was going well) with ideas. He finished *Tom Sawyer Abroad* and a short story, "The £1,000,000 Bank-Note." He performed a "literary Caesarean" on *The Extraordinary Twins*, giving birth to *The Tragedy of Pudd'nhead Wilson*, his last published novel set in America. He began work on the book he felt he would best be remembered for, a serious book, a book Susy heartily approved of, the story of Joan of Arc. Telling Livy, "I shall never be accepted seriously over my own signature," he first intended to publish it anonymously. Susy described it to her friend Louise, "Papa is progressing finely with his Joan of Arc which promises to be his loveliest book. Perhaps even more sweet and beautiful than the *Prince and the Pauper*. The character of Joan is pure and perfect to a miraculous degree. Hearing the M.S. read aloud is an uplifting and revealing hour to us all."

A hermit life not being for her, Clara returned to Berlin and Mrs. Willard's school to study her music, German, and French. She was missed sorely. "The house is empty, *empty*, EMPTY and it is very hard for Susy and me to settle ourselves to doing anything. We want to sit down and cry all the time," her mother wrote her. Susy concurred, "I have grown to dread so being left too much alone."

Much to the relief of both Susy and her mother, Grace and her sister Nan King came to visit for a month. Their presence helped brighten everyone's days. Susy recalled, "We enjoy her immensely. I never heard so brilliant a woman talker." Susy held a special place in King's heart because of Susy's interest in what life had been like for a southern lady before the Civil War. King found Susy frail, almost "ethereal," and thus unable to be away from home like the stronger Clara.

At first happy to have someone else to talk with, Susy began to long for the Kings to leave. "How aggravating and cantankerous they were the last part of their visit." Probably describing her own emotions more than those of their guests, she disliked their interference in her private angst. Seeming now to enjoy it, Susy wanted to get on with her isolation. "I am getting more and more expert in warding off loneliness. When the Kings go I shall be almost entirely alone because Mamma is on her sofa resting much of the time and Papa at work. I am going to be prepared." She would find comfort with a new gray kitten and by playing with the gardener's baby.

Susy confided to Clara that she was "lonely and anxious for a taste of 'the rage of *living.*' " Livy was equally anxious that Susy seemed so unhappy and isolated even with her dancing and singing lessons. "She has three or four pleasant young girl acquaintances but of course no close friends so I have to try to make up to her as well as I can for that."

Against doctors' orders, Livy was "at home" to receive visitors on Wednesday afternoons for Susy's sake. Susy disliked visiting people without her mother, so Livy hired a French governess, Mademoiselle Lanson, to help with the housekeeping and to go out with Susy on social calls. Livy regretted that her incapacitated state, for she was not to go out, restricted her daughter. "I feel that it is such a great sacrifice to Susy just at this time. She is very good and patient about it and assures me that this quiet is good for her; which I believe is true becaue she is not very strong."

Susy warned Clara, who from her letters obviously was tasting the rage of living, "Enthuse just as much as you *want* to about Berlin in your letters to *me* but not *quite* so much in your letters to *Mamma*." Clara's increasing autonomy reduced Livy to tears. When it appeared she would even stay away at Christmas, Livy wrote her, "I cannot bear to have you so far away from me and such a big piece of your life that I am not sharing it. It is the first Christmas in 18 years that you have not been with me and I do not like it at all."

Livy regretted she could not send Clara more money as she had requested, for an active social life demanded a wardrobe. As usual, their attempts at economizing were not very effective. There was the expense of running the villa with its five servants, and business conditions at home were not improving. "J. L. & Co are in no better shape than they were last year and there is no more prospect of having an income from them," Livy explained to her absent daughter. Her own financial difficulties were always on her mind, yet Livy felt compassion for others and recognized her own wealth. She told Clara how two people froze to death in Florence. "It seems so dreadful that of our abundance we could not have given warmth to those poor people." "I want you and Susy and Jean to be ever ready to help in all ways that you can with sympathy, with money, with work for others. A little money goes a good ways with poor people. How easily we could have warmed those freezing people if we had only known."

Susy envied Clara's activities in Berlin. "I am *heartily* tired of *books*, and *sewing* all day, of the echoes of this house, and the long long lonely evening when we read *again* by way of a *change*." Susy also envied Clara's distance from their father's moods and tempers, his "storms." "Still I feel constrained and he pierces me thru [sic] with his eyes as if he were determined to see whether I am embarrassed or not." Susy resolved to keep busy, avoid her father, eat in her room. But even in Berlin staying with distant relatives, the Von Versens, Clara could feel the heated glare of her father's disapproving eye.

RESA WILLIS

"Don't get used to being away from us my darling and have such a good time in Berlin that you feel content to stay away from us," Livy counseled Clara. But to her parents' distress, Clara was having "such a good time" with the braided coats and plumed helmets that continued to catch her fancy.

When Clara gleefully reported that she had been the only girl in a room of forty German officers at a Von Versens's ball, Clemens exploded. He wrote a long tirade to her that included:

> The average intelligent American girl who had never crossed the ocean would know better than to do that in America. It would be an offence against propriety there—then what name shall it be called by when done in Berlin—I mean, of course, by an American girl, for what European girl would dream of doing it? Are not the ways of American girls in Europe a matter of common talk over here? Is it possible that you have heard none of it? Of the forty officers was there one, old or young, who would have allowed his daughter or sister to stay in your place a minute? Was there occasion to add yourself to the list of American girls who bring their country into disrepute?

"And their well-known father?" was not directly stated, but the message was certainly there. Like Henry James, Clemens saw a role for the American girl in Europe, and he expected a certain conduct from his daughters. "There is not an American girl in Berlin who cannot better afford to make her conduct a matter of criticism than you."

Susy wrote for Livy, too ill to write for herself, trying to soften the sting of Clemens's wrath, yet fearful for Clara's and their own reputation.

> You mustn't misunderstand Papa's letter or think he's *severe* or *angry* or anything of the sort, for he was delighted that you had a good time at the Von Versen ball, and the only trouble is, he *cannot* make out *how* you happened to take your dinner *alone* with forty officers! Mama wants you to write me or her some explanation of it, and of how it came about, and then as she feels sure that it was entirely improper and will be talked about all over Berlin she thinks perhaps you had better take Papa's letter to Frau Von Versen and let her read it and say to her "Frau Von Versen, *did* I do anything out of the way at your house,

was it not comme il faut? etc.," so that she can see that *you* were innocent and meant no harm, and also that papa and mama have brought you up in the right way.

Livy scolded, "I felt that if you had gotten a little free from being away from my checking influence that all you needed was to be reminded." Clara could not have been ignorant of the situation she had gotten herself into. The middle child, she would always be the daughter who dared to assert her independence and defy her father. She was already trying to persuade her mother and father into allowing her to prepare for a career on the concert stage.

As Clara grew older, she pulled away all the harder each time her father grasped to keep her a little girl on his knee. Clemens was uncomfortable with his daughters becoming young women. When Livy had gone to Berlin to find living accommodations for the family the previous winter, Clemens had locked Clara in her room until her mother returned. Clara's crime? She had attracted a young German officer who had danced with her at a ball and tried to court her with visits and notes. On Livy's return and Clara's release, all Livy could do was laugh at the ridiculousness of the situation, much to Clemens's mortification. Still, he insisted his daughters be chaperoned everywhere they went, and Clara was until she married at the age of thirty-five. Once while living in Florence, Clemens and Clara stopped at a restaurant. He noticed some young men observing her. When they returned to the villa, he cut the artificial fruit from her hat, convinced its provocativeness had attracted the attention. Clara eventually lived in Europe, finding distance the easiest way to get along with her father in the last few years of his life.

Christmas in Florence was subdued, slightly melancholy. On Christmas Eve, the Clemens family toasted their friends at home in America, and Jean decorated the Christmas tree. Even with the language barrier of not being able to speak to the servants and their children, Susy found, "They were charmingly at ease and responsive." Clemens found an advantage to his reduced financial condition. Livy now had reason to "to give up that infernal Christmas-suicide."

"America looks further and further away recedes and recedes

till I am ready to *scream*," observed Susy. She, as well as the others, realized that because of the publishing business and Livy's health, returning home was not in their immediate future. The longer they stayed away, the harder it would be to go home. They were "getting accustomed to European life and growing to dread the *change* of going home with all our longing to return. Papa and Clara seem quite weaned." Livy, in bewilderment, wrote her daughter, "Clara, have you never any pangs of homesickness for our dear Hartford home?"

Livy felt pangs of separation with the twinges of her bad heart. To Alice Day she wrote of her fears of being ill abroad. "I say to Mr. Clemens sometimes 'think of the horror of dying over here among these new people.' I want to be with my own people or my own old friends when I go out of this world."

In her parents' concern for her two older sisters, twelve-year-old Jean was left to her own devices, which were always to make friends with animals, who gave so much and demanded so little. She stayed busy outdoors with her pets and busy indoors with her languages—French, German, Italian. All three Clemens girls had musical talent. Jean's manifested itself in her flair for languages. Wherever she want, Jean belonged to a humane society; if there wasn't one she started one. As a little girl at Quarry Farm in the summertime she had put signs up along the steep hill from Elmira that read, "Uncheck your horses going up here," meaning for drivers to unsnap the rein that held the horse's head upright, thus allowing the horse to pull more easily up the hill and easing the strain on its mouth. Not satisfied that her sign was enough, Jean watched for horse-drawn vehicles and stopped them if they did not obey her sign.

She and Clara went about Europe handing out blue cards from the Society for Prevention of Cruelty to Animals to any private or commercial driver they saw beating a horse. In the carriages they rode they instructed the drivers not to use the whip, which led to what Livy called "some pretty long, slow drives." Jean insisted they only ride in carriages with "the worst looking old horses" reasoning that the good-looking horses were well cared for and not beaten. "In that way we could protect the old bony horses," Livy said. Clemens sometimes lost patience with his daughters' humane efforts, especially when he was in a hurry and they were passing out their empowered blue cards. Once he asked his wife, "Do you know, Livy, that Clara holds up the entire Paris traffic with that blue card? Do you approve of that?" Livy supported, "Youth dear, you would do the same thing if the blue card was yours."

Concerned with Susy's isolation and Clara's celebration, Livy contemplated sending Susy to stay with her sister in Berlin. Even her father recognized that Susy needed a reprieve from "the dullness of eternal study." To Livy's relief, Clara wanted to come home. Susy, who had once said, "I am sorry not to love the place I am staying in," had found a reason to love Florence. "Florence has been gay lately," she wrote Louise. Susy discouraged Clara, reminding her of how constrained she would feel if she returned. "But I feel perfectly sure, perfectly certain that if you come to the Villa Viviani any sooner than you positively *have* to, you make a big, big, big mistake!!!!!!"

The big mistake was Susy's crush on a Byronic character named Count de Calry, and Susy didn't want to compete with her more vivacious sister. De Calry charmed every woman in his presence, including Livy, although she later recognized that he was polite only when it was advantageous to him. "He *is* a fascinating man altogether the most fascinating person I have met in Europe," Susy glowed. Even though he was married, he paid Susy some much-needed attention in a society that had for its main diversion "teas, teas, teas for ever and ever."

Susy began to long to see him. She measured the success of a social function by his presence. She lived for Wednesday afternoons when he might visit, but rarely did, during their reception day. When he didn't ask her to dance at the Princess Corsini's ball, she was crushed, but still rated it a triumph because it lasted until six in the morning when she was only used to attending "old people's teas."

De Calry's handsome face always "agitated" Susy even if she

recognized his flaws—his married state, his arrogant indifference—but the heart can't control the brain when the unattainable is the most desirable. Sadly, she concluded that she "might have known better for no one ever stays fascinated with me." "I do think it is hard to be young. One is so horribly *alive* and has so much *temperament* one can't bear things well, and oh dear one never gets any serenity."

Although Susy and her father had limited communication, he would have agreed that, young or old, serenity was a precious commodity as he prepared to sail again for America in search of his own desired unattainable.

CHAPTER 19

"Sombre days"

Spring came to Florence in February and, as spring does everywhere in the world, brought with it a sense of rejuvenation. It was balmy enough for the ladies to enjoy tea on the terrace and for Clemens to write outside. "The transformation is so sudden that it takes one's breath away," Susy recorded.

The Clemens family needed a new start, a transformation. A week after her father departed for America in late March, Susy gave a luncheon before she, her mother, and her sister left for Venice and yet another hoped-for beneficial change of scenery for Livy. After a season of going out on her own with Mademoiselle Lanson while her mother remained in bed, Susy felt, "I have really grown to be quite an adept at social intercourse." In fact, she felt daring, describing her gathering as "quite a social earthquake here as it's such a departure from the usual tea." Venice would see a new, bolder Susy Clemens. "I am going to make more of Venice this time and be out of doors—not in the hotel fuming and worrying as I was last time."

Fuming and worrying had become a way of life for her parents. Worry had sent Clemens back to America to check firsthand on their business ventures, both of which, the typesetter and the publishing house, needed a quick, massive infusion of dollars to survive. Paige was confident he had found investors in Chicago, so the machine might yet be manufactured and turn profitable. With such a delicate situation, Livy's letters to her husband charge him to not let his anxieties overcome his mouth. "Be nice and sweet to everybody—it is our *home* our place & we want to go there sometime."

Feelings of failure over his inability to provide for his family and believing that he had left them homeless consumed Clemens. Away from Livy his guilt intensified. She tried to comfort him across the miles. "My dear darling child you *must not* blame yourself as you do. I love you to death, and I would rather have you for mine than all the other husbands in the world and you take as good care of me as any one could do." Her duty was to support her husband, so she suppressed her fears. She told him that "while you and the children are spared to me in good health I have no reason to murmur."

In her duty as his editor, she expressed her opinions. "You did not tell me anything about sending an article or articles to the *Cosmopolitan.* Why did you do that? I should greatly prefer appearing in the *Century* or *Harper's* what made you do it?" Livy's priority was her husband's literary reputation, which she saw as part of her own, while Clemens's priority was making enough money for living expenses while in America.

At the opening ceremony of the World's Columbian Exposition in Chicago on May 1, President Cleveland praised American skill and intelligence and the "stupendous results of American enterprise." Eight days later a branch of the Chemical National Bank closed on the fairgrounds when the downtown bank failed. Feeling obligated to the foreigners who had deposited their money in the now-defunct branch, the president of Chemical National took up a collection from his wealthier friends to cover the visitors' accounts. Others would not be so lucky to have an angel watching over their money. Despite Cleveland's optimistic rhetoric, bad economic times were accelerating into the Panic of 93.

Clemens and Fred Hall traveled to Chicago where Paige had set up the machine with the hopes of getting the Chicago *Herald* interested in it. A cold kept Clemens in bed while Hall dealt with Paige, or Paige came to Clemens. With the beginnings of a depression out on the streets, Clemens lying safely in his hotel bed was still defenseless against Paige's entreaties. Clemens described Paige as a man who could not only charm fish out of the water but could get them to walk. After thirteen years, Paige's persuasive talents still worked, even if his typesetter didn't. Clemens admitted, "When he is present I always believe him; I can't help it."

Paige promised three million from Chicago investors. It was enough to manufacture the typesetter. They might even be able to exhibit one at the World's Fair. Manufacturing the machine so it could be sold or leased was the key to Clemens's future wealth. He believed that if one machine were made each day, then two, maybe even five, he would be rich.

Clemens wrote of his enthusiasm to Livy, and it made her "wild" in her reply. "It does not seem credible that we are really again to have money to *spend*." The thought made the conservative Livy, who was trying to pare living expenses from 375 to 350 francs a week, declare, "Well I tell you I think I will jump around and spend money just for fun, and give a little away if we really get some."

Clemens returned home on May 13 hoping all would be well. In June the stock market crashed, dropping from one hundred million dollars to thirty-seven million traded. The Panic of 1893 was on.

Just as John Marshall Clemens never recovered from the Panic of 1837, this panic nearly destroyed his son. It began who knows where but was aided by a drain on the gold reserve by foreign investors who sold their securities and withdrew them in gold from the U.S. The Sherman Silver Purchase Act, allowing gold to be used to purchase silver, further depleted the federal gold reserve by nearly one hundred million. Gold meant confidence. Without either, the dominoes began to fall. The stock market crash eventually took with it 160 railroads, five hundred banks and sixteen thousand businesses. It was estimated by 1894 that 20 to 25 percent of the work force was unemployed. Those with jobs went on strike to get decent wages as there seemed to be no money anywhere. Miners across the nation refused to work. Eventually the Langdon coal mines and Livy's income shut down.

It was not a good time to have two shaky businesses even for the most astute businessman. Too late, Clemens realized he was not that man. He advised Hall to do whatever was necessary to sell his interests. Livy concurred and wrote Hall, "I think Mr. Clemens is right in feeling that he should get out of business, that he is not fitted for it; it worries him too much." In an effort to help save the publishing firm, Livy requested Hall should send them no more money as things were so tight. She would get money from her brother until times were better at the publishing company.

Once Clemens returned to Florence he tried escaping into his work on Joan of Arc. Her distant past he could control, his own dubious present he couldn't. Livy closed the villa. She, Clemens, and Jean went to a cheaper Munich and the baths while Susy auditioned for the voice teacher Madame Marchesi in Paris.

The entire family counted each cent. Susy wrote Clara that "if we go bankrupt perhaps I can give instructions in singing." Jean, now thirteen, had spent her entire life hearing talk of the Paige typesetter. Growing up, she only knew that money went for "the machine." Livy sent Jean to purchase some cognac to mix with milk to help her sleep at night. When the milk curdled, Livy tasted the cognac to discover "the most wretched stuff that I have ever tasted." Jean had purchased the cheapest cognac she could find. "She evidently thought in the present state of our finances, I must get used to drinking what was well within the range of our purse," Livy surmised.

By August, Clemens could no longer live in Joan's world and ignore his own. The Webster Publishing Company had notes coming due that had been renegotiated too many times. Now with money in such short demand, they had to be paid. With the others to move from Germany on to Paris for the winter, Clemens along with Clara (Livy thought the ocean voyage would cure her bad cough) left for America.

Livy felt helpless in Europe. She could only try to reassure her husband, and try to keep expenses down.

So if this whole business fails, pack your bag and come back to us. We will give you some literary work to do and every evening we will be happy together hearing you read what you have written during the day. You know I can learn to economize even better than I have been doing, as I get more and more experience. You know we have an income of about $6,000 a year and with what you can comfortably earn in addition, without taxing yourself we can live perfectly well for our requirements. I write all this to let you know that if failure comes we shall not be cast down and you must not allow yourself to be.

To ward off further worry, Livy kept her husband ignorant of all she endured in the cheap Paris hotel—the cold, the bad food, the noise heard through thin walls—as she figured and refigured their income and outgo. She had chosen to live in Paris when so many Americans went home in the financial panic, and the cost of living there dropped. She admitted to Grace King in these "sombre days" that she dreaded complaining to the proprietor yet again about the conditions of her lodgings because she felt he was doing all he could.

"Poverty is hard!" she wrote Clara, who suggested it would be cheaper if she stayed in America since her mother insisted she pay board when visiting Aunt Sue in Elmira or friends. Livy said no. Besides, "There would be too much expense of longing for you to make it profitable." Livy's preoccupation with funds had extended into her communication with her daughter.

There would be no opera, theater, new clothes, extra lessons of any kind. Jean was placed in a public school. Livy hoped there would be enough money for Susy's singing lessons, for she was relieved that Susy, having found a purpose, was happier. Susy was willing to work very hard, for as Livy said, "She feels she has lost so much time, in fact all her time in Europe. I feel sorry for her in this respect."

Susy's late-developed singleness of purpose was not without problems. Madame Marchesi was appalled at her physical condition. The Madame believed Susy might have an operatic career as a soprano if she were stronger, with greater lung capacity. It scared Susy. She was "brokenhearted" that after only two lessons "my breath has been so short and weak that all my volume of voice has gone." The Madame discovered that despite Livy's hovering over her daughters, with her illness and the absence of Katy Leary, Susy had neglected her health. Susy adhered to the nineteenth-century ideal of a delicate lady with a picky appetite. Often in a state of what she described as "ennui," she slept little, was thin and anemic. With such high expectations for herself and from her parents, she was probably anorexic. Susy worried what Clara had told others back home of plans that she might not be able to fulfill. She wanted her father to know only of Madame Marchesi's praises of her voice. Susy would have to follow Madame Marchesi's strict health regimen or all the voice lessons in the world would be useless.

In this family where all too often secrets were kept among a few under the guise of protecting some other one, Clemens wrote Susy to keep her mother cheerful just as Livy was trying to keep worry from him. "Bear up mamma's hands and help her to endure our long separation as patiently as she can, for I absolutely must not budge one step from this place *until we are safe from the poorhouse.*"

While Clara returned to Berlin and her music lessons, Clemens was obligated to find that money to keep his family from the poorhouse. Webster Publishing was tottering, about to fall. When people are out of work and out of money, they do not buy books. Clemens remembered in his autobiography, "I emptied into the till twenty-four thousand dollars which I had earned with the pen." It was not enough to save the firm from the banks calling in their notes. He still needed eight thousand just to hold his ground.

He went to stay, as he told Livy, in "a cheap room" at The Players in New York. For his living expenses he depended on what he earned from selling a short story "The Esquimau Maiden's Romance" for eight hundred dollars to *Cosmopolitan*. For the serialized version of *Pudd'nhead Wilson* to appear in *Century*, he received seventy-five hundred to be sent to Livy for her expenses.

Even she suspended her editorial prerogative for cash. Ironically, when their former butler George called on Clemens at The Players, he appeared the only prosperous person in New York. He was doing well in the midst of a depression by cashing in on the same moonlighting skills he had used when in service to the Clemenses. Now he was making loans to white and black folk alike in these hard times and taking only gold and diamonds as collateral.

With "failure and ruin" everywhere, Clemens knew that obtaining eight thousand dollars would not be easy, but he didn't think it would be impossible. But after a week of going from bank to bank in New York and from friend to friend in Hartford, he found doors were shut everywhere. He "couldn't get anything." He contacted Sue Crane asking for money, "telling her I had no shame." All Charles and Ida Langdon could come up with was five thousand. At this low point, when "the billows of hell have been rolling over me" and the devils tearing at the soul of his pocketbook, Clemens found his angel. Clarence Rice, his sometime host and doctor, told him of an extremely wealthy man Clemens had met two years ago who admired the work of Mark Twain so much that he read it aloud to his family. Henry Huttleston Rogers had heard Clemens lecture years ago on the Sandwich Islands. He then, as he later told Clemens, went on to "read everything of yours since that I could get hold of."

Like Clemens, Rogers started life as a poor small-town boy, and it was that element in Twain's work with which Rogers so identified. In an era of colossi who could stride the American economy, Rogers had grown up to take his place with the likes of Carnegie, Morgan, and the Rockefellers. Only five years younger than Sam Clemens was when he went west to the Nevada territory and California, Rogers had saved enough money from odd jobs of selling papers and clerking in stores to go into partnership with another young man. They opened a small refinery in the Pennsylvania oil fields. By 1874 he was part of the group, along with the Rockefellers, who formed Standard Oil. He was on his way to becoming the outrageously wealthy man Clemens always wanted to be. Attaining wealth at any age is not without its taint of filthy lucre. Rogers had a reputation for being a tyrant to his colleagues, a cutthroat to his competitors, and a guardian to his friends.

Dr. Rice arranged a meeting for Clemens with Rogers at the Murray Hill Hotel. As with most important events in his life, Mark Twain liked to write of them with an aura of serendipity about them. He just happened to see young Langdon's image of Livy on the *Quaker City* in the Bay of Smyrna and was immediately taken by her. His fascination with Joan of Arc began when he was a young apprentice in Hannibal and happened upon a loose page from a book about Joan which was blowing down the street. So in his autobiography Twain described in 1909 his planned 1893 reintroduction to Rogers. "The meeting was accidental and unforeseen but it had memorable and fortunate consequences for me." Each man charmed the other with the natural talent that the other wished he possessed. Clemens told Rogers stories and Rogers talked of handling money. Later, Rice asked Rogers to look into the Gordian knot of Clemens's finances, for in Rice's understatement, "I am afraid they are a good deal confused."

By the 1890 reorganization of Standard Oil, Rogers had become a vice president and a director. Clemens was as bewitched with Rogers as he was with Paige, but with Rogers the spell never wore off. After Rogers's death Clemens paid him the highest possible compliment by comparing him to Livy. "In foresight, wisdom, accurate calculation, good judgment and the ability to see all sides of a problem, she had no match among people I have known, except Mr. Rogers." For to Rogers's credit he gave of his time and money management skills while preserving Livy's and Clemens's pride and demanding nothing of them but their cooperation. Clemens repaid him in equal loyalty. At a time when Webster Publishing could use the money, he refused to publish a book condemning Standard Oil saying Rogers was "the only man who is lavishing his sweat & blood to save me & mine from starvation."

Livy, the daughter of a self-made man, would not accept a direct gift from Rogers although eight thousand dollars was a pittance to him. She insisted they would pay back each cent. Rogers's first act to save the Clemenses' financial life was to rid the Charles L. Webster & Company of the *Library of American Literature* that was taking it into bankruptcy. Rogers arranged for his son-in-law William Evarts Benjamin to buy the ten-volume project for fifty thousand dollars. Charles Webster in his grave was not safe from Clemens's recriminations—it was all Webster's idea; Clemens never wanted the *Library of American Literature*. The move bought some time for Rogers to consider the economics of the typesetter. This delighted Clemens most of all. He wrote Livy, surprised that a stranger should be so generous to them, "I have got the best and wisest man of the whole Standard Oil groups—a multi-millionaire—a good deal interested in looking into the typesetter."

Clemens loved to loll around Rogers's eleventh-floor offices. In this "fortress," which overlooked the still-new Statue of Liberty, surely the American dream came true—money and power. Clemens marveled at Rogers's economic adeptness and energy. He wrote Livy, "It is beautiful to see Mr. Rogers apply his probe & his bung-starter & remorselessly let out the wind & the water from the so-called 'assets' of these companies." Wishing he could be more involved in his own finances, Clemens could do little but wait to be summoned to meetings. Yet he admired Rogers and loved to see him at work. "It's interesting to play games with a partner who knows how to play and what to play and when to play it." For Rogers's efforts, Clemens, who like his benefactor could love and hate with equal tenacity, called Rogers "the only man I care for in the world."

While Clemens waited for Rogers to straighten out his investments and debts, the best he could do was to try to keep busy by partaking of all the social activities New York could offer. In Clemens's words, "It rains invitations"—dinners, luncheons, the theater, balls. For his social rounds, he was dubbed the "Belle of New York." In Paris, Livy lived a quieter life as she waited for news from her husband. *Unberufen*, the German colloquial equivalent of "touch wood," became the word for all their troubles. He and Livy took turns in their letters repeating it to keep the luck it supposedly brought. *Unberufen* for Susy if she was better, *unberufen* for Livy's improved health, *unberufen* for Jean's teeth, *unberufen* for Clara's cough; and above all, *unberufen* for the machine.

Livy spent her forty-eighth birthday waiting alone. It was a cause for reflection for her. She wrote her friend, "Alice do you realize that we are middle aged women, isn't it *awful?* I cannot realize it, for in most things I feel quite as young as ever." To Clara she admitted, "Anniversaries are rather sad things when one has lost those who used to make much of them." Peculiarly American holidays are even more bittersweet when celebrated by yourself abroad. "We shall think as little about the old Thanksgiving days as possible. Four years this coming Thanksgiving that Susy first gave her play. Three years since Grandmamma lay so low."

Susy, in a fret to rival both of her parents, was in a vicious cycle. She had to sleep, tried to sleep, but couldn't. She was too tired to even attend her voice lessons. Another doctor suggested massage and gymnastics to overcome her anemia and increase her stamina. With Susy and their "financial perplexities" on her mind, Livy admitted, "Sometimes it has been hard to keep cheerful."

Clemens urged Livy to find a Christian Scientist experienced in mind cure to help Susy. George Warner had recommended one for Clemens to treat his bad cold and cough. Although the mind cure specialist stared at the wall while Clemens walked, talked, and smoked, Clemens thought he felt better, although he was also taking some powders. "I tried the mind-cure out of curiosity. That was yesterday. I have coughed only two or three times since. Maybe it was the mind-cure, maybe it was the powders." The Clemenses had experimented with mind over matter years before, and now there was so little they could control in their lives, if they could think themselves to health and prosperity, why not try?

Just as thousands of Americans in the late nineteenth century searched their own minds for the cause of their ailments, Alice Day also recommended Christian Science. She sent Livy some pamphlets to read. Clemens wrote Livy that William James of Harvard, according to Elinor Howells, said mind cure and hypnotism were really the same. Because Dr. Charcot was in Paris, Clemens pressed Livy to take Susy to him or one of his "pupils and disciples" (Charcot's most famous successor, one who had broken from his influence, was, of course, Sigmund Freud). "Don't lose a minute," he said, but Livy did not immediately rush out as her husband desired. She feared charlatans. She also disliked the "bad taste" of the way the pamphlets spoke of Mary Baker Eddy. It "offends one's taste" that they advertised to sell Eddy's pictures, while showing pictures of her summer home. For Livy it was far too "commercial" if they were just "trying to make an honest penny."

In a journal where Livy sporadically jotted down quotations and thoughts, she included some from her readings on mind cure. For this reader of Carlyle and Emerson, the passages that caught her attention emphasized the positive strengths we carry within us. From Helen Wilman's chapter entitled "I can and I will" in a book on mental science, Livy copied out segments on the "living fountain." "It is the only voice within you that you should ever listen to." Livy wrote out things in her own hand to think them through as she wrote. "Every time you turn away from the cries of weakness sent up by your exterior self—your body—and say 'I will not give up I will conquer,' you have come a step nearer the living fountain within." Not entirely convinced of being responsible for all her healing, Livy began electrical treatments, a standard and well-used method of treatment that had been around since her youth.

Livy needed to believe that thinking could make things good or ill as she sat, as she had for years, waiting for news on Paige. Although it was close to Christmas, she insisted Clemens, despite his guilt, stay in America until Paige signed a new contract with Clemens that would see the machine manufactured by the fall of 1894. Clemens told Livy that upon this contract, negotiated by Rogers, "depends our very bread & meat." With each week Clemens informed her that all would be well the following week. She wrote Sue Crane in January, "On the 5th of this month I received a cable, 'Expect good news in ten days.' On the 15th I received a cable, 'Look out for good news.' On the 19th a cable, 'Nearing success.' " He assured her he would never dabble in business again and do what she wanted him to do. "I will live in literature, I will wallow in it, revel in it; I will swim in ink!"

Livy received her twenty-fourth anniversary present on February second. The cable read, "Wedding news. Our ship is safe in port. I sail the moment Rogers can spare me."

The seeming conclusion of the Paige problem flooded Clemens with relief. Too agitated to sleep, cry or laugh, he wrote Livy, "Suddenly & without warning the realization burst upon me & overwhelmed me: I and mine, who were paupers an hour ago, are rich now & our troubles are over!" He told her to assemble the family and drink to Rogers's health.

Clemens felt confident enough of their financial situation after seven months' absence to go home for Susy's birthday. To his sister Pamela he wrote that he had left Livy "to fight her way long enough among strangers in indifferent health & with a sick daughter on her hands. Susy's health—but she hasn't any; it has all wasted away." Livy and Clemens had endured the longest separation of their married life.

He stayed with her for three weeks and returned to New York in early April to again take up quarters at The Players. Livy wanted to return with him but did not want to interrupt her electrical treatments and lose all the ground she had gained. There was really nothing either one could do in New York, for their relief was short-lived. While Clemens had devoted all his attention to Paige, the publishing company hadn't gone away.

Mount Morris Bank demanded a ten-thousand-dollar payment on its notes held against Webster & Company. Clemens informed Livy, "Mr. Rogers has been at Websterco's several times & kept close watch upon its affairs." Rogers had hoped to close out the business or at least get Clemens out of it in time, but Rogers wanting something wasn't always enough. A new president and board at the bank wanted their payment now.

After sleeping on the situation, Rogers gave Clemens the hard choice of coming up with a lot of money to keep the company going or going into voluntary receivership, something he had considered since January. Clemens had discussed it with Livy on his return home, but she was against this move. After years of doing without to keep their business interests going, she saw it as quitting, giving up. Rogers understood her beliefs and asked Clemens to tell her there was "not even a tinge of disgrace." It was the best thing to do. "If you don't do it you will probably never be free from debt, and it will kill you and Mrs. Clemens both."

On April 18, Clemens entered into bankruptcy. Rogers represented Clemens at a meeting of ninety-six creditors. Rogers, who had been called "a pirate" in many of his own business deals, judged some of these creditors as particularly ruthless. They were "bent on devouring every pound of flesh in sight and picking the bones afterward." Reminiscent of Clemens's vindictiveness toward the bookkeeper Scott who had pilfered twenty-five thousand dollars from the Webster till seven years ago, they wanted the Hartford house in addition to Clemens's copyrights and other assets. Rogers identified Livy as the chief creditor of the firm; it owed her sixty thousand dollars invested from her personal fortune. The house was in her name, and Rogers declared the copyrights were also hers. This shrewd move on his part saved Clemens's sanity and Livy's pride. Remembering it in 1909 Clemens wrote, "I am grateful to his memory for many a kindness and many a good service he did me but gratefulest of all for the saving of my copyrights—a service which saved me and my family from want and assured us permanent comfort and prosperity."

Rogers taught Clemens to refer to all their assets as Mrs. Clemens's—her books, copyrights, stock, her house. Clemens admitted to Livy, "I got the hang of it presently. I was even able to say with gravity, 'My wife has two unfinished books, but I am not able to say when they will be completed or where she will elect to publish them when they are done.' "

Livy expected the inevitability of bankruptcy, but the reality of it distressed her. She wrote Sue Crane, "But I have a perfect *horror* and heart-sickness over it. I cannot get away from the feeling that business failure means disgrace." Certain in this shame that her life was over and everything "impossible," she stated, "I should like to give it up and die." But what she admitted to her sister and the brave, comforting front she put on for her husband were two different faces. The only thing she could think to do was perhaps mortgage their Hartford home. Clemens wrote her words in his autobiography as he remembered it, "This is my house. The creditors shall have it. Your books are your property—turn them over to the creditors. Reduce the indebtedness in every way you can think of—then get to work and earn the rest of the indebtedness, if your life is spared. And don't be afraid. We shall pay a hundred cents on the dollar yet." She never wavered on this belief.

In an effort to convince herself as much as Alice Day, she wrote of their bankruptcy, "The two most important things, that there was nothing dishonourable about the failures, and that the debts will all be paid." Although because times were hard the other creditors had settled on being paid fifty cents out of a dollar, Livy insisted all would be paid back in full. Rogers agreed with her for he believed "a literary man's reputation is his life; he can afford to be money poor but he cannot afford to be character poor; you must earn the cent per cent and pay it."

The years of struggle had taken their toll on Livy. "Sue, if you were to see me you would see that I have grown old very fast during this last year. I have wrinkled."

Declaring bankruptcy was not an end, only a beginning. Clemens made what he called another "flying trip" back to the States after spending most of May, June, and July with his family moving about France in search of healthier cures and climes for Susy and Livy. Clara escaped into her music lessons in Switzerland.

Summoned by Rogers, Clemens arrived in New York on July 14 for a month. As much as Clemens delighted in watching Rogers harass their creditors, Livy was horrified.

What we want is to have those creditors get all their money out of Webster & Co. and surely we want those debts paid and we want to treat them all not only honestly but we want to help them in every possible way. It is money honestly owed and I cannot understand the tone which both you & Mr. Rogers seem to take—in fact I cannot understand it at all. You say Mr. Rogers has said some caustic and telling things to the creditors. (I do not know what your wording was) I should think it was the creditors [sic] place to say caustic things to us.

My darling, I cannot have any thing done in my name that I should not approve.

Livy had learned her ethics from a rare source—a scrupulous businessman, her father. Rogers was from a generation of businessmen who believed in the Darwinian philosophy of the survival of the fittest. Clemens invoked her father's memory to appease her and justify Rogers's methods. "Suppose father had been here in Mr. Rogers's place? Would he have advised me differently? Indeed, no." He promised, "I am not going to wrong anybody."

Clemens rejoined his family in Étretat in August before they all returned to Paris for the winter. Both Livy and Susy had brightened. Livy's electrical treatments benefited her so much that she intended to resume them in Paris. At Livy's suggestion, Clemens should postpone what he had feared for so long, returning to the lecture platform for money. She urged him to finish his labor of love, his book on Joan of Arc. Susy was right: "The world looks so attractive when one has something to *do!*" Clemens had a story to tell, Livy had manuscripts to proof, and Susy resumed her singing lessons.

The waters were temporarily calm for the Clemenses, but tragedy now struck Rogers, who lost his wife in May 1894. Another frail wife of a prominent, wealthy man, Abbie Rogers's heart was so weak that sometimes Rogers had to carry her up steps when there was no elevator. Yet she died of a tumor. Before the operation that ended her life, Rogers proudly related to Clemens that ever the businessman's wife, she had made out checks to pay her bills. The event prompted Clemens to say to Livy, "May we die together."

By December, with six months of learning to accept bankruptcy, Livy and Clemens were informed by Rogers of another financial blow. After a test run in October and subsequent breakdowns, the Chicago *Times-Herald* had lost interest in the Paige typesetter.

It had taken Rogers one year to see what Clemens refused to see in fifteen, that the machine would never work. It was useless to throw more money into it. Deep down, Clemens expected the news and was almost relieved. "Lord, it shows how little we know ourselves and how easily we deceive ourselves." He planned to leave for America the next day until Livy persuaded him to calm down and write Rogers. She knew there was little he could do; he should simply let Rogers bury the machine and all their hopes and dreams.

After three years' absence from her Hartford home, she had begun to long to see it again. She was reluctant to admit what her husband recognized: "We shall try to find a tenant for our Hartford house; not an easy matter, for it costs heavily to live in. We can never live in it again; though it would break the family's hearts if they could believe it." Susy had come to the same decision months before when she wrote her friend Louise, "We cannot now afford to live in Hartford."

If she must rent her home, Livy insisted on friends occupying it. As if providence guided her wishes, Alice Day and family had returned home to Hartford after Europe. Their own home had been rented out for the past seven years, and they didn't wish to upset their tenants. Alice, aware of Livy's predicament, wrote asking to rent her friend's house. At first Livy did not want to admit that she might never live on Farmington Avenue again. She used several concerns as excuses. She was reluctant to say they could have it for longer than six months as Clemens would be in Hartford for business and might need to stay there. Also, "The house has stood unused so long that there will be a good deal to do to it, plumbing, etc."

Finally, confronting reality, she agreed if Alice would promise to care for the contents of the house and servants who had so faithfully watched over them. "There are so many things in that house that father and mother gave me and that I can never replace, so I am entirely unwilling to risk their being handled by careless servants or used by unloving hands," Livy instructed Franklin Whitmore who was acting as the rental agent in her absence. It was agreed. The Days would stay until December and then the O'Neills would once again occupy it on their own as they had for years.

On their twenty-fifth wedding anniversary, Livy and Clemens were nearly one hundred thousand dollars in debt. Clemens marveled, "Nothing daunts Mrs. Clemens or makes the world look black to her—which is the reason I haven't drowned myself."

The groom was nearly sixty; the bride nearly fifty. At a time when they should have been thinking of retiring, living an easy life on all they had built together over the years, looking forward to grandchildren, they had to start over with less than they had had as newlyweds. Clemens gave Livy a silver five-franc coin saying, "It is our silver-wedding day, and so I give you a present." Within a week he had finished the story of Joan of Arc and read it aloud to the family. Susy recorded, "To-night Joan of Arc was burned at the stake." They all cried, but they were weeping for more than the death of a martyr.

CHAPTER 20

"The bondage of debt"

Clemens, back in the States in March, wrote Livy that at first he thought he never wanted to live in Hartford again, that he didn't want to cross the threshold of their house. Knowing the power their home had over him, he feared surrendering to it. Livy empathized, for she had written Alice Day of spring on Farmington Avenue. "I think there is no season of the year when the place is so charming as during April, May and June," she sadly commented when she agreed to rent her house. Once inside, Clemens was overcome with memories: "It took my breath away." Katy Leary and the O'Neills had the house in order for the Days. "Katy had every rug and picture and ornament and chair exactly where they had always belonged." It was as if they had never left. Time melted away; Livy must be upstairs with the children. Momentarily he knew security and peace for the first time in years, and he wanted to prolong the feeling. "I was seized with a furious desire to have us all in this house again and right way, and never go outside the grounds any more forever—"

For Clemens, "It seemed as if I had burst awake out of a hellish dream." But the nightmare was all too true. Livy was not upstairs, and all he could afford of this house was its memories. He was about to embark on what he had dreaded for so long. To Mrs.

Fairbanks he acknowledged he would "have to mount the platform next fall or starve." Although he had praised Rogers for saving him from this "unendurable toil," Clemens always knew he could return to it when he needed money. James B. Pond, who had arranged his last tour with Cable in 1884, had proposed a tour two years ago when the panic had first begun. Now Clemens felt the necessity. This time the world would be his stage.

Hartford longed to welcome Livy. "Words cannot describe how worshipfully and enthusiastically you are loved in this town; and the wash of the wave reaches even to me, because I belong to you." Livy wanted to visit old friends, but knew it would be too painful to see her house if she could not live in it. She planned their itinerary; they would go from New York to Elmira, bypassing Hartford.

Clara and Susy too had misgivings about returning home. Though homesick for so long, both had become accustomed to life abroad. Susy had admitted to Louise Brownell two years previously, "I was afraid of this fatal result of staying over here too long."

Clemens sailed to Europe and brought his family back to America in May 1895. They stayed a few days in New York at the Everett House before moving to Quarry Farm. Charles Langdon had asked them to be his guests at the new Waldorf, but Livy declined because "it wouldn't look modest for bankrupts." Because she felt strong and was concerned about their finances, Livy did not see a physician in New York. Livy was happy to be home, and her health had rarely been better.

In the four years since Livy had been to Quarry Farm, it had changed little except that vines now covered Clemens's gazebo study. All that she loved was still there—the hush of the hills, the earthy scent of the pines, the early morning mists off the Chemung River, the crickets in the evening. The sights and sounds and smells caused her to reflect on family who were gone. Livy admitted, "It is, in a way, hard to go home."

Major Pond joined them at the farm for three weeks to work with Livy and Clemens on the tour. Since Clemens was in bed with a carbuncle, much of the planning was done by Livy and Pond. The carbuncle was so fierce that Clemens feared he wouldn't be able to stand, let alone tour. Lancing the boil helped, but he had lost time. Instead of having three readings prepared, he only had one. With Livy's help in selecting readings, he would have to make up the others as they traveled. This thirteen-month "lecturing raid" would be grueling on a man half his age. He would open in Cleveland, travel across the United States to the Pacific and sail to perform in Australia, New Zealand, India, South Africa. He would conclude in England by writing a travel book of their experiences before they came back to Hartford. For the first time in months, husband and wife began to talk of the future. When their travels were over, debts paid, they would go home to live once again in their house. By Livy's calculations it would take four years to pay off their debts.

Livy, excited about the journey, realized it would probably be her only chance to see the world. It was the first time she would see the vast expanse of the western United States. Yet this was more than just a holiday excursion for her. Paying these debts was a matter of honor to her, and she would support her husband in earning the money. She would take on the responsibility of the business side of the journey, keeping the accounts and doing the correspondence, which included passing on the gate receipts to Rogers minus Pond's share. Given purpose, her health flourished, although Clemens worried about her ability to make the journey.

This time they waited for the doctor to say Clemens, not Livy, was fit to travel. Livy wanted all three girls to accompany them. Susy and Jean elected to stay behind with Aunt Sue in Elmira. Clara, the most adventuresome and healthiest of the three, would go along to help her mother. Livy was torn by the prospect of being separated from her two daughters for over a year, but she knew Clemens needed her on this tour. Susy disliked the sea as she suffered severely from seasickness. Besides, Madame Marchesi had prescribed a year of healthy farm life, "on a hill," to increase Susy's lung capacity. With a healthy diet, fresh air, and exercise, she could properly begin to train for the opera. Jean preferred to stay with the animals at Quarry Farm, and at fourteen had not finished school. Livy enrolled her in preparatory school in Elmira. Katy Leary would help Sue see that Susy lived a healthy existence and that Jean got to school every day.

The Clemenses accompanied by Major and Mrs. Pond left Elmira by train July 14, 1895. It was ten-thirty at night. As the train pulled out, Livy and Susy waved to each other, crying and blowing kisses until neither could see the other. As Susy's figure, under the station lights, receded into the distance, it reminded Livy of when she left her on the railway platform at Bryn Mawr.

From Cleveland, they "lectured and robbed and raided" their way across a sweltering United States. Livy was overwhelmed at their reception. Everywhere they were greeted with flowers, dinners, ovations, plaques, and gifts. The audiences were full. The American public came to see their favorite author, for they had heard of his plight and his vow to pay off his creditors. They wished Mark Twain well; if he could start over, so could they. Before sailing from the West Coast he told his admirers what they wanted to hear:

> From my reception thus far on my lecturing tour I am confident that if I live I can pay off the last debt within four years, after which, at the age of sixty-four, I can make a fresh and unincumbered [sic] start in life. I am going to Australia, India and South Africa, and next year I hope to make a tour of the great cities of the United States. I meant, when I began, to give my creditors all the benefit of this, but I am beginning to feel that I am gaining something from it, too, and that my dividends, if not available for banking purposes, may be even more satisfactory than theirs.

The adulation boosted his crippled pride and his health. "Lecturing is gymnastics, chest-expander, medicine, mind-healer, blues-destroyer, all in one." He insisted, "I am twice as well as I was when I started out" although he continued to suffer from weariness, rheumatism, and a perpetual cold that sometimes delayed his lecture a day or two. He also thought the trip was good for Livy and Clara. "My wife and daughter are accumulating health and strength and flesh nearly as fast as I am." Susy wondered to Clara how their "little modest Mamma" was putting up with the "splurge"? Clara agreed with her father it was good for Livy because she always prospered by a change of scenery, and on this trip they were seeing much of that. All her life, Livy was able to take catnaps at any time and any place, so she was getting plenty of rest. Livy's good health made it easier on Clara, who considered it part of her job to see that her mother didn't overextend herself. Having made it this far with no problems, Clara was certain she could go on easily to Australia.

Clemens felt so good from his public's response that he wanted *Joan of Arc* published under his name, not anonymously. He had told Rogers, "Possibly the book may not sell, but that is nothing—it was written for love." His enthusiastic crowds now persuaded him the book could also bring him money as well as love. The book had begun serialization in *Magazine,* and after a few issues readers guessed the author from his style. Clemens wrote Harper's requesting the change in plans, thinking that his name on it might help with the sales. Livy, convinced of her husband's own argument that if readers knew Mark Twain wrote it, the book would not be taken as a serious work of literature, said no. He had his own way, but dedicated it to Livy for "her years of valued service as my literary adviser and editor" even if he didn't follow her advice.

Leaving the Ponds in Vancouver, Livy, Clemens, and Clara sailed for the land down under. A cholera quarantine kept them from going ashore at the Sandwich Islands. Clemens was disappointed he could not lecture in the land he had visited as a young man and that he had so often spoken about to Livy. They had to content themselves with gazing from a distance at "the silky mountains . . . clothed in soft, rich splendors of melting color, and some of the cliffs were veiled in slanting mists." On board their ship was a woman who had crossed with Clemens from California to Hawaii twenty-nine years previously. She and others who lived on the islands went ashore. Livy, troubled about sending these people to a disease-infested island, pondered, "We shall probably never see one of them again in this life." In this life, she also noted that Clemens lost a minimum five-hundred-dollar profit by not being able to speak. The calm sea and lack of breeze made the air stifling. Livy and Clara looked for relief by trying to sleep in the ladies' lounge. Nothing helped, so they returned to their stateroom.

Even if the weather could be uncomfortable, the voyage was full of strange new natural sights not known to Elmira, Hartford, or even Europe. In the month it took to sail from Hawaii to Australia, they saw meteorites, a total eclipse of the moon, and flying fish. Porpoises dived and resurfaced, dived and resurfaced, racing the ship toward the equator. When her father pointed out the horizon of the blue Pacific and said it was the equator, Clara, along with some other passengers, took a photograph of it.

After stopping a few hours on the Fiji Islands, they landed in Sydney on September 16, 1895 to another enthusiastic reception. Livy was relieved that for the first time in three weeks they could get letters from home. She wrote Susy, "People are good and kind to us everywhere, and we get a most lively interest in them, and dislike leaving them." Crowds were good in Australia; a thousand came every night to hear and see Mark Twain. "And so it goes, it is constant unceasing adulation of Papa and most appreciative words about him. They know his work well out here, in fact they seem to know most of it by heart."

No matter what the size of the audience, Clemens had two constant faithful followers—Livy and Clara. Livy wanted to hear how his material was going and to make suggestions about ordering it and what to include or exclude. She knew the material so well that she gained her humor not from him but from watching the crowds. She helped Clemens vary his lecture each time he gave it. If he gave two lectures in the same place, he gave two entirely different readings. She gauged an audience as to how good a story was by how quickly they got the point and how long and loud they laughed. "They made me laugh most heartily," she wrote Susy, "much more at them than at Papa's talk, as that really was not all new to me."

Clemens appreciated how his wife and daughter "would afflict themselves with my whole performance every night when there was no sort of necessity for it in order that they might watch the house when that pause came; they believed that by the effect they could accurately measure the high or low intelligence of the audience." Clemens, the master storyteller, knew how to work the audience with the pause. "For one audience the pause will be short, for another a little longer, for another a shade longer still; the performer must vary the length of the pause to suit the shades of difference between the audiences."

Clemens admitted, "I used to play with the pause as other children play with a toy." Two stories of his depended on the effect of the pause as observed by Livy. One was "The Golden Arm" story that had so frightened and humiliated Susy. The other was "His Grandfather's Old Ram" in which an Irishman falls from a ladder on a stranger and not on a dog. Which is special providence? To save the dog, to save the Irishman, or kill the stranger? The pause Livy waited for followed the part of the story, "Why wa'n't the dog app'inted? Becuz *the dog would 'a' seen him a-comin'*."

If Clemens got the timing just right, the laughter could be "a crash." If the audience was sharp, they immediately picked up on "the logic which recognizes a dog as an instrument too indifferent to pious restraints and too alert in looking out for his own personal interest to be safely depended upon in an emergency requiring self-sacrifice for the benefit of another, even when the command comes from on high."

They sailed to New Zealand on what Clemens called "a cattle-scow" and Livy called "perfect pandimonium [sic]." Instead of the intended 125 passengers on board they estimated two hundred. Livy wrote, "Every corner of the ship was turned into a sleeping room. People slept on the tables, under the tables and in all the passage ways." There were no towels, pillows or sheets, but they did have extra women in their tiny room. They couldn't move for bags and trunks all about the floor. Livy and Clara constantly had to shake their clothes to get the cockroaches out of them. Livy accepted the situation philosophically. "We comfort ourselves now that if we should at any time be compelled to go steerage it could bring us little experience that would be new."

Livy and Clara stayed in Palmerston North in New Zealand while Clemens toured and lectured with his Australian contact Mr. Smythe. Livy took the opportunity to learn more about a people that she had read of before their voyage. She was interested in the plight of the Maori, a Polynesian tribe threatened by their proximity to white culture. They had resisted British colonization by waging an eight-year war when their lands were seized. When they lost, the British set about to westernize them; fortunately for them or not, the Maori later adapted and survived. Hearing of her interest, their hosts the Kinseys gave them Maori gifts—a necklace for Livy and a wife-beater for Clemens.

One day Livy and Clara went to visit one of their villages and were fascinated with the Maori's bushy hair and tattooed lips. After seeing the village and taking some fleas back with them, Livy remarked of her interest in these primitive peoples, "I have been very much interested in the Maoris since we came here, and have been anxious to see more of them, now I have had enough I shall not seek their dwellings any more."

Livy could write, "In spite of the fact that our lives are not now all luxury we enjoy ourselves *very much*." Faraway places still could not make her totally forget the purpose of their voyage. Although her husband sometimes despaired of paying their debts, Livy was hopeful. "I am sure if his life & health are spared to him that it will not be long until he is out of debt. Won't that be one joyful day," she wrote her sister.

Clemens lost time in New Zealand with his third troublesome carbuncle of the trip. They also both celebrated their birthdays. He turned sixty, and she confided to Sue, "I do not like it one single bit. Fifty years old—think of it; that seems very far on." Her birthday made her reflective. "I wonder if we ever shall get our debts all paid, and live once more in our own house. Today it seems to me as if we never should. However, much of the time

I believe we shall, but it is a long way." She asked that Sue send her some financial news for "I have had no word since I left America regarding any of the business affairs." She was particularly interested in how it would affect the cost of living in their home again.

They spent Christmas in Melbourne. With four months into their trip and nearly nine more to go, Livy began to realize they would not return to England by spring but more like late summer or fall. "Everything takes longer than we expected," she wrote Susy. The sooner they got back to England, the sooner they would see Jean and Susy and the sooner they could live in their home again, which made any discomfort she lived through now worth it. "We have done steadily our work all the time, we have not loitered *one day* for sight-seeing." In fact, she feared Clemens would not have enough for a book as they had passed by so much for lack of time and seen "almost nothing of the wonder of this land that we ought to see."

To Susy, Clemens blamed the carbuncles and colds he battled on "a diseased mind, and that your mental science could drive them away, if we only had . . . you here to properly apply it." Both Livy and Clemens were pleased with Susy's study of mind cure in their absence. Livy wrote, "I am very glad indeed that Susy has taken up Mental Science, and I do hope it may do her as much good as she hopes." It was all the rage in polite society so Susy heard of it in the few luncheons and balls she attended in Elmira and Hartford. She was practicing her music but still consumed with her own restlessness. She thought mind cure would be the answer to her "spoiling and frittering away my life." In Hartford she contacted her former governess Lilly Foote who had introduced the family to mind cure. "I have become determined to get hold of a philosophy that will if possible straighten me out morally, mentally, and physically and make me less of a burden to myself and others," Susy wrote Clara.

She felt it helped her in social situations, where she was often shy. She had learned from the Christian Scientists and Spiritualists she met in New York that all people had positive and negative aspects that must be kept in balance. "One doesn't have to control one's *external* manner; it may be quiet or talkative, but the *inner* attitude must be right and then the real poise is felt." It gave Susy's creative mind an outlet, for if she dwelt too much on everyday things her sensitive nature led her to be deeply depressed. At Quarry Farm she practiced her mental science treatments on John Lewis's daughter, also named Susy, and her cousin Julia Langdon.

After two days in Ceylon and delays due to illness in India, Clemens began his two-month tour of the country. He was so popular he often had to give three lectures a day to accommodate the crowds, and sometimes people were turned away. They were collecting so many gifts that Livy wondered how she would get them all home. While Clemens's health often suffered from the exhaustion and the stresses of the trip, Livy boasted to Jean, "Don't you think I must be pretty strong and well?" She also noted they were "royally treated everywhere we go." In India they had servants who followed them about, even waiting on them in someone else's home and sleeping at their doorsteps. The servitude of the lower classes, which included men pulling jinrikishas, even if they were paid, bothered the egalitarian Clemenses. In a reverse discrimination that amused them, they stayed as houseguests of a maharaja, but they had to take their meals alone, as the maharaja wouldn't eat at a table with inferior white people.

Livy went to a museum where only women attended at certain times, "so Hindu ladies can go in without being afraid of being seen by men." Livy found "I was as great a curiosity to them as they were to me. They crowded about me and chattered and examined me and followed me about." Livy so liked their colorful silken saris, "their gorgeous dressing," that she had one made for Susy.

Surprisingly, Clemens wrote Twichell, "Livy and Clara enjoy this nomadic life pretty well; certainly better than one could have expected they would." He added, "They put up with the worst that befalls with heroic endurance that resembles contentment." This included shaking clothes for cockroaches, looking under beds for snakes, fighting off mosquitoes and other insects, and trying to survive the heat. The wind burned Livy's face, but if she tried to stay out of the wind she remarked, "You suffocate with the heat."

Clemens was not enduring or content. Livy tried to encourage him as much as possible but it was difficult to buoy herself up sometimes. Her goal that kept her strength up was to live in her house again, but sometimes that seemed "far in the distance." She wrote Alice Day that while she was happy to know she was in the house she was also "jealous." "I love that house and the things it contains as I could never love another one, but I know if I were able to go back to it that I should feel very much the grind of the work that it is to keep such a house, and also the worry of having to live there more economically than formerly." Livy spent much of her time with pencil and paper on this tour making "acres of figures" trying to figure out how they could live in their house on one thousand dollars a month as they had done in Paris.

She wrote her sister of her dream, "You know I have pretty good courage, but sometimes it comes over me like an overwhelming wave, that it is to be bitterness and disappointment to the end." It took all her strength to get her "poor old darling" husband on the stage. In his blackest times he raged that he never wanted to return to America. "He does not believe that any good thing will come, but that we must all our lives live in poverty."

In South Africa, Clemens became so discouraged he considered taking the post of American consul in Johannesburg as he had once considered applying for a diplomatic post in China in February 1868. Then he had just met Livy at the Christmas *Quaker City* reunion. Now she was his wife, and she firmly refused. She wanted to return home one day.

Once on the stage, he enjoyed the attention "but all the rest of the time it grinds him, and he says he is ashamed of what he is doing." Sometimes all he could do was take to his bed, but ten days of rest cost him nearly two thousand dollars, Livy estimated. By the time they were ready to sail to England, Livy's account books showed they still needed forty to fifty thousand dollars to pay off their "bondage of debt," which she admitted to Sue "is a very large sum of money to try to earn."

South Africa was their last stop, and she became a bit more

optimistic, for she could see the end. "We feel now the back of our journey is broken, and that we are starting toward home, at least toward England which will be so much nearer home."

Livy and Clara stayed in Durban while Clemens lectured throughout South Africa. Even by letter, Livy kept her role of advisor and admirer. She loved and missed him and cautioned him, "But you must continue to miss me and to think that you do not get on as well without me as you do with." Although she could not physically be in his audience, she advised him on his lectures by mail as she had done when they were engaged twenty-seven years previously. He must make sure his presentations were long enough for the audience. "I want them to feel that they have had the worth of their money." She advised including the "Jumping Frog" or "Buck Fanshaw" to lengthen his program. "I should think if a reader could make it go, you could make it go much better."

After two months in South Africa, they headed for Southampton on July 14, 1896, exactly one year since they had left Elmira. They had sailed round the globe and toward the twentieth century. In India the young Gandhi had been their guide at a Hindu temple. Livy had worried about the intrusion of western culture on what would become known as the third world. In South Africa, Clemens visited British prisoners taken by the Boers in the Jameson Raid.

When Livy and Clemens started their journey, he was an American literary figure, but he would return a world literary figure. His journeys and speakings popularized Mark Twain's works on a shrinking earth that made him then and still the best-known American writer in the world.

Livy was not thinking of posterity. She was happy to be heading home to see her other two daughters and looking forward to occupying her house again in Hartford. Everywhere Livy had traveled in circumnavigating the globe, she met kind people she hated to leave. "So I went, wondering as I daily wonder, whether I should see them ever again," she repeated in different words at each stop on the journey. Ironically, she had not had these thoughts when she left Susy in Elmira.

CHAPTER 21

"I cannot find Susy & I cannot find the light."

S usy missed her family. Absence had heightened the good times for her and dimmed the troubled ones. She had written Clara, "We *are* such a congenial family. It seems to me no one ever understands us as we understand each other. We *do* belong together." In pet names whose origins were as personal and special as the sisterly bond, Susy wrote to her sister Black Spider, Blackie, or Spider. Clara wrote to her sister Pigg, Porc Pigg, Pea, or Sweet Pea. Susy had even taken to playfully calling her father the gray *grenouille*, French for "frog." As the time grew closer for their reunion, all became more excited. Looking forward to the time they would be together in London, Pigg and Spider repeated to each other in their letters, "Won't it be nuts?"

Lonely at Quarry Farm, Susy visited for three weeks in New York before going on to stay in Hartford with the Days in her family's own house and then with the Warners. She found Hartford not as intellectually stimulating as New York, but she fought her bouts of depression by telling herself, "When we are all together all will be well." Every day Susy practiced her voice in the house she grew up in to the delight of the neighborhood and proof of her talent. Katy Leary remarked, "Well, there was always a crowd outside in the street listening to Susy sing, for she had a wonderful voice and really we had a concert every afternoon."

Livy and company arrived in England on July 31. Since she had sprained her ankle on shipboard, it was difficult for her to inspect prospective lodgings. She found this particularly frustrating for she could not cable her girls to join her until she found a house. She quickly took one in Guildford in London with the idea of finding something better at a later time. Livy wrote Sue Crane not to let Jean, Susy, and Katy sail for England until she cabled them and to be sure they came over on an American line. Livy was so anxious that she underlined the instructions to an elder sister who was not lacking in common sense.

Livy cabled for Susy, Jean, and Katy to start on Saturday, August 5. Katy rushed to Elmira to ready Jean for the voyage and returned with her to Hartford. She then went to the Warners on Friday morning to fetch Susy, so they could leave the next day. Susy, pale and flushed, said to Katy, "I don't think I can start now. Couldn't we wait till evening, when it's cooler?" Hartford was in the midst of its summer heat, but Susy burned within.

By the afternoon, Susy's fever was worse, but because of her belief in mental science, she insisted, "I don't want any doctor or any medicine." Even if Susy's parents approved of mind cure, Katy and her no-nonsense Irish pragmatism did not. She sensed Susy had not been well since she returned from New York with her head filled with "darn lies." When one of the Spiritualist healers, who used to pass her hand over Susy's throat to make her a strong singer, insisted to Susy that her dead husband attended a concert with her, Katy said, "Rats!" She refused to let Susy see the woman again. Susy had continued what she called "absent treatments" every day when she would sit and concentrate on another healer a "Miss B—" who would, in turn, be thinking of her. Now, in her fever, Susy insisted this was all she needed. Katy disagreed, went for Dr. Porter, and sent word to England that Susy was too ill to travel.

"Nothing serious," said the letter, further information to follow. Porter diagnosed that Susy had been working too hard. She should rest. Feeling uneasy, Livy told Clara to start packing. They would take the next ship for New York. Clemens cabled for more news. Katy's reply, "Wait for cablegram in the morning." Clemens stayed at the Guildford post office until midnight, but still no word. Clemens, Livy, and Clara sat quietly until one in the morning. They tried to sleep but couldn't. The morning of August 15, Clemens took his wife and daughter to the boat train. Before it left, a cablegram reached them saying, "Susy's recovery will be long but certain." Clemens was relieved, but Livy was frightened. She wanted to care for her Susy.

Susy did not improve. Her Uncle Charlie and Aunt Sue came from Elmira when Katy telephoned them. They moved her from the Warners' home into the guest bedroom on the first floor of the Clemenses' Hartford home. Joseph Twichell joined them from the Adirondacks. The doctor diagnosed spinal meningitis the same day that Livy and Clara left England for New York.

Susy's fever and delirium seared her body and mind. She spent the last thirteen days of her life in pain and misery. Livy and Clemens would later insist that Katy tell them the details of these days over and over again in an attempt to share their daughter's final hours.

In her delirium, Susy wandered from room to room and would have no one nurse her but Katy. She found an old dress of Livy's, buried her head in it, and cried and cried, thinking her mother dead. She dressed and sat writing. She imagined she was the friend of La Malibran, a famous singer who had died very young. She criticized her own ambitions, "You will never follow far enough in her footsteps artistically to dominate the artistic world with light." She wrote, "In strength I bow to Mme. Malibran Mr. Clemens Mr. Zola. . . . " Looking out the window, she commented, "Up go the trolley cars for Mark Twain's daughter. Down go the trolley cars for Mark Twain's daughter." Clemens would later grasp at these words as proof of his daughter's love and approval.

When at last Susy lay down to die, the infection spread to her brain and she lost her sight. "I am blind, Uncle Charlie, and you are blind." Susy's last gesture and words broke Livy's heart, for she later said, "I was not with her. . . . I can never forgive myself this desertion." Susy reached out, touched Katy's face, and said, "Mamma." She lay unconscious for two days before she died on a Tuesday evening, August 18.

When Clemens wrote of Susy's death in his autobiography, he took great solace in this last action of hers. "How gracious it was that in that forlorn hour of wreck and ruin, with the night of death closing around her, she should have been granted that beautiful illusion—that the latest vision which rested upon the clouded mirror of her mind should have been the vision of her mother, and the latest emotion she should know in life the joy and peace of that dear imagined presence." Clemens was in Guildford, in the dining room, in his own words, "thinking of nothing in particular, when a cable-gram was put into my hand. It said, 'Susy was peacefully released today.' "

"It is one of the mysteries of our nature that a man, all unprepared, can receive a thunder-stroke like that and live." He noted Susy was twenty-four years and five months old. He immediately thought of Livy and Clara, three days at sea and in troubled but blessed ignorance. In his anguish and loneliness, he had begun to write letter after letter to Livy the moment she had left, more for himself than to her, alternating between blaming himself and looking for shreds of comfort. Before they knew Susy was dead, both had expected the worst. On August 16, Clemens wrote Livy, "I could not tell you how deeply I loved you nor how grieved I was for you, nor how I pitied you in this awful trouble that my mistakes have brought upon you. You forgive me, I know, but I shall never forgive myself while the life is in me." He did not yet know Susy was dead, and he had begun to blame himself as he would to his own deathbed.

Later, in stunned grief, he irrationally reasoned that if only he had agreed with his sister Pamela not to let Annie marry Charles Webster, he would never have gone bankrupt and left Susy alone as they traveled round the world. His greatest pain was that he could not be with his wife to comfort her: "My grief is for the mother—for myself I am thankful; my selfish love aside, I would not have it otherwise." He searched through letters looking for anything Susy had written him and could find "oh, not so much as a line." Seeking absolution for something which no one could be blamed or forgiven, Clemens, who needed guilt and forgiveness, had met his challenge. Mentally, he whipped himself: "—but I neglected her as I neglect everybody in my selfishness." Without Livy to moderate his emotions, he condemned, tried, and sentenced himself, "my crimes made her a pauper & an exile." The only thing that kept him going was Livy. "I eat—because you wish it; I go on living—because you wish it; I play billiards, billiards, and billiards, till I am ready to drop—"

Alternating between gloom and optimism, Livy and Clara sailed across "the unending Atlantic Ocean." They were due to land in New York on the twenty-second of August. As Clara was on her way to the salon, a steward told her the captain wished to see her. Before she could reach his quarters, he found her in the companionway. The captain showed her a newspaper with the headlines MARK TWAIN'S ELDEST DAUGHTER DIES OF SPINAL MENINGITIS. Her immediate thought, "How can I tell Mother?" When Livy saw Clara's face there was no need to tell her. Livy swooned, "I don't believe it!"

Joseph Twichell, Charles Langdon, Dr. Rice, and Katy met them in New York. Clemens had cabled Rogers to have them meet the ship but not en masse. He knew the sight of all of them would overwhelm Livy with grief. They must tell Clara first. They too wondered how they could face Livy, who unbeknownst to them already knew. Those who greeted her just made the unbelievable believable to Livy. Katy commented, "Such grief is terrible to see. I could hardly bear to look at Mrs. Clemens just at first." All Livy could say was "Susy's gone—Life has killed her!"

In ironies that a writer recognizes, Clemens noted that Livy and Clara arrived in Elmira on "the same train and in the same car which had borne them and me westward from it one year, one month and one week before." Katy had taken Susy to Elmira, to the house where she was born, to lie in her coffin in the same parlor in which her mother had been married and where the coffins of her Langdon grandparents and her brother Langdon had lain.

Clemens, unbearably alone in England, envied Livy, "You will see her." There was no use that he sail for America; he would not arrive in time for the funeral. He felt horribly left out. He looked for word from anyone of details of Susy's death for he only knew she had died of "brain congestion and meningitis." He wrote Livy, "I sit back & try to believe that there are any human beings in the world, friends or foes, civilized or savage, who would close their lips *there*, & leave me these many, many, many days eating my heart out with longings for the tidings that never come." Livy found only the strength to send a cablegram inquiring as to his health. In his despair, Clemens stated, "I wish there were five coffins." "How lovely is death; and how niggardly it is doled out."

Livy, unbearably alone with her family about her, envied Katy. "Oh, Katy, if it could only have been *me* instead of you!" Standing at Susy's coffin calmed Livy, and she remarked at her daughter's beauty. Cruelly, as Clemens would see at Livy's demise, death restores the ravages of illness. Livy kept a vigil at her daughter's coffin, refusing food and sleep until Susy's funeral.

"On the 23rd her mother and her sisters saw her laid to rest— she that had been our wonder and our worship," Clemens wrote. On the hillside Elmira cemetery where Susy had often visited with her family and played as a child among the headstones and the trees, she was buried with her little brother and her grandparents. On her headstone, Livy and Clemens engraved lines from a poem Livy had found. They later identified it as written by the Australian author Robert Richardson when people tried to credit it to Mark Twain. They changed northern to southern as below the equator warm wind comes from the opposite direction.

> *Warm summer sun, shine brightly here,*
> *Warm Southern wind, blow softly here,*
> *Green sod above, lie light, lie light,*
> *Good night, dear heart; good night, good night.*

Livy tried to take comfort that Susy had died quickly, not lingering like Winifred Howells, and that it was better for Susy to have died than to have survived without her mental faculties. Clemens tried to take comfort that Susy had died in her own house. "If she had died in another house—well, I think I could not have borne that," he wrote Twichell.

A few months before, Livy had written a letter of condolence to Mrs. Whitmore on the death of her child. How prophetic her words were, "Why, Why—we must constantly ask—are we allowed to love and rear these children and then have to sit by helpless when they are taken away from us." Night and helplessness had descended upon Livy and brought with it isolation. She was not only separated from her Susy, but from her other daughters and her husband. She could barely hold herself together, let alone the husband and family so dependent on her. She would eventually echo her husband's sentiments, "I long to be with Susy."

At twenty-one years of age, Susy had written a remarkable rule for herself, "The less we *feel* the better off we are, and the more good we can do. It's a *horrid repulsive* conclusion, but really I believe it. I think that I live better when I don't feel." If she could only have passed this belief on to her family, who were now immobilized with grief and obsessed with their loss.

Livy, Clara, Jean, and Katy returned to England, and the family moved to a house in a section of Chelsea, 23 Tedworth Square, to hide away that forlorn autumn. Clemens wrote Howells that he was "indifferent to nearly everything but work." For eight or nine hours at a stretch, he "buried" himself in writing the travel book that would become *Following the Equator*. Livy, he wrote, was "always so quick to recover herself before, but now there is no rebound, & we are dead people who go through the motions of life." For hours at a time while Clemens worked, Livy sat by herself, speaking to no one, trying to reason what had happened and why. "What a mystery it all is? What a heartbreaking mystery." Sometimes she copied out a poem or a quotation in an attempt to console herself. From an unidentified source: "There comes a time when one's grief becomes a closed chapter to the world and the heart goes on bearing it alone." When she wrote a friend, it was on the black-rimmed mourning paper she used the rest of her days, black rimmed as her heart was. Katy Leary recognized that Livy never got over Susy's death. "It was always on her heart."

Her letters became expiations of grief as in the mourning process she moved from shock to anger. "Now my world is dark," she wrote Alice Day. "I cannot find Susy & I cannot find the light." No one would understand her pain. "No one knows, and only Mr. Clemens and Clara can suspect what Susy was to me." Now Spiritualism was a "terrific evil influence" and why had those around Susy let her succumb to it? Why hadn't they sent for Livy's brother and sister, Susy's "natural and wise protectors"? Susy was "badly managed" in Livy's absence. Death raises all types of rhetorical questions and comments for those who remain alive. Livy voiced them. "Yet, I cannot take it in I am alive and *Susy* dead!" With a loss so great she asks, "What saves such from committing suicide?"

She received a letter of condolence from Howells that so touched her, because he too had lost a daughter, Livy placed it in her New Testament. Yet this woman so kind and gentle and always considerate of others until now replied of the Howellses, "What do *they* know? They have lost a daughter, but they have not lost a Susy Clemens."

Clemens lashed out in anger at the "damned human race." "It is an odious world, a horrible world—it is Hell; the true one, not the lying invention of the superstitious; and we have come to it from elsewhere to expiate our sins." He would take Clara and Jean for walks along the Thames or through Regent's Park and expound on the flaws of human nature, the same flaws he damned himself for—all people were selfish, easily corruptible, incapable of change. Clara argued with her father over these pessimistic views. Neither could Livy be so extreme. In pity, not hate, she said, "poor, poor human nature." Clemens expanded his bitterness on paper, which led in 1897 to what he called his gospel, his Bible, "What is Man?" Livy hated the book, would not hear of it, and forbade him to publish it. He did not publish it until after her death, and then published it anonymously and not for sale.

For those mourning, it seems impossible that life goes on outside the shell. The raw spots can't bear any contact, and so it is easier to stay within. "My family are hermits & cannot see any one," Clemens declared. Since they were still in need of money, it made for an excuse not to go out. Clara had to practice her piano daily. Jean's epilepsy had manifested itself in seizures during the round-the-world tour. Now they were becoming more frequent, so it was best they stay at home with her.

The Clemenses were so isolated that rumors began to circulate that Mark Twain was deserted by his family, sick and impover-ished. For Clemens this was further proof of man's vile nature. "This would enrage and disgust me if it came from a dog or a cow, or an elephant or any other of the higher animals, but it comes from a man, and much allowance must be made for man." The New York *Herald* began a fund with one thousand dollars for the payment of his debts. Andrew Carnegie offered another thou-sand. The *Herald* asked for any amount as little as five cents per person from all over the world. Livy put a stop to it all, and Clemens wrote to the *Herald* stating his family would not allow him to accept aid as long as he could still care for them. "I am sorry such exaggerated reports went to America regarding our condition," Livy wrote.

When Dr. James Ross Clemens, a nephew of Frau Von Versen of the St. Louis Clemenses, living in London, became ill, news-papers believed it was Mark Twain. A reporter found Clemens at Tedworth Square, with the instructions to write five hundred words if Mark Twain was ill and a thousand if he was dead. Clemens made his famous statement, "Just say the report of my death has been grossly exaggerated."

Neither Livy nor Clemens could bear the other's grief, but sep-arately they had come to the conclusion that in their devotion only the loss of the spouse could be worse. To Mrs. Fairbanks Livy wrote of Susy's death, "This is of course the first terrible staggering blow that we have had and I realize that for me there can be but one worse."

Thanksgiving passed, Livy's birthday passed, Clemens's birthday passed—all without notice. Christmas morning "We three sat & talked as usual, but the name of the day was not mentioned. It was in our minds, but we said nothing." Without Susy, lungs might breathe, hearts might beat, but life had stopped. If Susy was not there to smile upon the occasion, this family who once made excuses to hold festivities would celebrate nothing, not even Jean's or Clara's birthdays, in the years to come.

Livy was grateful for Clemens's industriousness, for it gave her something to do. She read his manuscript, got out her editor's pencil, and once more applied her standards of correct grammar, accuracy of detail, tact, and taste. He "finished" *Following the Equator* three times, each time making her suggested revisions. Neither minded, but were glad of any diversion. Paine gives a selection of their give-and-take as writer and editor that survives on this manuscript. Livy's comments follow the page numbers.

> Page 1002. I don't like the "shady-principled cat that has a family in every port."
> Then I'll modify him just a little.
> Page 1020. 9th line from the top. I think some other word would be better than "stench." You have used that pretty often.
> But can't I get it in *any* where? You've knocked it out every time. Out it goes again. And yet "stench" is a noble, good word.
> Page 1038. I hate to have your father pictured as lashing a slave boy.
> It's out, and my father is whitewashed.
> Page 1050. 2nd line from the bottom. Change breech-clout.
> It's a word that you love and I abominate. I would take that and "offal" out of the language.
> You are steadily weakening the English tongue, Livy.

Once her work on *Following the Equator* was finished, the curtain of depression descended upon her again. The faith of her childhood had long ago been undermined by life's harsh realities. Now her husband's tirades against God further chipped away at this foundation of her life and sanity. Katy recalled, "He'd say hard, severe things about religion, and Mrs. Clemens, although she hated to hear him talk that way, said she'd made up her mind when they first married, that her husband was going to be *free* to *say* anything and everything that he wanted to no matter what it was; that he wasn't ever going to dread her criticizing him—" Clemens had once remarked to Grace King that while he didn't believe in hell, his mother's fundamentalist religion had made him fear it and made him certain he was going there. To this Livy had replied, "Why, Youth, who, then, can be saved?"

Now Livy wanted proof of an afterlife, that she would see her Susy again. She began to attend séances, and even talked Clemens into going with her. They made no contact with Susy on the other side. Livy read up on Spiritualism, and they became friends with an editor of a publication on psychic research. Individually they made appointments with a renowned Hindu palmist. Separately, he told Livy she would be a widow within a year and Clemens a widower within the same year. Each was upset until they revealed their "futures" to each other. They should have listened to Katy. She insisted if he had not been Hindu (which she doubted), did not have a mystical-looking dwelling, and did not charge so much (a guinea or five dollars), no one would go to him. They then acknowledged there was probably no credibility in the occult, at least if the prediction was negative, although they continued to dabble in it from time to time. Clemens did like the prophecy that he would be wealthy by the time he was sixty-eight. When Livy could complete her husband's sentences or say what he was thinking before he said it, they took it as proof of telepathy, "telegraphy" Clemens called it. They must not have recognized that living together for over twenty-five years might produce a similar way of looking at the world.

Never free of Susy's spirit, Livy tried to contact her again in May 1900 by taking a brooch of hers to Mrs. Thompson, an English medium. Mrs. Thompson fell into a trance and Mrs. Myers, her assistant who was unconvinced that a true contact had been made, wrote a transcript of the answers Susy made to Livy's questions. "Susy" requested that her manuscript, which could only be her biography of her father, not be incorporated in another book by "someone belonging to her." Livy wanted to believe it was her daughter, for at Susy's death Clemens had lamented to his wife at the loss of her literary powers, the books she could have written and particularly "in all these years I have never wholly ceased to hope that some day Susy would take up my biography again." He later included portions of her biography of him in his own autobiography. Livy tried to reach Susy once more in 1901 through a New York medium, but Susy remained as elusive and ethereal in death as in life.

The celebration of Queen Victoria's Jubilee, her sixty years on the throne, brought Sue Crane and Julia Langdon to London to visit in June 1897. Clemens wrote of the celebrations for the American newspapers. The girls were delighted to watch the parade from Trafalgar Square, and Clara attended a theater benefit where she saw Sarah Bernhardt.

They summered in Switzerland in the town of Weggis near Lake Lucerne. Clemens had considered sending the women on alone and returning to the United States to lecture. As they still owed money, why not lecture to an audience that could pay enough to pay off his debts? A group of millionaires could afford to pay him twelve thousand dollars to speak on one occasion. When Livy heard of his scheme, she vetoed it. He would have to lecture as he always had done and at "ordinary prices." Pond contacted him to do this very thing—fifty thousand dollars plus expenses for 125 nights. It would pay the debts, but Clemens refused. He knew Livy did not have the strength for this marathon, and she felt so guilty that she had not been with Susy in her illness and death that Livy decreed unless the entire family could go together no one would go anywhere.

The morning of August 18, 1897, the anniversary of Susy's death, Livy rose early to find Clemens in his study. Without speaking to anyone, she put on her hat and coat, took a small bag, and left the house. Her family saw her leave but were afraid to ask what she was doing. She took a lake steamer to a small inn, rented a room, and spent the day reading and rereading what Clemens had searched for when he got word of Susy's death. Livy had described the letters Susy wrote her to Alice Day as "much more like a lover's letters than like a daughter's." By evening when Livy returned, Clemens waited distraught and fearful for her at the Weggis landing. When Livy returned to her room, she found lying on a chair a poem, "In Memoriam," that he had written in Susy's memory. He published it in *Harper's Magazine* in November 1897. In the poem he describes Susy as a spirit "made all of light!" dwelling within a temple that is destroyed leaving "the priests" "speechless" and lost. On the anniversary of her death in 1898 he wrote another poem that so touched Livy that she couldn't tell anyone of it, not even Jean or Clara. In this poem he wrote "in a most beautiful way I think, three or four pictures of Susy's life from her young childhood until the day of her death." Clemens was trying to say what he couldn't in life. "I loved Susy, loved her dearly; but I did not know how deeply, before," he had written Livy at Susy's death.

Clemens, Livy, and their girls had once delighted in his burlesque of the graveyard school of poetry and the oversentimentalizing of grief in the Emmeline Grangerford episode of *Huckleberry Finn*. After all, Emmeline's poetic "tributes" had given Huck the "fantods." The Grangerfords had canonized Emmeline, preserving her memory in her poetry and drawings as they preserved her room. What once amused the Clemenses now haunted them.

The devoted Katy Leary, who worked for the Clemens family for thirty years.

The Langdon summer home, Quarry Farm.

Mark Twain in his gazebo at Quarry Farm. Here, overlooking the Chemung River, he wrote some of his greatest works.

Clara, Livy and Clemens at Dollis Hill, near London, in 1900.

A view of the Hartford home from Farmington Avenue, about 1874.

Livy, Clemens and Clara in 1895 on Mark Twain's world-wide lecture tour that he undertook to pay off his debts after declaring bankruptcy the previous year.

Livy and Clemens in 1895 on his lecture tour.

One year before her death, Livy sits with her husband on the porch at Quarry Farm before moving to Italy for her health.

Livy's adopted sister, Susan Langdon Crane.

Mark Twain's billiard room on the third floor of his Hartsford home.

The dining room of the Twain home in Hartford.

Olivia Lewis Langdon in the library of the Clemens home in Hartford.

A view from the library in the Hartford home, looking into the dining room, about 1875.

Mark Twain's neighbor, Harriet Beecher Stowe.

Henry Huttleston Roberts, Mark Twain's financial savior.

William Dean Howells, Mark Twain's friend and editor.

CHAPTER 22

"If I looked into the eyes of a friend I might talk."

From Switzerland, the Clemenses moved to Vienna, the city of Strauss, for Clara's musical career. She wanted to study piano with the celebrated but demanding Theodor Lesche-tizky, who had taught Paderewski. He agreed to take her as a student if she did more technical training first. Clara spent three months practicing three to four hours daily until he accepted her. In Leschetizky's classes Clara met her future husband Ossip Gabrilowitsch.

Slowly the family had begun to come out of their metaphorical mourning clothes. Clemens noted, "Jean's spirits are good; Clara's are rising. They have youth—" then characteristically in his nihilistic frame of mind he added, "the only thing that was worth giving to the race." As Livy did not yet wish to venture out, Clara accompanied him to social functions.

Clemens was a celebrity in Vienna, his popularity having grown tremendously after his round-the-world lectures and the notoriety he had gained from his financial reversals. They received many invitations, or as Katy said, "They had a grand time and was [sic] invited everywhere by Royalty and everybody else." A Vienna newspaper announced, "He has been feted and dined from morn till eve." Although Livy wasn't ready to leave their suite at the

Hotel Metropole, she did have teas and occasionally invited people for dinner in an attempt to repay the many invitations her husband received. At one point Livy described to her sister the assembly in their parlor. "Such funny combinations are here sometimes: one duke, several counts, several writers, several barons, two princes, newspaper women, etc." After two years in Vienna, the Clemens salon was a second American embassy, and Clemens noted he was the "self-appointed ambassador-at-large of the United States of America—without salary."

Two deaths, that of a dreamer and a survivor, darkened their cloud of mourning that never really lifted. Orion Clemens died December 11, 1897, plotting his latest caper at seventy-two years of age—a biography of Judas. Or if his brother didn't like that, Clemens could write a novel about him, "a fool character . . . that would grow up to be a great man and go to Congress." Livy characterized Orion: "Although he had been unsuccessful in his life he was most fortunate in his death." At least he had done something right for once, for he died quickly, writing at his desk. At almost the same time, they heard of the death of their former butler George. Jean was most upset at the passing of her childhood playmate, her safari tiger. The news nailed closed another shutter on their Hartford home and their happy past.

Livy's greatest diversion, for which she got "millions of delight" was subtracting their payments from their total debt. With each letter from Rogers informing them of what he had paid and what investments he had made for her, she marked through the creditors' names and recalculated when they would be financially free. She set her goal to have their debts paid off by January.

In January 1898 the newspapers in the United States were declaring that the economy had recovered from the Panic of 1893. Livy had finally reached her goal, for so had the Clemenses. Toward the end of January, Rogers sent word that the last payment had been made, and they even had twelve to thirteen thousand dollars to spare. In the next few months Rogers sent the various thank-you letters he had received from their creditors to Livy. She read them over and over again, and Clemens reported her as declaring that "this is the only really happy day she has had since Susy died." Clemens experienced "abundant peace of mind again—no sense of burden." Clemens was now hopeful that he could get his wife, for her own good, to take part in Viennese society. He used the pretext that he needed her, for her German was better than his.

At one of his readings, Clemens and Livy were introduced to the sister of the Austrian archduchess Maria Theresa, the Countess Bardi. Court etiquette required they visit the palace at a later date to sign the register of visitors. When they arrived at the palace and informed the *portier* they wished to sign the book, he insisted they were expected. The more Livy protested, the more he insisted they were to wait in the drawing room. Livy fretted over the embarrassment of the situation. The princess was expecting some other Americans, not them. Clemens as usual found it amusing:

> I was hoping and praying that the Princess would come and catch us up there, & that those other Americans who were expected would arrive and be taken as imposters by the *portier* & be shot by the sentinels & then it would all go into the papers & be cabled all over the world & make an immense stir and be perfectly lovely.

Imagining the supreme embarrassment of being the wrong people in the wrong place and at the wrong time, Livy tried to get her husband to promise to tell no one of their social faux pas. Like the little boy who put his hand in the cookie jar and got away with it, Clemens wanted to gloat, but he didn't get the opportunity. "Seems a kind of pity we were the right ones." A royal invitation had been sent. They just hadn't been at their hotel to receive it; they had been expected at two o'clock. In relating the tale to her sister, Livy was mortified that she was so shaken by the whole situation that she forgot to curtsy and to prompt Clemens to kiss the royal fingertips. She knew ladies who practiced curtsying days beforehand, and she hadn't at all.

Any event caused Livy to sigh and think how she would have liked to tell Susy about it. She wrote John and Ellen O'Neill to send pink and white roses from her garden to Elmira, "so they could be put on Miss Susy's grave the 19th of March—her 26th birthday."

When the United States and Spain went to war over Cuba, Livy feared, "I know we shall soon find ourselves hated." Austria was allied with Spain through imperial marriages. At first supportive of the action, Clemens declared the United States had "stained the flag" by taking the Philippines. The war Teddy Roosevelt allegedly described as "not much of a war, but the only war we had" ended in August 1898. The following month the Clemenses watched the funeral procession of Empress Elizabeth of Austria, Queen of Hungary, assassinated by Italian vagabonds. The world was rehearsing for the next war which would be quite a war, the one to end all wars.

After Jean and Livy took the baths at Kaltenleutgeben outside Vienna, the family took a few excursions into the countryside, the trip marred only by a cinder in Livy's eye that after two days had to be removed. The Clemenses were ready to return to Vienna for the fall and winter. Livy began looking for better lodgings than the Metropole which was roomy but whose food Clemens disliked. In a new hotel called the Krantz, Livy found Clemens's picture in the lobby. "We don't know who made it nor when, but we recognize that it is a hotel that has taste," he wrote Rogers. Livy was so used to economizing, she would not move there until they agreed to drop their prices. They needed a parlor, a dining room, a music room for Clara, a study, four bedrooms plus their meals. The Krantz wanted the Clemenses as good advertisement, so when they agreed to charge only sixty dollars higher than the Metropole, Livy took it.

Livy was homesick, but she could not write her friends back in America as much as she used to. She found her spirit too heavy to reveal what she wanted although she longed to unburden herself with "expression." She wrote Mrs. Cheney, "I sometimes feel if I looked into the eyes of a friend I might talk." Another death left them further from home and the past: one of Clemens's chief confidantes, Mary Mason Fairbanks, had died December 8, 1898, a sad ending to an already sad year. Livy could not write a letter of condolence for months. "I . . . kept trying to think of some way by which I could reach you," she wrote Molly Fairbanks, "but you, before this, know the reason of our silence." The Clemenses lacked an address and the heart to consider her demise.

In January 1899 Livy calculated, as Clemens said, "for her own satisfaction, not mine, & found that we own a house & furniture in Hartford." Livy saw that their account books were sufficiently in the black, perhaps enough to go home in the spring of 1899. That plan was postponed because Livy didn't want to interrupt Clara's musical career. As her elder sister had done, Clara gave up the piano. She declared her hands too small to stretch and reach an octave. Susy's decision had upset Livy, for she saw the years of lessons a waste. This time Livy didn't have the energy to protest. Now she stated Clara's decision would probably be better for her if it meant not such hard work. They began the search for a suitable voice teacher. One German opera singer so irritated Clara that after being screamed at for days by her, Clara hit the woman on top of the head with a mirror and left in a fit of temper to rival her father's.

At the end of May 1899 they left Vienna followed by a cheering crowd, dignitaries, and notables to send them off at the station. Livy once more mused that their Viennese friends were like so many people she had met in her travels—"we shall probably never see again in this world."

The Clemens family settled in London after visiting Budapest, Prague, and Cologne. This time Jean precipitated their move. Jean's epilepsy was becoming worse. Her momentary lapses of awareness were increasing, and the Clemenses were seeking a cure. Her health had not improved in three years despite the doctors, the drugs, the baths. She had been taking bromide up to three times a day in an attempt to help what Clemens and Livy called her "absent-mindedness" or her petit mal seizures which occurred as many as twenty times a day. They were ready to try anything now "except Christian Science" Clemens said.

Poultney Bigelow, an American journalist, told the Clemenses of Dr. Jonas Henrick Kellgren and his Swedish Movement Cure practiced at his Swedish Institution in London. Prior to the treatments, Bigelow had been in bed seven months suffering from dysentery and too many doctors. Clemens was impressed that in one day Bigelow was out of bed without the benefit of medicine.

After visiting Kellgren's London gymnasium, Livy, Jean and Clemens went to summer in Sweden to take Kellgren's cure in his sanatorium by the lake. Clara remained in London where she sought out Susy's old voice teacher Madame Marchesi, who gave her the same recommendation that she had given Susy—rest, build strength and lung capacity, and then begin training. With this advice Clara joined her family in Sweden for a rest cure. Clemens believed Kellgren's method had stopped his bronchial cough. He admitted to Rogers, "The fact is I *want* the thing to succeed, for I don't like medicines—and moreover I have but a pale and feeble confidence in them." Livy took the manipulations for her rheumatic hip which ached so much at night that it kept her awake. For twenty minutes each morning they submitted to the massage treatments which delighted Clemens. "It is vigorous exercise, and *other people do it for you*," he wrote Rogers.

Jean was improving. She stopped taking the bromides and her daily bouts of absentmindedness were reduced to twice a day although Kellgren warned the Clemenses that her bad attacks could return. Clemens commented on his and Livy's relief, "For the first time in 3 years we go to bed untroubled, and get up the same." For a little over a month Jean had been troubled with no more than slight losses of awareness for a minute or two in the morning, but no grand mal seizures for over a month. They might yet return home in the spring at the rate of Jean's recovery.

Although Clemens now called himself a capitalist, he admitted that after years of scrimping it was difficult to change. He had found out that Livy had not taken all the treatments she should have in Sweden in an attempt to save money.

Clemens announced to his friends, "I am tired to death of this everlasting exile," but going home was again postponed. Jean's recovery would not be complete in six months but might take up to twelve. They returned to London in the fall to live at Albert Gate, close to Kellgren's gymnasium where Jean and Clara went daily for treatments.

At first Clemens had asked Rogers to keep the fact of Jean's "ailing" a secret. It was not until February 1900 that Clemens admitted to him it was epilepsy. He told Rogers that Jean had struck her head when eight or nine years old and seven years ago her personality had started to change; their sweet child had become moody, irritable, and irritating. At the time Clemens had grumbled that this was the true Jean, the sweet daughter had only existed because of "parental restraint and watchfulness." A full seizure at school four years later in 1895 had terrified her. New York doctors diagnosed epilepsy. Livy and Clemens returned home from the world tour to this news in addition to the tragedy of Susy's death. Clemens again mentally beat himself for his lack of sensitivity, and Livy suffered for not being with either daughter when they needed her.

Clemens had confidence in the Kellgren method. When Livy came down with the flu, Clemens talked her out of calling for a doctor, which he believed would have sent her the way of other flu patients "booked for the season or the grave." He even believed it could have cured Susy, because her doctors had killed her. "It was assassination through ignorance." Considering the health record of Clemens, Livy, and their children, he admitted after Livy's death perhaps two such emotionally high-strung people shouldn't have had children.

Clemens was again toasted and feted in London like royalty as he had been on the Continent. He often dined out and gave speeches at various clubs—the White Friars, the Vagabonds, the Savage, the Beefsteak, and the Authors. This type of life, which fed Clemens's ego, caused Howells to lament years later that he wished his friend was dining out less and writing more. Livy preferred entertaining in their apartment at Wellington Court, "a quiet talk with two or three congenial people to me is the best sort of social intercourse." Dr. James Clemens and his wife were the main people she saw for teas and luncheons. At the birth of their daughter, Livy went to visit "the new little kinswoman" and "bid her welcome to this rather sad world." Now even the hope she once associated with the birth of a new baby became a reminder of a gloomy everyday life without Susy.

Livy's bout with influenza early in the year and his interest in Kellgren led Clemens to Plasmon. Clemens inquired of James Clemens where he could buy what he called "the Vienna albumen" that he had used in 1898. He thought Livy should take it to fortify her strength. He had wanted to invest in it in Vienna. Now that he found there was a London branch for Plasmon, Clemens began cheerleading for it as a cure-all for everything to everyone he came across. This milk-protein powder could be mixed in liquids, foods, or taken on its own as a food substitute. Livy insisted he tell those he recommended it to that they should mix it with water and boil it before adding it to foods.

In Livy's name, Rogers had built up nearly sixty thousand dollars, and Clemens invested twenty-five thousand of it in Plasmon. Rogers's silence on Clemens's enthusiasm could be interpreted as skepticism, perhaps disappointment. Livy didn't hesitate to offer her opinions on literary matters, but she still left business ventures to her husband even after his disastrous past performances. His passion always overcame her protests in these areas. Not having learned from Paige, he was still looking for the scheme to make him a millionaire in the same league with his friend Rogers. In 1898 in Vienna after just paying off all his debts, he had become enamored of another inventor, Jan Szczepanik, and his machine. This time the machine would revolutionize carpet weaving. After many zealous letters to Rogers of schemes and dreams that rivaled those penned by Orion, Clemens dropped the idea when Rogers reported it would not work. There were not enough jacquard looms in America to make it worthwhile investing in a machine to produce the instructions for that particular loom. Plasmon was different; it could feed the world's hungry and cure the world's sick. Undaunted, in April 1900 Clemens was elected to the board of the Plasmon syndicate. His fervor for Plasmon lasted until 1906 when he refused to invest further in it because he believed the

American branch would go bankrupt. Like Huck Finn, he had been there before.

Another spring arrived, and they still hadn't returned home. Livy recognized of her husband, "The poor man is willing to live anywhere if we will only let him 'stay put.' " Clemens had tired of nearly five years of packing and moving. Livy remained ambivalent. One moment all she wanted was to live in her Hartford house and the next she feared she couldn't take care of it. She wondered if emotionally she could survive "going into the house in Hartford?" she asked Sue. Then in her indecision she added, "I feel if we had gotten through the first three months all might be well, but consider the first night." The thought of managing such a large establishment bothered her. "When I was comparatively young I found the burden of that house very great." Echoing what she had said as a young woman, she admitted she didn't like housekeeping, the servants could be problems. "I hate the correcting of them." When they returned from Sweden, she had to hire two new servants as the ones behind who were to care for their apartment had left without notice. "I don't think I was ever fitted for housekeeping," Livy said. Yet she had done it for years and in many places and circumstances, even when ill. If she felt she wasn't fitted for it or that she did a poor job of it because she didn't like "the practical part of it," no one inside or outside her family agreed with her.

Kellgren announced that Jean's treatment "has turned a corner." Livy and Clemens did not want to disrupt their daughter's treatments after her progress. Clemens had been trying to find out if osteopathy in the United States was as good as "Kellgren's method." Since he didn't have the time and energy and couldn't justify "cross[ing] the ocean" to find out, they decided to stay on in London over the summer. The whole situation made Clemens rage against a God who would create a human race that was "a nest of disgusting & unnecessary diseases."

Clemens sent his nephew Samuel Moffett with a list of questions to the osteopath Dr. George J. Helmer in New York. Moffett was to write down the answers and send them to his uncle. Clemens swore Moffett to secrecy because only Sue Crane and Helmer knew of Jean's epilepsy. They had even considered returning to Sweden. As Clemens told Howells, who was ignorant of Jean's condition, "Mrs. Clemens is strongly inclined to put in a good deal of time gadding around over Sweden & Norway." Jean's better health could be maintained with treatments in London, so by July they had moved into Dollis Hill House, a country home with six acres of "hay and sheep" outside London. Livy loved the "beautiful & peaceful" country spot that reminded her of Quarry Farm. Only a few miles from London, Jean returned daily for her treatments. Livy once again had to contend with housekeeping and servants. Livy spent as much time outside as possible on the lawn, under the trees where the girls played tennis late into the light English summer nights. Clemens described himself as "the only person who is even in the house in the daytime but I am working & deep in the luxury of it."

Certain that osteopathy was the same as the Kellgren method, and that Jean could receive treatment in New York, they sailed on *The Minnehaha* arriving October 15, 1900. Livy had pondered, "I realize more and more how great we are going to find the changes in Hartford when we return." Clemens had begun to realize they probably could never return to their former residence in Hartford or as he called it, "Heartbreak."

CHAPTER 23

*"We are going to give up
our Hartford home."*

America opened its arms to Mark Twain and embraced him
in welcome. The author, who would come to be considered
the most quintessential American, had come home after
nearly a decade of residing abroad. More than just a literary figure,
Twain was a public hero who had conquered adversity and financial ruin. In the celebration of Samuel Clemens, the myth of Mark
Twain began. After his death, Twain's life and works would be
read, studied, discussed until his books would fit his own defi-
nition of a classic—"A book which people praise and don't read."
Clemens was partly responsible for his own legend, for he continued creating the persona of Mark Twain. Now Mark Twain, in
his triumphant homecoming, had opinions on everything and was
happily expressing them.

At sixty-four and fifty-four, Clemens and Livy in their "renewed
youth" looked ten years younger to Howells. Her husband's vigor
reminded Livy of "a fighting cock." Clara, an attractive twenty-
six, was looking more like the Clemens side of the family. At
twenty, Jean appeared in good health to those unaware of her
epilepsy. Clemens attributed their fitness to Plasmon, but maybe
it was because they were home and secure. The Clemenses were
financially stable. They had had their share of tragedies, now behind them. They were confident of a comfortable future.

Settling first in the Earlington Hotel, Livy began looking for a house, as she said, "our hiding place for the winter," close to Jean's doctor. As Livy and Clemens aged, their years became filled with the funeral processions of friends. Within a week of their return, Clemens was asked to be a pallbearer at the funeral of his friend and coauthor of *The Gilded Age*, Charles Dudley Warner. "How fast the friends are going. So many that we looked forward with pleasure to seeing and taking by the hand have joined the great majority," Livy said. It meant a trip to Hartford, and Clemens refused to let Livy go. "I cannot trust myself to go to Hartford," she agreed. Independently, they both had realized they could not enter their house again. Livy believed, "I am not sure that we shall ever be strong enough to endure that strain." Yet she couldn't accept selling it. Clemens tried to convince her to at least consider it, but she couldn't even bear the thought of advertising the home. Livy once again sent word to John O'Neill to send flowers from her greenhouse that she hadn't seen in nearly ten years. Still a neighbor in spirit, she would share her blooms with the Warners.

Livy was once again busy establishing a residence. She hired a cook and two maids, which prompted Clemens to say, "We are all fixed for housekeeping—lacking the butler—but we are short of one minor detail—a house." They took a furnished home found for them by Frank Doubleday at 14 West Tenth. After Livy's death, Clemens berated himself for allowing housekeeping to be a cause of her demise, since she would not have a housekeeper. "She had resisted, and successfully resisted, all my persuasions in that direction from the day that we married. Social life was another heavy tax upon her strength."

In the parlor, Clemens once again held court as he had in Europe. When not at home, he was celebrated as if at an endless wedding reception. He received so many invitations that it kept himself, Livy, Clara, Jean, and a secretary busy refusing, accepting, and thanking. Jean learned to type to help with the correspondence. "I declined 7 banquets yesterday (which is double the daily average) & answered 29 letters," Clemens reported. He laughed about the man "who killed himself trying to do all the dining and speeching," but at Livy's insistence he knew he had to slow down the spin of his social whirl. He began attending banquets at the point of his remarks and leaving immediately afterward. He vowed not to speak at all in the New Year of 1902, a resolution he kept as well as most New Year's resolutions are maintained.

Livy described their activities as a "rushing life," but she did not attempt to keep up with her husband's schedule. Livy quietly entertained, giving teas, luncheons, attending them and the theater. Clara continued to prepare for the concert stage. Determination and hard work guided her. For the past year she had not allowed herself any "festivities." Her music came first, which alternately pleased and displeased Livy. To Clara she could state, "Indeed I am glad that you keep up your music and it is right you should. I want you to have this great resource in this sadly changing world. I hope great good will come to you through it." But to her friend Grace King, she admitted that she and Clemens were relieved that Clara was giving up her concerts for the winter. "We do not oppose her, for of course that is not best, but we are very sorry indeed that she wants this public life." Livy attended Clara's debut in Washington, D.C. It was scheduled but had to be postponed until January 22 as her accompanist Marquis de Souza was ill. Her second recital was in Hartford. Other performances would be canceled this season and in the future due to her throat problems and management difficulties. "Agents seem to be slippery beings," said Livy. Clemens avoided these stage attempts on his daughter's part to assert her individuality, to be more than what had haunted Susy—Mark Twain's daughter.

It was Mark Twain's opinion, sought on everything, that kept him in the limelight. Publicly, he expounded his views on the damned human race—the Boer War in South Africa, suppression of natives in the Philippines, violence done in the name of Christianity. He introduced the twenty-six-year-old Winston Churchill, who had fought in and reported the Boer War, to a New York audience and took the opportunity to remark that England and America were partners in sin; for England's war in South Africa and America's war in the Philippines.

When Clemens offered his views on missionaries he was attacked with a vehemence equal to the love that had been poured out only a month earlier on his arriving home. He wrote "A Greeting from the Nineteenth Century to the Twentieth Century," appearing in the New York *Herald*.

> I bring you the stately nation named Christendom, returning, bedraggled, besmirched, and dishonored, from pirate raids in Kiao-Chou, Manchuria, South Africa, and the Philippines, with her soul full of meanness, her pocket full of boodle, and her mouth full of pious hypocrisies. Give her soap and towel, but hide the looking-glass.

In February he continued his attack in the *North American Review* with his "To the Person Sitting in Darkness." Once again he spoke of "Christian missionaries who marched to distant land to conquer in the double sign of the cross and the black flag." He kept up his criticism in another piece "To My Missionary Critics." What had spurred his heated pronouncements? Clemens had read the remarks of the Reverend W. S. Ament of the American Board of Foreign Missions about collecting damages from the Chinese for injuries done to the Christian converts—"three hundred taels for each murder," payment for Christian property destroyed and fines of thirteen times the damages. The money to be used to further spread the word. Violence and greed clothed in sanctimony aroused Clemens to inspired levels of anger.

It is always a risky business to attack Christianity in public, but in private people often agree. Mail poured in from all over the United States and even from other parts of the world. Livy noted to Grace King that although many of their friends didn't approve of his angry words, the letters were running ten to one in their favor. Despite the controversy, Livy was glad her husband was working, his activity helped her keep up with his stamina: "Mr. Clemens is my will & vigorour [sic]." Her fighting cock strutted in controversy.

That June they began their summer holidays in a rustic log cabin, "The Lair," which Clemens found great joy in referring to as "The Liars" on Lower Saranac Lake near Ampersand in the Adirondacks. Clara joined them later from New York, where she continued her voice lessons. Following Langdon's death twenty-nine years ago, they had gone to New Saybrook, Connecticut. Now sitting by a lake again brought back a "frightful sadness of melancholy" to Livy.

Enclosed in the quiet woods, they were shut off from the rest of the world. "The air is delightful & the lake most beautiful" for Livy. They had few callers, nor wanted any. "Rowing & bathing & a little tennis are the only amusements," Livy told Alice Day. Jean typed for her father and tried to entice the squirrels ever closer with food. Clemens worked on "A Double-Barrelled Detective Story" in a tent staked close to the cabin.

In August, Clemens accompanied his friend Rogers on a yachting cruise to New Brunswick and Nova Scotia. Not totally away from the missionary controversy he had stirred, he wrote his friend Twichell who, not surprisingly, hadn't supported Twain's attack. "We caught a Chinee missionary and drowned him."

Livy occupied herself that summer with a ghost from the past that after all their other financial difficulties makes her interest in it curious. One would think she would want to keep this bogus golden arm buried. Sam Moffett told her that even though the Tennessee land had long been sold there was an error in the title that could cause it to revert to them or, at least, they might own the mineral rights to it. "I do wish something could come out of the Tennessee land! I have great faith in it but your Uncle Sam has none," she wrote Moffett. She shared her dreams with Clara: "How strange it would be if there should anything ever come out of the Tennessee land. For more than fifty years—in fact I suppose for more than sixty the family have expected riches from it." She based her excitement on the certainty that Orion, who was so seldom conscientious, had reserved the minerals "but the thing was to find the papers that prove it." "How I wish some of it could revert to us by some mistake in its being sold or something. One has a sentiment about land that has been so long in the family beside its intrinsic value. What a *shame* that it was ever allowed to go. *Do* find something to our advantage in the (copy) abstract of title," she urges Moffett. By January of 1902 she was still interested in this phantom. Since Clemens was not interested, she asked Moffett to be careful and discreet.

Livy had remarked to Grace King, "How foolish it is to think much about the future for so many things are decided for us." At the same time that Livy was pursuing the Tennessee land, and in equal stealth, Clemens was trying to decide their future. Clemens was keeping his activities from Livy concerning the house in Hartford. In August he contacted Franklin Whitmore to take bids on the home even if he had to sell at a loss, but not to let Livy know. He figured the land and house were worth $111,000, but he would take $60,000. Livy was still against even advertising the home and would remain so Clemens knew until "there was some other place that she preferred."

Livy remained involved with her house in Hartford. She often sent instructions to Ellen and John O'Neill. Little notes of maintenance—to polish furniture, rehook rugs, clean windows. It was her responsibility to maintain it whether for them to return one day or for someone else to occupy it.

After Ampersand, although Livy "dreaded" the memories, they spent a week in Elmira before they moved into a house at Riverdale-on-the-Hudson. She wrote Alice Day, "I feel that it is rather too large and too expensive for us, but Mr. Clemens and the girls were so pleased with it that they wanted to take it."

It was airy and roomy and they even considered buying it, but Livy decided it was beyond their means. The rent was no more than living in the city, but the upkeep of this mansion was more expensive. Livy's health had remained good since their return home, and the guests that passed through Riverdale rivaled the old days of entertaining in Hartford. In 1885 Livy had taken a guest book and turned it into a journal; now she took a journal and made it a guest book. Livy noted:

> We rented 1st of October for a year the Appleton Homestead. We have very much enjoyed our stay here. The girls and Mr. Clemens wanted to be *near* but not *in* New York this winter so we came out here. I have intended to put down the name of

friends and acquaintances who have come to us here but have failed to do so. Now I am going to write those that I can remember.

In a week early in 1902 they had guests for seventeen of their twenty-one meals and three out of every seven nights. Nearly every day someone took luncheon or tea "with us." The constant entertaining, as shown in her guest book, continued with her good health through nearly the end of June.

One of those guests was Marie van Vorst, who is significant only in that she prompted an incident that shows the relationship between Livy and Clemens remained much as it had been from their newlywed days. A few months previously, Livy had written a friend congratulating her on her daughter's marriage and expressing, "I hope she will have as much happiness in her married life as I have had in mine." Every marriage has as much aggravation as happiness for both partners. An undated message from Livy to Clemens that looks as if it were hurriedly and passionately written begins, "Youth darling, have you forgotten your promise to me? You said that I was constantly in your mind and that you knew what I would like & you *would not* publish what I would disapprove. Did you think I would approve the letter to Marie van Vorst?"

Marie van Vorst was a writer in her thirties who visited at Riverdale in March 1902, even spending the night several times. At some point she must have inspired Clemens to write one of his outraged and outrageous letters that was probably more slanted toward the foibles of "the damned human race" than her in particular. Livy suppressed many of his letters, like this, written in a heated moment, to protect his own reputation. Those he felt strongly enough about, such as his opinions on the missionaries, he got into the newspapers anyway. Her words to him in the rest of the letter show her weariness of his continued pessimistic campaign.

I am absolutely wretched to-day on account of your state of mind—your state of intellect—why don't you let the better side of you work? Your present attitude will do more harm than good. You go too far, much too far in all you say, and if you write in the same way as you have in this letter people forget the cause for it and remember only the hateful manner in which it was said. Do darling change your mental attitude, *try to change it.* The trouble is you don't want to. When you asked me to try Mental Science I tried it and I keep trying it. Where is the mind that wrote the Prince & P. Jeanne d'Arc, The Yankee, &c, &c, &c. Bring it back! You can if you will—if you wish to. Think of the side I know; the sweet, dear, tender side—that I love so. Why not show this more to the world. Does it help the world to always rail at it? There is a great noble Work being done. Why not sometimes recognize that? You always dwell on the evil until those who live beside you are crushed to the earth and you seem almost like a monomaniac. Oh! I love you so & wish you would listen & take heed. Yours Livy

It is not a new message from Livy; she had often reminded him to find good in the world just as she had done with his feud with George Washington Cable or Bret Harte. Following Susy's death it had been harder for Livy to get her Youth to "listen & take heed."

While Clemens was on another trip with Rogers, this time to the Caribbean, Livy made a down payment of twenty-five thousand dollars on the purchase price of forty-five thousand on a house owned by Flora Casey in Tarrytown on the Hudson River. Nineteen acres went with it. To Katherine Clemens she sadly wrote, "We are going to give up our Hartford home. We do this partly because we want Jean to be where she can have more outdoor pursuits." Livy would never be certain that she was doing the right thing. "Sometimes I feel as if we were making the mistake of our lives in selling our well beloved home and leaving the dear friends (I know we shall never find any like them) but we cannot afford to keep it any longer and we cannot make up our minds to go back to it now," she would write to Franklin Whitmore a year later when the house was sold to the president of the Hartford Fire Insurance Company.

Neither Livy nor Clemens could enter let alone live in the house where Susy had died. At Susy's death, her father had written:

To us our house was not unsentient matter—it had heart & a soul & eyes to see us with, & approvals & solicitudes & deep sympathies; it was of us, & we were in its confidence, & lived in its grace & in the peace of its benediction. We never came home with an absence that its face did not light up & speak out its eloquent welcome—& we could not enter it unmoved. And could we now? Oh, now, in spirit we enter it unshod.

Until the Hartford house was sold, Livy could not do the remodeling she planned on their new home. The asking price was seventy-five thousand. By late May, Rogers was advising Clemens to get rid of it even if the price had to drop to forty-five thousand. Livy, too, became concerned that the house might never sell. She began to kindly pester Whitmore through his wife because "waiting is very trying." She suggested that perhaps he could get an offer and hold "that over the others [to] push them up a bit." She adds in her usual method of getting someone to do something her way with self-effacement, "However he knows his business and I don't."

Clemens returned to Missouri in May 1902. He had begun to think he was doing things for the last time, and this was one of them. He was reunited in St. Louis with the man who had taught him the Mississippi, Horace Bixby. He spent five days in Hannibal where he met with old friends, even his childhood sweetheart Laura Hawkins, and placed flowers on the graves of his relatives. Wherever he went and spoke he was applauded. The native son had gone home again to a Hannibal and a Missouri more of the mind than reality. He traveled to Columbia where on June 4 he received an honorary laws doctorate from the University of Missouri. Back in St. Louis he attended the opening of another world's fair. Livy would have liked to accompany "my good man" on his trip, but he insisted the heat would be too much for her. Perhaps sentimental journeys should be made alone. "Don't let him stay long," Livy wrote Katherine Clemens in St. Louis, "for I find life very lonely when he is away."

In Clemens's absences, Livy tried to cope with her own mental and physical condition as well as that of her daughters. The selling of the Hartford house weighed heavily on her mind. She still suffered from her "gouty condition." Heart palpitations bothered her so much she sat propped up at nights to breathe. Jean still had spells of being "absent," and the headstrong Clara had gone to Europe with her voice teacher for three months after being reunited with Ossip Gabrilowitsch when he toured the United States in 1901. Clara had vowed not to marry, but when she suddenly went to Paris where Gabrilowitsch was, her protective parents could not help but worry. Livy and Clemens tentatively planned to visit Venice in the summer of 1902. Perhaps the threat of this was enough to make Clara promise to return home in August. Like Jean's epilepsy, Clara's behavior seemed to be a family secret. Clemens never mentions it, and Livy only remarks on it three times. She records in her journal-guestbook when on April 22, "Clara sailed without us for Europe to be gone three months!!" The "without us" seems to be the part meriting exclamation. Livy wrote Katherine Clemens that Clara had gone with her singing teacher to study. And in a letter to Mrs. Whitmore, "We shall all be very thankful when it is over and she says she shall never do it again. I hope she will never need to. She has been very homesick." "It" presumably studying abroad—whatever Clara might be studying.

Hoping a change of scenery would help them all, they left July 1 for a cottage in York Harbor, Maine on Rogers's yacht the *Kanawha*. Jean had a massive seizure on the yacht. Clemens was relieved they were not on a more public train. "It would have been equivalent to being in hell." Livy spent two sleepless nights with Jean, but another seizure convulsed Jean's body after their arrival. Clemens told Rogers that he had only witnessed this devastating scene three times in five years. "It comes near to killing Mrs. Clemens every time, and there is not much left of her for a day or two afterward. Every three weeks it comes. It will break her down yet."

Clemens was convinced Jean's condition would destroy his wife. "Mrs. Clemens's five years of constant anxiety and periodical shocks and frights on Jean's account are bringing a break-down."

He didn't voice this fear to Livy. The pattern of their lives was to hide the truth of these stressful times in the hopes the other wouldn't know. The other always knew. In trying to protect each other, they only deceived themselves. At their summer cottage Livy's heart "alarmed her" and she dreaded leaving the house. When they drove out, she clung to Clemens, insisting the driver walk his horses slowly. "I am alarmed about her, and she suspects it, tho [sic] I lie the best I can in the circumstances, and so does the doctor," Clemens wrote Rogers.

Livy wanted to observe the celebrations of the two hundred and fiftieth anniversary of municipal self-constituted government as displayed by the villages around York Harbor. In watching the fireworks, parades, and musical performances Clemens remembered, "She was overexerting herself, overtaxing her strength, and she began to show it." The afternoon of August 11 Clemens called "the last she ever spent in this life as a person personally and intimately connected with this world's affairs." Livy entertained at tea a woman with a letter of introduction from the Queen of Romania asking Clemens to find music classes for her to teach.

Livy started to crumble the morning of August 12. She told her husband, "I am dying." She couldn't breathe, her heart palpitation was severe. The doctor was present within a half hour of her heart attack. By the next day she had two doctors, an MD and an osteopath. The best medicine seemed to be the return of Clara that same night of her attack. (Her knowledge of Clara's return that day may have added to Livy's anxiety.) Clemens stayed by his wife's side while a procession of doctors and nurses came and went under Clara's commanding eye. Sue Crane joined them to help care for her sister. The summer holiday home became a convalescent one with quiet the number-one rule. Clemens pinned notes to the trees outside Livy's window entreating the birds to sing softly.

Clemens, Clara, and Jean were frightened. Their center of gravity was wavering. "But the worst of all is, that Mrs. Clemens feels doubtful all the time. She was never like this before, in her life." Clemens blamed Jean's condition, the Hartford house, the new house. Whatever the cause, "The illness drags along." It was weeks of "up & down & down-&-up"; then Livy hit bottom again on September 20 and three doctors were summoned in three days. Clemens wished Kellgren from Sweden could treat her. He found another osteopath, Helmer, who gave Livy a "treatment" that made her "sore and lame and she slept but little." Her medical doctor suggested Helmer not be brought back until Livy was strong enough for his treatments, but Clemens insisted it was the treatment that allowed her to take food. On the twenty-third, they thought the end was near.

With "no light in her eyes" she broke down the family's defenses, and they admitted she might be dying. With that and the encouragement of Katy Leary she said, "*I intend to get well*." She rallied to return to her role as "what she always was: boss," telling doctors what she would and wouldn't do, showing disapproval of the nurses selected for her. Clemens admitted she "detests Plasmon," but she ate it, probably as much to please her husband as to build her strength. Only with the doctor's permission could Clemens show Livy letters from friends and offers for the house in Hartford. Eventually the doctors recommended he and other members of the family be kept away from her to allow her to rest. In her strength, they had always gone to her. Now in her illness, their demands on her attention could be fatal. Jean remained without seizures for nearly ten weeks, the longest stretch in four years. Clara remained so upset about her mother's condition that it only added to her father's worries.

The doctors began to say Livy's illness was due to heart disease and nervous prostration, the catch-all term for this era's ailments. Her hyperthyroidism diagnosed in Nauheim in 1891 would account for the nervous condition that strained her heart further. Clemens wanted to believe it was nervous prostration as he wrote Muriel Pears, a young Scots correspondent of his, and Howells. The chances of survival were greater with nervous prostration since it was an ailment of the mind, not of organic damage. His words to Howells must have tweaked Howells's memories of his daughter Winifred whom they too had refused to see was physically suffering when diagnosed with nervous prostration. In his autobiography Mark Twain stated that "Mrs. Clemens had never been strong." "She had the spirit of a steam engine in a frame of flesh." According to his autobiography she had been diagnosed as dying for many years. "Twelve years before, two Hartford physicians of high repute had ordered her to the baths of Aix-les-Bains and had told her that with care she would live two years." "Physicians of repute in Rome, Florence and Berlin had given her the usual two years—" A physical in Nauheim said she could live a good long time. Writing of her death two years after the incident Clemens wanted to remember she had not had a heart attack but a nervous breakdown.

By October the physicians thought Livy could leave York Harbor. Clemens arranged for a private invalid railway car so she could be transported with family and medical attendants to Riverdale. He paid for special locomotives to be waiting to cut down on the travel time. Livy's bed was slung from the ceiling like a hammock to reduce the jerks and shocks of the moving train.

Livy was carried upstairs to her bedroom on October 16 where she remained for seven months. The closed door kept Clemens and Jean out. Her doctor came twice a day, a nurse and Clara were constantly at her side. Clemens wrote Twichell that her condition changed little; "Livy drags along drearily." It is sometimes harder on the partner not ill, for he added, "I wish I could transfer it to myself."

Livy was only allowed to see her husband a few minutes each day, but he put a love letter under her door each night. She replied to his letters—"at first at some length, but as the months dragged along and her strength grew feebler, she put her daily message of love in trembling characters upon little scraps of paper, and this she continued until the day she died." Katy remembered, "Mr. Clemens could only see her two minutes at a time every day, and oh! he was always waiting at her door long, long before he could get in. He just stood there waitin'! And sometimes when he couldn't stand it any longer, he used to write little notes and push them under her door. That seemed to comfort him a little."

Sometimes he waited in "great disappointment." "I was sitting outside Livy's door waiting. Clara came out a minute ago and said Livy is not well, and the nurse can't let me see her today." When Clemens saw his wife for the first time in three and a half months, it was only for two minutes with "the trained nurse holding the watch in her hand." Clemens was kept from Livy for fear he would tell her of Jean's returning "fainting" spells. As much as he wanted to see his wife, he didn't even trust himself not to alarm her. "With a word I could freeze the blood in her veins!" he wrote Twichell.

At the top of a letter he wrote Livy on November 30 from Elmira, he cautioned, "Clara dear, this is to your mother, but you must not risk showing it to her without reading it first yourself." He had attended the wedding of Julia Olivia Langdon and Edward Loomis held in the Langdon parlor where he and Livy had been married. It evoked many memories, "33 years blew away from my life, & it was our wedding over again." He wanted her to know that he had heeded her instructions given to him so many times over the years. "I was [thoughtful] careful, & watchful of my conduct & manners." But the beautiful memory was tinged with a melancholy because she couldn't share it with him; "lord God, what a sad thing a wedding is!"

In her illness, Livy was as Clemens said when he supposedly saw her picture for the first time in the Bay of Smyrna—never out of his mind. George Harvey of Harper Publishing gave him a sixty-seventh birthday banquet in New York City. He could only think of her.

> Now, there is one invisible guest here. A part of me is not present; the larger part, the better part, is yonder at her home; that is my wife, and she has a good many personal friends here, and I think it won't distress any one of them to know that, although she is going to be confined to her bed for many months to come from that nervous prostration, there is not any danger and she is coming along very well—and I think it quite appropriate that I should speak of her.

He appreciated this celebration for both of them. "And now my wife and I, out of our single heart, return you our deepest and most grateful thanks, and—yesterday was her birthday."

On Christmas Eve Jean caught "a chill" which developed into pneumonia. It was left to Clara to tend to their mother and to hide the truth of Jean's illness. In an effort to keep Livy calm, Clara told "holy lies," Clemens recorded. "She had never told her mother a lie in her life before, and I may almost say that she never told her a truth afterward. It was fortunate for us all that Clara's reputation for truthfulness was so well established in her mother's mind. It was our daily protection from disaster. The mother never doubted Clara's word." Livy, who even in illness had to have news of her family, daily asked Clara of Jean's activities. "Clara furnished the information right along in minute detail—every word of it false, of course." When Clara ran out of descriptions of Jean's wardrobe, "she got to adding imaginary clothes" until Livy protested the expense.

Clemens, the creator of two boys who took great pleasure in telling "stretchers," almost envied Clara's position. "Clara could tell her large improbabilities without exciting any suspicion, whereas if I tried to market even a small and simple one the case would have been different. I was never able to get a reputation like Clara's."

Jean was burning with temperatures of up to 104. The doctor ordered a change. Katy and Jean's nurse took her to Old Point Comfort in Virginia for a few weeks, but to Livy, Jean was carrying out her usual activities. Clara practiced "these ingenuities" the rest of her mother's life. "We guard her against feelings & thinkings all we can," Clemens said. The subterfuge included the entire family. Livy had a severe relapse in November that Clara kept from her father until she learned he planned a trip to Hartford. Clara's task also included keeping any bad news about Livy from Jean.

Ironically, in the Christmas 1902 issue of *Harper's Magazine*, Mark Twain had a story published called "Was it Heaven? or Hell?" Livy had been too ill to edit it and so Clemens looked to Howells and Clara. The story uncannily had predicted the events of the past weeks. In the story, a mother and daughter both lie ill and in ignorance of each other's illness while two aunts tend them and lie about the situation. In writing this story, Clemens had predicted the future for his own family using deception in an attempt to save each other anxiety.

In honor of their thirty-third wedding anniversary, Livy was allowed five minutes with her husband. Their years together must have seemed to have passed as quickly as those few minutes. Much has been said about their relationship in subsequent years by friends, family, scholars, and biographers, but one certainty can be stated—Livy and Clemens genuinely loved each other.

CHAPTER 24

"We will save each other
in Florence I think."

L ivy felt well enough in February to take her "blue pencil" to Clemens's letters. Her time with her husband increased to fifteen minutes every day, and she could be told when Jean and Clara came down with measles and the house quarantined. Riverdale was still more hospital than home. Clemens, ailing from bronchitis, rheumatism, and toothaches, was in bed nearly five weeks from April to May. Livy was reading again and dictating letters to Isabel Lyon, the secretary hired on recommendation of Mrs. Whitmore and who had begun working for them since October.

As Livy steadily improved, she sent notes to her bedridden family. Livy's notes to Clara express her desire to nurse her as tenderly as the daughter had done for the mother. Livy was more understanding of her daughter's affections for Ossip Gabrilowitsch than Clara's father. Where Clemens doesn't mention the man's name, Livy teases her daughter about his photo in the room. "It seemeth to me that during the passing of the last two days there has been in the face, particularly in the eyes, a look of mild reproach as if mine were not the company most desired, and that as measles had no terror for him he greatly desired to be allowed to go elsewhere."

By April "a conspiracy of physicians" decided Livy must be in a moderate climate for the winter. Both California and Italy were discussed, but with her fond memories of Florence, Livy favored Italy. At her present rate of progress, her doctors agreed she would be able to endure the ocean voyage by fall. Knowledge of her planned trip lifted her spirits. However, the cost of Riverdale, the remaining legacy of the bankrupt and lean years, troubled her. Clemens informed Rogers, "She is not deceived about our expenses here, in spite of all our lying." Clemens figured her illness increased their living expenses by eight to nine thousand dollars a year.

By May, Livy was sunning on the terrace and could be moved downstairs. She was walking about a little as long as she had help. She was concerned for her husband's health and felt well enough to encourage him to leave her for a while. Clemens told Rogers, "To-day, of her own accord, she proposed to let me go up and spend a night at Fairhaven some time when the yacht is going. *That* shows she is getting healthy—it's the surest sign I've seen. Heretofore she has not been willing to have me outside the house a night lest her anxieties give her a nervous setback."

The sale of the Hartford house was finalized on May 11. It was sold to Richard M. Bissell for twenty-eight thousand, well below the low price of forty-five thousand that Rogers had suggested just to be rid of it. Tying up the loose ends and details of the house occupied Livy's best moments. As she was forbidden to write letters, she had Isabel Lyon send details to Whitmore, or she wrote them herself, against doctor's orders because "no one else seems to understand these things." Livy sent Whitmore lists of furniture she wanted to keep, what was to be sold, and what went with the house. She hoped Mr. Bissell would keep John and Ellen O'Neill on in his service.

Livy sent Katy to help the packer from Tiffany's crate up her glass and china and to supervise the other packers. She wanted her Tiffany stained-glass windows and the large mirror that had come from the Buffalo house. While the shades, screens, and gas fixtures could stay with the house, the price of the house was so low she couldn't allow "these expensive items" to remain. She wanted to keep Gerhardt's statue of Eve and the statue of Peace, also from the honeymoon Buffalo home. The other statues could adorn the homes of friends. Gerhardt's Mercury went to Mrs. Whitmore to "keep for us." The bust of Henry Ward Beecher should go to Mrs. Hooker. The seaweed in Susy's room was to be carefully packed away. Livy desired the mantelpiece to be removed and certain pieces of furniture to go to the O'Neills.

Her house was gone. She was leaving the United States probably forever. Howells felt the Clemenses would never return. Livy wanted to spend one last summer at Quarry Farm before leaving for Italy. Clemens and Livy sailed on July 1, 1903 on the *Kanawha*, through Rogers's kindness, to Hoboken and then took the train to Elmira. Jean and Clara remained at Riverdale.

The restorative powers of Quarry Farm once again healed Livy. Her appetite improved. She spent most of the day on the porch where she could look out over the hills and pines of the valley below where Elmira bent about the Chemung River. Clemens returned to his octagonal study to do some writing. Livy took a few carriage rides with her sister and her nurse and could be wheeled a short distance down East Hill in a wheelchair. Clemens described her—"in the matter of superintending everything & everybody, has resumed business at the old stand." She even edited an interview of Clemens to appear in the *Ladies' Home Journal*.

As much as Livy loved Quarry Farm, she wrote Clara, "I must confess however to a great feeling of pathos and sadness. Everything here is so full of the past—the cherry tree, the air, the odors, the sounds of summer every thing is so suggestive of a time long ago, that one feels overwhelmed with a cloud of sorrows. At night it seems almost unendurable." When the memories were too much, she began sleeping on the porch because she slept "but poorly & brokenly in the house." In another letter to Clara suffering from a carbuncle and tonsil problems, she looked to the future and stated, "We shall save each other in Florence I think."

Livy still had bad days. "I don't expect to die today, as I felt I might on Tuesday," she wrote Clemens, who was away visiting in New York. Her spells left her frightened and contemplating an afterlife. In what Howells called an "heroic lie," Clemens wrote his wife when he was away preparing for their passage to Italy that he believed in an afterlife. Howells felt that "her keen vision pierced through his ruse." Yet from her words his remarks seemed to comfort her.

> I am truly thankful that you "more believe in the immortality of the soul than disbelieve in it." Why are you "vexed" at this I should think you would be most pleased, now that you believe or do not disbelieve, that there is too much that is interesting to work for. An immortality already begun seems to make it worth while to train oneself. However you don't need to "bother about" it, "it" will "take care of itself."

It was the sound of his voice reading aloud to her that moved her to the sublime and probably the most certainty she had of an afterlife. "How much immortality you have in your dear blessed self," she told him.

On October 3, Clemens placed flowers from both of them on Susy's grave for what he thought was the last time. He read the words on her headstone to himself, "Good-night, dear heart, good-night."

On October 5, they left Quarry Farm to stay at the Hotel Grosvenor before sailing on the *Princess Irene* on October 24. They landed in Genoa on November 6, after stopping at Naples. Despite a few bad spells, Clemens felt Livy made the voyage "marvelously well." On November 9, Livy, Clemens, Jean, Clara, Katy, and the nurse Miss Sherry moved into the Villa di Quarto. Isabel Lyon was to follow later.

Livy's bouts of breathlessness continued, leaving her depressed and weakened to withstand the next. She accidentally burned herself with carbolic acid at the villa, probably when her mind wandered during one of her spells. Yet she insisted she felt well enough to send Miss Sherry home in December 1903.

On February 4, Livy remembered that thirty-five years ago today "I was engaged to Mr. Clemens." By the end of February her family thought she was dying until a "subcutaneous injection of brandy saved her." It was an accomplishment when Livy could sit up for fifteen minutes without gasping. She knew the severity of her illness. She remarked to Clemens, who informed her sister Sue, "I suppose they think I am frolicking around Florence!"

Clara made her Florentine singing debut on April 8, 1904, which caused her father to remark that her performance "astonished the house—including me—with the richness and volume of her voice, and with her trained ability to handle it." Livy was so excited about her daughter's "triumph" that she awoke at midnight to send for Clara to tell her all about it. Two days later the excitement took its toll when Livy "had another of those frightful attacks of breathlessness and strugglings." Again they expected her death, and the injection of brandy saved her. Clemens remarked to Rogers, "This has been an awful 3 months, with these periodic frights."

Her end came on June 5, 1904, "after 22 months of unjust and unearned suffering," Clemens recorded. He had feared the loneliness of her passing since Susy's death when he wrote her, "I know what misery is, at last, my darling. I know what I shall suffer when you die."

Two years before her death, Livy had written, "I feel one thing strongly & perhaps more and more as the days go on, that our loved ones who go escape so much." Livy escaped the misery of her family trying to cope without her. In language reminiscent of how Susy's death hit him, Clemens wrote Rogers, "It is a thunderstroke." Numb, he could make no plans for Livy, who had made most of his in their married life. His daughters would have to make the arrangements. He couldn't think beyond "We shall carry her home and bury her with her dead, at Elmira."

A few days later, on Clara's birthday, Clemens wrote Livy's brother, Charles, that thirty years ago Livy held the baby Clara in her arms while Susy, the admiring big sister, looked on. "And now Susy is gone, the happy mother is gone, & Clara lies motionless & wordless—and has so lain ever since Sunday night brought our irremediable disaster."

Livy's final journey began when the survivors left the Villa di

Quarto on June 20. They stayed four days in a Florence hotel waiting for a dressmaker to finish mourning dresses. Clara and Jean were alternately sick. All joined Livy's coffin on the *Prince Oscar* and sailed for home on June 28. On a freighter to the United States traveled two gray mares, Livy's last gift to her daughters. They were accompanied by Clemens's Italian butler and maid, for with Livy's passing these animals had become "the most precious horses in the world, now."

Clemens kept track in his notebook of the number of hours, days, weeks, since his wife's death. After five weeks he wrote, "But this funeral march—how sad & how long it is!"

The *Oscar* docked the evening of July 12 in New York. A special directive came from President Theodore Roosevelt to allow the Clemens family immediately through customs without delay.

On July 14, 1904 a private funeral was held for Livy in the Langdon parlor that had been the scene of so many family weddings and funerals. It was a bright, sunny, warm Elmira day and the grounds and the street in front of the Langdon home were crowded with silent spectators honoring the passing of another of the Langdons.

Clemens recorded in his notebook the sad irony. "Where she stood as a bride 34 years ago, there her coffin rested; and over it the same voice that had made her a wife, then committed her departed spirit to God, now."

Twichell's was that same voice. He closed his remarks with a quotation from Robert Browning, a favorite of both Livy and Clemens, on living out a life alone. "And so good-by. Good-by dear heart! Strong, tender and true. Good-by until for us the morning break these shadows fly away."

Dr. Eastman, who had followed Beecher as minister of Park Congregational Church, said a closing prayer, and they played "Nearer, My God, to Thee."

The graveside service so grieved Clemens that he vowed, "I would never endure that horror again; that I would never again look into the grave of any one dear to me." Clara was so distraught she cried out and might have jumped or fallen into her mother's grave, but her father caught her and held her in his arms.

Clemens had engraved on Livy's headstone from the German language they so prized, *"Gott sei dir gnädig, O meine Wonne!"* She could have translated it, "God be gracious, Oh, my Bliss!"

Livy was gone, and Clemens's loss was tremendous. He lost not only a beloved wife and companion, but a talented editor and his inspiration. Clemens put his most poignant tribute to Livy into the mouth of the first husband in "Eve's Diary." Standing at Eve's grave, Adam declares, "Wheresoever she was *there* was Eden."

NOTES

ABBREVIATIONS IN CITING SOURCES:

EB	Elisha Bliss	IBH	Isabella Beecher Hooker
LB	Louise Brownell	EH	Elinor Howells
CC	Clara Clemens	WDH	William Dean Howells
JC	Jean Clemens	GK	Grace King
MC	Mollie Clemens	CL	Charles Langdon
OLC	Olivia Langdon Clemens	JL	Jervis Langdon
OC	Orion Clemens	OLL	Olivia Lewis Langdon
SLC	Samuel Langhorne Clemens	IVL	Isabel Lyon
Susy	Susy Clemens	PM	Pamela Moffett
SC	Sue Crane	JHT	Joseph Twichell
AHD	Alice Hooker Day	GW	George Warner
MMF	Mary Mason Fairbanks	LW	Lilly Warner
FH	Fred Hall	CW	Charles Webster
BH	Bret Harte		

Neider, Auto   Twain, Mark. *The Autobiography of Mark Twain*. Ed. Charles Neider. New York: Harper and Brothers, 1959.

GKP   Grace King Papers, Louisiana and Lower Mississippi Valley Collections, LSU Libraries, Louisiana State University, Baton Rouge, LA.

HHR   Leary, Lewis, ed. *Mark Twain's Correspondence with Henry Huttleston Rogers, 1893-1901*. Berkeley: University of California Press, 1969.

NOTES

L1   Branch, Edgar Marquess, Michael B. Frank, Kenneth M. Sanderson, eds. *Mark Twain's Letters, Volume 1, 1853–1866.* Berkeley and Los Angeles: University of California Press, 1988.

L2   Smith, Harriet Elinor, Richard Bucci, Lin Salamo, eds. *Mark Twain's Letters, Volume 2, 1867–1868.* Berkeley and Los Angeles: University of California Press, 1990.

LBSP   Louise Brownell Saunders Papers. Hamilton College. Clinton, New York.

LL   Wecter, Dixon, ed. *The Love Letters of Mark Twain.* New York: Harper & Brothers, 1947.

MFMT   Clemens, Clara. *My Father Mark Twain.* New York: Harper & Brothers Publishers, 1931.

MTBM   Webster, Samuel, ed. *Mark Twain Business Man.* Boston: Little, Brown, 1946.

MTE   DeVoto, Bernard, ed. *Mark Twain in Eruption.* New York: Harper and Brothers, 1940.

MMF   Wecter, Dixon, ed. *Mark Twain to Mrs. Fairbanks.* San Marino: Huntington Library, 1949.

MTHL   Smith, Henry N., and William M. Gibson, eds. *Mark Twain–Howells Letters.* 2 vols. Cambridge, Mass.: Harvard University Press, 1960.

MTL   Paine, Albert Bigelow, ed. *Mark Twain's Letters.* 2 vols. New York: Harper and Brothers, 1917.

MTM   Mark Twain Memorial, Hartford, Connecticut.

MTN   Paine, Albert Bigelow, ed. *Mark Twain's Notebook.* New York: Harper and Brothers, 1935.

MTP   Mark Twain Papers. University of California at Berkeley.

Paine   Paine, Albert Bigelow. *Mark Twain, A Biography.* 3 vols. New York: Harper and Brothers, 1912.

Paine, Paine, Albert Bigelow, ed. *Mark Twain's Autobiography.* 2
  Auto   vols. New York: Harper and Brothers, 1924.

SDP   Stowe-Day Papers, Harriet Beecher Stowe Center, Hartford, Connecticut.

S&MT   Salsbury, Edith Colgate, ed. *Susy and Mark Twain.* New York: Harper & Row Publishers, 1965.

NOTES

ABBREVIATIONS USED IN CITING
FROM MARK TWAIN'S WORKS:

CSS   Twain, Mark. *The Complete Short Stories of Mark Twain.* Edited by Charles Neider. New York: Doubleday & Company, 1967.

CY   Twain, Mark. *A Connecticut Yankee in King Arthur's Court.* New York: Harper & Row, Publishers, 1917.

GA   Twain, Mark, and Charles Dudley Warner. *The Gilded Age.* 2 vols. New York: Harper and Brothers, 1901.

TS   Twain, Mark. *Adventures of Tom Sawyer.* New York: Harper & Brothers Publishers, 1920.

HF   Twain, Mark. *Adventures of Huckleberry Finn.* Boston: Houghton Mifflin Company, 1962.

Speeches   Twain, Mark. *Mark Twain's Speeches.* New York: Harper and Brothers, 1923.

Other works quoted from are cited in the bibliography.

INTRODUCTION

PAGE

xi   Twain once remarked, . . .: Clemens to F. M. White, quoted in Wagenknecht 165.

xii   "I am reading . . .": OLC Journal, June 7, 1885, MTP.

xii   Mark Twain says in his autobiography, . . .: Neider, *Auto* 3.

xii   He wrote Mrs. Fairbanks, . . .: *MMF* 123.

xiii He once remarked to . . . Sue Crane, . . .: K. Leary 307.

xiii Concerning his autobiography, . . .: K. Leary 307.

CHAPTER 1

PAGE

1   Clemens described Livy . . .: Paine, *Auto* 1:215.

2   "For from that day . . .": Paine, *Auto* 2:103–5.

2   "The Countess is none other . . .": IVL Diary, Nov. 7, 1903, MTP. With permission of the Isabel Lyon estate and John Seeyle.

3   As Isabel Lyon stated, . . .: IVL Diary, Nov. 7, 1903, MTP.

3   Clemens would seek restitution . . .: Autobiographical dictation, "Villa di Quarto," 1904, MTP.*

3   Clemens described the three-storied villa . . .: *MTHL* 2:775.

NOTES

PAGE

3   "huge confusion . . .": Paine, *Auto* 1:204.

3   "tortured into . . .": IVL Diary, Nov. 7, 1903, MTP.

3   This location allowed . . .: Paine, *Auto* 1:206.

4   From mid-May when she . . .: Paine, *Auto* 1:215.

4   "persistent inspiration . . .": *MTL* 1:389.

4   Despite the priest's reassurances . . .: K. Leary 224–26.

4   As a young wife . . .: OLC to SLC, Nov. 20, 1871, MTP.

4   He had written in January . . .: *MTL* 1:390.

5   After twenty months . . .: Paine 3:1216.

5   His constant fear . . .: MTL 2:756.

5   The choking sessions . . .: LL 348–49.

5   She frightened her husband . . .: *LL* 348–49

5   Katy admitted later, . . .: K. Leary 224–26.

6   He was only to see her . . .: K. Leary 227.

6   In 1885 Livy had written . . .: OLC to SLC, Apr. 9, 1885, MTP.

6   "Mrs. Clemens is an exacting critic, . . .": *MTHL* 2:778.

7   "Youth my own precious Darling:": MTM.

7   The three of them . . .: Neider, *Auto* 343.

7   Clemens described his wife . . .: Paine 3:1216.

7   In the last few hours . . .: K. Leary 228.

7   Clemens wrote, "She wanted . . .": *LL* 348.

7   After her death, in an attempt . . .: SLC to CL, June 13, 1904, MTP.

8   "She was bright . . .": Neider, *Auto* 344.

8   As he left her room, . . .: Neider, *Auto* 344.

8   In his "deep contentment" . . .: Neider, *Auto* 344.

8   Livy admitted . . .: Paine 3:1217–18.

8   Katy recalled . . .: K. Leary 228.

8   "Last night at 9:20 . . .": *MTHL* 2:785.

9   "She asked me to go on, . . .": Neider, *Auto* 344.

9   Lyon recorded . . .: IVL Diary, June 5, 1905, MTP.

9   "Livy was sitting . . .": Paine, *Auto* 3:1218.

9   "young and sweet": K. Leary 229.

9   "How sweet she was in death, . . .": *MTL* 1:395.

9   "unresponsive to my reverent caresses . . .": *MTL* 1:395.

9   "I was not expecting this. . . .": *HHR* 569.

10   "She has been dead . . .": Neider, *Auto* 343.

10   "Poor tired child . . .": Neider, *Auto* 344.

10   Eventually he would be able to admit . . .: *LL* 348.

10   Only two years before, . . .: OLC to Laura Schulz, June 2, 1904, MTP.

10   In his notebook . . .: Paine 1218.

11   He wrote Howells, . . .: *MTHL* 1:375.

11   "I wish I were with Livy": *MTL* 1:393.

NOTES

PAGE

11   Clemens paced . . .: Paine 3:1219.
11   In a strange repetition . . .: *MTHL* 1:377.
11   As Clara's despair grew . . .: *MTL* 1:394.
11   A year later . . .: IVL Diary, June 5, 1905, MTP.
11   Howells declared, . . .: *MTHL* 1:377.
11   "The family's relation . . .": LL 349.
11   In his tribute, Twichell . . .: Hartford *Courant*, June 12, 1904, MTP.
12   Friends and family . . .: Neider, *Auto* 345.

CHAPTER 2

PAGE

13   New England had always been . . .: Langdon 51.
14   As a boy, Jervis . . .: Funeral oration by Thomas K. Beecher, MTP.
14   Jervis remained on the family farm . . .: Langdon 51.
14   On July 23, 1832 . . .: Funeral oration, Jan. 11, 1891, MTP.
14–15   "He suddenly woke up . . .": Neider, *Auto* 23.
15   "Ill fortune . . .": Neider, *Auto* 23.
15   The experience would cause . . .: Neider, *Auto* 24–25.
15   In Millport, Jervis Langdon . . .: Langdon 52.
15   "The house that was to be . . .": Towner 614.
15–16   Susan had been born . . .: Files, Quarry Farm.
16   They were so close . . .: Funeral oration, Jan. 11, 1891, MTP.
16   In their new constitution . . .: *Centennial Album* 46.
16   When Clemens was working on *Huckleberry Finn*, . . .: *MTHL* 2:509–10.
17   He told Beecher, . . .: Eastman 136–37.
17   The unconventional "TKB" . . .: Eastman 138–39.
17   Friends described Langdon . . .: *Saturday Evening Review*, Jan. 1, 1905, MTP.
17–18   It was valued . . .: Towner 614.
18   Expressions like "What are . . .": OLC to GK, Feb. 2; 25, 1890, GKP.
18   The Elmira Seminary, . . .: *Circular and Catalogue of Elmira Seminary*, 1858–59.
18   At the age of nine, . . .: Files, Quarry Farm.
18   The catalog reads, . . .: *Catalogue* 1858–59.
19   The training of a lady . . .: *Catalogue* 1854–55.
19   A lady must have . . .: *Catalogue* 1854–55.
19   Her education was to prepare . . .: *Catalogue* 1858–59.
19   So while it was . . .: *Catalogue* 1858–59.
19   In 1857 out of a total . . .: *Catalogue* 1857.
19   . . . Livy's roommate . . .: Wisbey 7.

NOTES

19   In order to be admitted, . . .: *Catalogue* 1858–59.
20   Her father paid . . .: Wisbey 7.
20   "A habit of reading . . .": *Catalogue* 1854–55.
20   It boasted, . . .: *Catalogue* 1858–59.
20   "the best development . . .": *Catalogue* 1858–59.
20   A total environment . . .: *Catalogue* 1858–59.
21   "a daily practical lesson . . .": *Catalogue* 1858–59.
21   The Bible was required . . .: *Catalogue* 1855.
21   "Young ladies . . .": *Catalogue* 1858–59.
21   to "make or receive calls . . .": *Catalogue* 1858–59.
21   The first graduating class . . .: Wisbey 7.

CHAPTER 3

PAGE

23   "In reading authors . . .": OLC, Commonplace Book, MTP.
24   "She became . . .": Neider, *Auto* 183–84.
24   It was a frustrating malady, . . .: Gleason 177.
24   In men and women . . .: Beard 204.
25   Gleason believed . . .: Gleason 179.
25   Gleason agreed . . .: All quotations are from *Gleason's Talks to My Patients* 14–17.
26   Mark Twain wrote his fiancée . . .: *LL* 131.
26   By 1873, Dr. Silas Weir Mitchell's rest cure . . .: Mitchell 7; 41.
26   Physicians believed . . .: Gleason 14.
27   Another paralysis victim . . .: Burr 156.
27   In Mark Twain's recounting . . .: Paine, *Auto* 2:103.
27   "Now we will . . .": Paine, *Auto* 2:104.
27   Twain's rendition . . .: Paine, *Auto* 2:105.
27   Gleason believed that "many women . . .": Gleason 178.
28   Twain writes that Newton . . .: Paine, *Auto* 2:105.
28   Olivia Lewis Langdon's entries . . .: OLL Diary, Feb. 11, 1865, MTM.
28   Livy's mother records . . .: OLL Diary, June 3, 1865, MTM.
28   "Yesterday Livia . . .": OLL Diary, Apr. 23, 1866, MTM.
28   She also records . . .: OLL Diary, Apr. 23, 1866, MTM.
28   "She enjoyed it . . .": OLL Diary, Apr. 5, 1866, MTM.
28   "Livia seems . . .": OLL Diary, Apr. 12, 1866, MTM.
28   "beautiful watch & chain": OLL Diary, May 3, 1866, MTM.
28   Olivia Lewis Langdon records writing . . .: OLL Diary, June 7, 1867, MTM.
29   All quotations from OLC, Commonplace Book, MTP.

CHAPTER 4

31	"the heart free laugh": Neider, *Auto* 185.
32	His worried mother records . . .: OLL Diary, June 7, 1867, MTM.
32	"But still we . . .": OLC to AHD, June 7, 1867, SDP.
32	This trip as well . . .: OLC to AHD, Nov. 1, 1869, SDP.
32	"But if I only grow . . .": OLC to AHD, Nov. 28, 1867, SDP.
32	"We became very much excited . . .": OLC to AHD, May 26, 1867, SDP.
32	"We read King Henry V . . .": OLC to AHD, Oct. 30, 1867, SDP.
33	"I saw her first . . .": Neider, *Auto* 183.
33	He had to meet her.: Paine 1:339.
33	He reported in his newspaper, . . .: Neider, *Auto* 174.
33	Clemens wrote his mother, . . .: *LL* 7.
33	In January 1862 . . .: *L1* 145.
34	He desired enough money . . .: *L1* 145.
34	"Marry be d—d.": *MMF* 8.
34	Shortly before he met . . .: *MMF* 8.
34	He said of his mother, . . .: Neider, *Auto* 33.
34	In a particularly poignant story . . .: Paine 1:75.
35	He described her in a letter . . .: *LL* xxii.
35	He praised her . . .: *MTL* 1:217–218.
35	"Don't be afraid . . .": *LL* 37.
35	In a letter to Livy, . . .: *LL* 112.
36	"Your reproofs . . .": *L2* 148–49.
36	"I know I never, . . .": *L2* 171.
36	Apparently not yet . . .: *L2* 172.
37	Charles, knowing the propriety . . .: Paine 1:367.
37	Years later Clemens . . .: SLC to SC, Sept. 9, 1904, MTP.
37	His own family . . .: Neider, *Auto* 185.
38	"My own cousin Olivia . . .": *LL* 17–18.
38	Hattie may have had . . .: OLC to MMF, Jan. 15, 1869, MTP.
38	At the end of the week, . . .: Paine 1:368.
39	"For I do not regret . . .": *LL* 14.
39	Livy would one day . . .: *LL* 14.
39	"I ask that you will write . . .": *LL* 18–19.
40	"I will so mend . . .": *LL* 27.
40	"Mr. Clemens spent two days . . .": OLC to AHD, Sept. 29, 1868, MTP.
40	Years later in his . . .: Neider, *Auto* 187.
40	"It pushed my suit . . .": Neider, *Auto* 187.
40	He wrote her from Hartford . . .: *LL* 22.

NOTES

PAGE

41   "I have not had anything . . .": *LL* 23.

41   He admitted to Samuel Webster, . . .: *MTBM* 101–2.

41   Clemens was at the Langdon door . . .: Jerome and Wisbey 69.

41   "Wednesday night . . .": *MMF* 51.

42   "I cannot, and need not, . . .": OLL to MMF, Dec. 1, 1868, MTP.

42   At the same time, . . .: *L2* 295.

42   "six prominent men . . .": Neider, *Auto* 189.

42   In his autobiography . . .: Neider, *Auto* 189.

42   "Why didn't you refer me . . .": Neider, *Auto* 189.

42   Clemens didn't because . . .: Neider, *Auto* 189.

43   Livy confided . . .: OLC to AHD, Mar. 3, 1869, SDP.

43   She writes . . .: OLC to MMF, Jan. 15, 1869, MTP.

43   "I want the public . . .": OLC to MMF, Jan. 15, 1869, MTP.

43   Clemens could happily . . .: *LL* 64.

43   It was not entirely unexpected . . .: *L2* 295.

43   Livy had to wait . . .: MMF to OLL, Feb. 15, 1869, MTP.

44   Livy called the ring . . .: *LL* 72.

44   "Of course, every thing . . .": OLC to AHD, Mar. 3, 1869, SDP.

CHAPTER 5

PAGE

45   For Clemens, Livy . . .: *LL* 87.

46   "I grow prouder . . .": *LL* 75–76.

46   If she wished . . .: *LL* 75–76.

46   Neither should she . . .: *LL* 75–76.

46   She had already read . . .: *LL* 75–76.

46   "Few women understand . . .": Haller and Haller 90.

47   " . . . I shall treat smoking . . .": *LL* 134–36.

47   A year after his marriage, . . .: *MTL* 1:179.

48   He could always tell Livy, . . .: *MMF* 112–13.

48   By November 1869 . . .: *LL* 112.

48   "I suspect . . .": *LL* 110.

48   "But now I never swear; . . .": *LL* 65.

49   His plans for the future . . .: *LL* 67.

49   Clemens appreciated . . .: *LL* 68.

49   "I take as much pride . . .": *LL* 68.

49   "In the beginning of our engagement . . .": Neider, *Auto* 190.

49   "I feel like a . . .": *MMF* 57.

50   "well and happy . . .": *LL* 89.

PAGE

50   "I am afraid I never shall . . .": *LL* 80.

50   So if he can't get along . . .: *LL* 80.

50   Livy had delayed . . .: OLC to AHD, Mar. 3, 1869, SDP.

51   All his life . . .: *LL* 108.

51   Clemens took possession . . .: OLC to AHD, Nov. 1, 1869, SDP.

51   His royalties . . .: Paine 1:382.

51   "I am so grateful . . .": *LL* 102–3.

51   He will wear a flower . . .: *LL* 106.

51   Livy writes the Twichells, . . .: OLC to JHT, Oct. 31, 1869, MTP.

51   The date seemed . . .: OLC to JHT, Nov. 1, 1869, MTP.

51   Livy's prenuptial jitters . . .: OLC to JHT, Oct. 31, 1869, MTP.

52   She writes Alice, . . .: OLC to AHD, Nov. 1, 1869, SDP.

52   "I am glad . . .": OLC to AHD, Nov. 1, 1869, SDP.

52   Even Livy did not like . . .: *LL* 119.

52   "*Don't* let your sister . . .": *LL* 120.

52   Livy offers her assistance, . . .: OLC to SLC, Nov. 13, 1869, MTP.

52–53   Even the Hookers . . .: *LL* 123.

53   "All I should get for it . . .": *LL* 123.

53   Langdon's involvement, . . .: *MMF* 116.

53   "It is just a year to-day . . .": *LL* 130.

53   Clemens concluded . . .: *LL* 141.

CHAPTER 6

PAGE

54   "quick" and "quiet": OLC to AHD, Nov. 1, 1869, SDP.

54   "with only relatives . . .": OLC to JHT, Oct. 3, 1869, SDP.

54   Clemens had sent the fare . . .: Varble 284–85.

55   The wedding date was changed . . .: *MMF* 108, 113.

55   The time of the wedding . . .: Paine 1:394.

55   The only wedding trip . . .: *MMF* 114; Paine 1:394.

55   It should be a boarding house . . .: Neider, *Auto* 186.

56   The driver finally stopped . . .: Paine 1:394.

56   Clemens was dumbfounded, . . .: Neider, *Auto* 186.

56   Livy's reply was, . . .: Paine 1:395.

56   Livy later remarked . . .: OLC to JL and OLL, Feb. 6, 1870, MTP.

56   Jervis Langdon presented . . .: Neider, *Auto* 186.

56   Mrs. Fairbanks recorded . . .: Paine 1:395–96.

57   Controlling his tears, . . .: Paine 1:395–96.

NOTES

PAGE

57   She saw the whole incident . . .: *MMF* 121–22.

57   "But there is no romance . . .": *MMF* 123.

58   ". . .this morning . . .": *LL* 143.

58   "I am very glad . . .": *LL* 148.

58   "I wish I could . . .": OLC to JL and OLL, Feb. 6, 1870, MTM.

58   "I enjoy house keeping . . .": OLC to AHD, Mar. 17, 1870, SDP.

59   "The girl that I . . .": OLC to SC, Apr. 16, 1870, MTP.

59   "But I had rather . . .": *LL* 143.

59   Livy also handled . . .: OLC to JL and OLL, Apr. 16, 1870, SDP.

59   "I am beginning to yearn . . .": OLC to JL and OLL, May 13, 1870, SDP.

59   "I felt a little desire . . .": OLC to AHD, Mar. 17, 1870, SDP.

59   She records with horror . . .: OLC to AHD, Mar. 17, 1870, SDP.

60   "I think I shall get the name . . .": *MMF* 129–30.

60   "Mr. Clemens is splendid . . .": *MMF* 129–30.

60   After letters to her parents . . .: OLC to JL and OLL, Apr. 17, 1870, SDP.

60   She misses . . .: OLC to AHD, Nov. 1, 1869, SDP.

60   Very much in love, . . .: Neider, *Auto* 185.

60   Clemens wrote . . .: Neider, *Auto* 185.

61   "I guess I am out . . .": Paine 1:409–10.

61   When she had not yet . . .: OLC to JL and OLL, Feb. 6, 1870, MTM.

61   "We need the prayers . . .": OLC to JL and OLL, Feb. 6, 1870, MTM.

61   He wrote the happy couple . . .: Paine 1:415.

61   "Samuel, I love your wife . . .": Paine 1:415.

61   After six weeks . . .: Paine 1:415.

62   "Truly a great light . . .": OLC Commonplace Book, MTP.

62   "He was my . . .": OLC to AHD, Jan. 25, 1871, SDP.

62   Thomas K. Beecher . . .: "In Memoriam," *Saturday Evening Review*, Aug. 13, 1870, MTP.

62   In her commonplace book . . .: Commonplace Book, MTP.

62   Whittier's "God is Love" copied by Livy, Commonplace Book, MTP.

63   In delirium ravings, . . .: *Daily Advertiser*, Sept. 30, 1870, Chemung County Historical Society.

63   "I try to picture . . .": OLC to AHD, June 6, 1870, SDP.

63   In October . . .: *MMF* 139.

63   Despite the fact that Clemens . . .: SLC to OC, Nov. 11, 1870, MTP.

PAGE

63   In his own paper, . . .: Commonplace Book, MTP.
63   To the Twichells . . .: Paine 1:417.
64   Nothing fits . . .: *LL* 156–57.
64   Young Langdon described . . .: Paine 1:417.
64   By January Livy could write, . . .: OLC to AHD, Jan. 25, 1871, SDP.
64   "I have had a great aversion . . .": OLC to AHD, Jan. 25, 1871, SDP.
64   She wrote Alice, . . .: OLC to AHD, Jan. 25, 1871, SDP.
65   "Sometimes I have hope . . .": Hill 55–56.
65   By mid-March . . .: SLC to SC, Mar. 14, 1871, MTP.
65   "We leave for Elmira . . .": *MMF* 150.
65   He would sell the house . . .: Paine, *Auto* 2:119.
65   All he wanted to do . . .: Paine 1:433–34.
65   He vowed he would . . .: Paine :433–34.
66   For Mark Twain, . . .: Paine 1:433–34.

CHAPTER 7

PAGE

67   Her strength improved . . .: *MMF* 153.
67   "My stock is . . .": Paine 1:440.
67   "His writing went so well . . .": *MMF* 154.
68   Clemens had written . . .: Paine 1:434.
68   "I mean to take . . .": SLC to OC, Mar. 10, 1871, MTP.*
68   Clemens wrote her from Hartford . . .: *LL* 158.
68   Clemens chose to rent . . .: Andrews 3–5.
69   All summer, . . .: *MMF* 155.
69   Clemens settled . . .: Andrews 24.
69   "speaking face": OLC to SLC, Nov. 28, 1871, MTP.
69   Langdon could respond . . .: OLC to SLC, Dec. 30, 1871, MTP.
70   "no need of coming": OLC to SLC, Dec. 29, 1871, MTP.
70   Upon visiting . . .: OLC to SLC, Nov. 28, 1871, MTP.
70   "Do you pray for me . . .": OLC to SLC, Nov. 28, 1871, MTP.
70   "Mr. Twichell's prayer . . .": OLC to SLC, Dec. 2, 1871, MTP.
70   On seeing the congregation . . .: *LL* 165.
71   So she prayed . . .: OLC to SLC, Jan. 7, 1872, MTP.
71   She enjoyed . . .: OLC to SLC, Dec. 20, 1871, MTP.
71   So she set to investigating . . .: OLC to SLC, Dec. 30, 1871, MTP.
71   "Youth in certain . . .": *LL* 165.

NOTES

CHAPTER 8

NOTES

PAGE

80   This division of labor . . .: Krauth 107.
80   Her harsh treatment . . .: *GA* 1:123.
80–81   "Her wealth attracted . . .": *GA* 2:323.
81   "They both pleaded . . .": *MMF* 171–72.
81   "If I could only . . .": *GA* 2:40–41.
81   Livy admired Potter's flamboyant originality . . .: Paine
        1:481.
82   Livy told her mother, . . .: OLC to OLL, Jan. 19, 1873, MTP.

CHAPTER 9

PAGE

83   Clemens, now with Livy . . .: Paine 1:483–84.
83–84   Livy wrote her sister, . . .: Paine 1:484.
84   The responsibilities . . .: OLC to MC, June 23, 1873, MTP.
84   "The trouble is . . .": OLC to OLL, July 7, 1873, MTP.
84   "I feel quite in the dark . . .": OLC to OLL, July, 1873,
        MTP.
84   "If I was *sure* . . .": OLC to OLL, July, 1873, MTP.
84   By the time they reached . . .: Neider, *Auto* 194.
85   "sweet and winning face": Neider, *Auto* 195.
85   "worshiper and willing slave": Neider, *Auto* 194.
85   Brown called her . . .: Paine 1:487.
85   Susie hid . . .: Neider, *Auto* 196.
85   Any separation . . .: Paine 1:488.
85   Livy had vowed . . .: OLC to OLL, Aug. 1873, MTP.
86   If their bankers . . .: OLC to OLL, Sept. 1873, MTM.
86   "I do think . . .": OLC to OLL, Sept. 21, 1873, MTP.
86   The London fog . . .: OLC to OLL, Sept. 1873, MTM.
86   "a more enviable reputation": Paine 1:489.
86   "His reputation . . .": Paine 1:489.
86   "dreadful fog": *LL* 185.
87   "I made a speech . . .": *LL* 186.
87   Livy was the more . . .: *LL* 186.
87   "I *do* feel it, . . .": *LL* 186.
87   "Expedition's . . .": *LL* 186.
87   "Livy, my darling, . . .": *LL* 190.
88   Clemens told his wife, . . .: Paine 1:502.
88–89   The incidents with Lilian Aldrich are chronicled in her book
        Crowding Memories 127–130; 160.
89   "I was always . . .": Neider, *Auto* 185.
90   Like a little boy . . .: Paine, *Auto* 1:358.
90   It was a welcome . . .: OLC to MC, Jan. 11, 1874, MTP.
90   Just prior . . .: SLC to OLC, Mar. 18, 1874, MTP.*

NOTES

90   Clemens called her . . .: *MTL* 1:219.

90   For her brother-in-law, . . .: Paine 1:507–8.

90   "It is a cozy nest . . .": Paine 1:507–8

91   "Mr. Clemens thinks of Huck . . .": Files, Quarry Farm.

CHAPTER 10

PAGE

92   While Clemens coached . . .: SLC to OC, Sept. 21, 1874, MTP.

92   "It's so queer.": *MTBM* 123.

92   Details and quotations concerning the building of the Hartford home from Paine 1:520–26.

94   The plumber . . .: Interview, *Hartford Times*, Nov. 1, 1935.

94   From the library, . . .: *MMF* 203.

95   The conservatory . . .: Harnsberger 2–3.

95   "On the third floor . . .": Paine 1:526.

95   "In his cozy, sunny . . .": Files, Mark Twain Memorial, Hartford.

96   "I can write . . .": *MMF* 191.

96   Clemens told Howells, . . .: *MTHL* 1:72.

96   With pride she extended . . .: OLC to WDH, Dec. 6, 1874, MTP.

96   Livy immediately . . .: OLC to OLL, Mar. 14, 1875, MTP.

96   Impressed by the Clemenses' hospitality . . .: *MTHL* 1:70–71.

96–97   Susy celebrated . . .: OLC to OLL, Mar. 21, 1875, MTP.

97   The celebration . . .: OLC to OLL, Mar. 21, 1875, MTP.

97   "Clara continues to grow . . .": OLC to OLL, Mar. 21, 1875, MTP.

97   She couldn't leave . . .: *MTHL* 1:76.

97   Clemens described Clara's fifth wet nurse . . .: *MTHL* 1:72.

98   On occasion . . .: OLC to OLL, May 6, 1877, MTP.

98   She wrote her husband . . .: OLC to SLC, June 1874, MTP.

98   Clemens recalled . . .: *S&MT* 55.

98   Clemens went to Cambridge . . .: *MTHL* 1:79.

98   The two men had . . .: *MTHL* 1:74.

98   Clemens could report . . .: *MTHL* 1:74.

99   In Livy's words, . . .: *MTHL* 1:76.

99   Elinor also suffered . . .: *MTHL* 1:141.

99   As delicate wives . . .: *MTHL* 1:103.

99   "Of course I didn't expect . . .": *MTHL* 1:103–4.

100   "Can't you tell her . . .": *MTL* 1:239.

100   By 1877 . . .: *MMF* 205.

PAGE

100   The manuscript . . .: *MTHL* 1:107.
101   She was pleased . . .: *MTHL* 1:107–8.
101   Clemens told his friend, . . .: *MTHL* 1:107–8.
101   "Livy Darling, . . .": Paine 1:561.

CHAPTER 11

PAGE

102   Clemens remarked to Howells . . .: *MTHL* 1:107.
102   May was a tense time . . .: *MTHL* 1:136.
102   "However the little girl . . .": *S&MT* 52.
102   Clemens recorded Livy's diligence . . .: Paine 2:115–16.
103   She once remarked . . .: *MMF* 197–98.
103   "She shall always go . . .": SLC to LW, June 17, 1880, MTP.
103   The girls continued . . .: *MFMT* 6.
103   At one week old . . .: Paine 1:577–78.
103   By August, . . .: *MMF* 201.
104   So when her mother . . .: *MTHL* 1:143.
104   "I wish I could . . .": Paine 1:577.
104   He wrote Howells . . .: *MTHL* 1:144–45.
104   This time . . .: *MTHL* 1:171.
104   In his autobiography . . .: Neider, *Auto* 125.
105   Puzzled as to how . . .: Andrews 104.
105   "Harte, your wife . . .": Paine, *Auto* 1:296–99.
105   The exact insult . . .: BH to SLC, Dec. 16, 1876, MTP.
105   A year later, . . .: OLC to SLC, July 28, 1877, MTP.
106   The next day . . .: LL 203.
106   Despite Clemens's high hopes . . .: *MTHL* 1:206.
107   He admitted . . .: Andrews 86–87.
107   Isabella, sensing her host's anger . . .: Andrews 86–87.
107   Livy, knowing her husband's dislike . . .: Andrews 86–87.
107   Although she committed to her diary . . .: IBH Diary, 193–95.
107   "Miss Kassie": Andrews 58.
108   "the queerest looking lot": Andrews 58–61.
108   She wrote her mother, . . .: OLC to OLL, Feb. 2 & 4, 1877, MTP.
108   She dreaded a visit . . .: OLC to OLL, May 6, 1877, MTP.
109   She described . . .: OLC to OLL, May 6, 1877, MTP.
109   "particular eater": OLC to MC, Aug. 21, 1874.
109   It was Livy's desire, . . .: OLC to OLL, 1874, MTP.
109   Clemens liked to say . . .: Paine 2:572–74.
109   George once told Livy, . . .: Paine 2:572–74.
109   That summer from Quarry Farm . . .: Paine 2:572–74.

NOTES

PAGE

109	Despite her discharging . . .: Paine 2:572–74.
110	Before Katy Leary's mother . . .: K. Leary 50; 55–56.
110	All the new husband . . .: *LL* 199–201.
110	Clemens often left instructions . . .: *LL* 195.
111	Livy wrote her husband, . . .: *LL* 204.
111	"Susie, don't you want . . .": OLC to SLC, Aug. 12, 1877, MTP.
111	Livy would not allow . . .: *MTHL* 1:189.
111	At the urgings of Livy . . .: Paine 2:597.
112	It was Livy who noticed . . .: *MTHL* 1:196.
112	When Clemens reached . . .: *MTHL* 1:196.
112	Clemens described it . . .: *MTHL* 1:196.
112	This event served . . .: *MTHL* 1:199.
112–113	"The Story of a Speech" appears in *The Great Short Works of Mark Twain*, ed. Justin Kaplan (New York: Harper's Perennial Classics, 1967), 129–38.
113	Finally, he wrote Howells, . . .: *MTHL* 1:212–13.
114	The gesture showed . . .: Paine 2:606–9.
114	Although husband and wife . . .: *MTHL* 1:212.
114	By February Clemens . . .: *MMF* 217.
114	Twenty-eight years later, . . .: *The Great Short Works of Mark Twain* 138.
114	He was "afraid . . .": *MMF* 218.
114	He planned . . .: *MMF* 218.
114	Clemens felt . . .: *MMF* 222.
114	Clemens told . . .: *MMF* 222.
115	Elinor Howells . . .: *MTHL* 1:224.
115	She roamed . . .: *MTHL* 1:219.

CHAPTER 12

PAGE

116	She also found . . .: OLC to OLL, Apr. 26, 1878, MTP.
116	Livy wrote . . .: OLC to OLL, Apr. 26, 1878, MTP.
116	Even though . . .: OLC to OLL, Apr. 26, 1878, MTP.
116	Susie, being Susie, . . .: *MTHL* 1:237.
116–117	Clara, being Clara, . . .: *MTHL* 1:237.
117	"What a paradise . . .": *MTL* 1:328.
117	Susie wrote her Aunt Sue, . . .: Paine 2:622.
117	Although she had Rosa . . .: OLC to OLL, May 7, 1878, SDP.
117	In another three months . . .: OLC to OLL, May 26, 1878, MTP.
117	Livy wanted . . .: OLC to OLL, Dec. 7, 1878, MTP.

NOTES

PAGE

117   Her husband's frustrations . . .: OLC to OLL, Aug. 18, 1878, MTP.

117   Susie did become . . .: *MTL* 1:343–44.

117   "He has been making . . .": OLC to OLL, May 7, 1878, SDP.

118   Livy paid . . .: OLC to OLL, May 26, 1878, MTM.

118   She recorded . . .: OLC to OLL, May 7, 1878, MTP.

118   She told her brother . . .: OLC to CL, July 21, 1878, MTM.

119   She wrote, "Mother, . . .": OLC to OLL, Apr. 26, 1878, MTP.

119   Often Livy's letters . . .: OLC to OLL, Nov. 20, 1878, MTP.

119   "No one in the hotel . . .": OLC to OLL, May 7, 1878, MTP.

119   She enjoyed buying . . .: OLC to OLL, Aug. 4, 1878, MTP.

119   "Write me . . .": OLC to OLL, Sept. 1, 1878, MTM.

119   Livy found . . .: OLC to CL, July 21, 1878, MTM.

119   Quarry Farm . . .: OLC to OLL, 1878, MTP.

120   "How I wish . . .": OLC to OLL, June 9, 1878, MTP.

120   Clemens felt optimistic . . .: *MTHL* 1:236–37.

120   Years later . . .: Blair 50–51.

120   By August 1 . . .: OLC to CL, July 21, 1878, MTM.

120   From a woman . . .: OLC to OLL, Sept. 15, 1878, MTP.

121   "It is so fascinating, . . .": OLC to OLL, Oct. 13, 1878, MTP.

121   "We have bought . . .": OLC to OLL, Oct. 13, 1878, MTP.

121   These pieces included . . .: OLC to OLL, Oct. 13, 1878, MTP.

121   Livy disagreed.: OLC to OLL, Oct. 13, 1878, MTP.

121   Clemens in his autobiography . . .: Paine, *Auto* 2:73.

122   For being an anonymous . . .: Paine 2:613.

122   She believed . . .: OLC to OLL, Oct. 21 & 27, 1878, MTM.

122   He wrote Howells, . . .: Paine 2:634–35.

122   And he didn't mind . . .: Paine 2:634–35.

122   Livy informed . . .: OLC to OLL, Oct. 21 & 27, 1878, MTM.

122   Livy kept meticulously detailed notebooks of her purchases . . .: Notebooks, MTP.

123   Clara Spaulding . . .: OLC to OLL, Nov. 24, 1878, MTP.

123   He described . . .: Paine 2:636–37.

123   For additional practice . . .: OLC to MC, Dec. 15, 1878, MTP.

123   Livy found . . .: OLC to MC, Dec. 15, 1878, MTP.

123–124   Livy described, . . .: OLC to OLL, Dec. 28, 1878, MTP.

124   Livy confided . . .: OLC to OLL, Dec. 22, 1878, MTP.

124   Clemens informed Howells, . . .: *MTHL* 1:246.

124   "I at once . . .": OLC to OLL, Jan. 19, 1879, MTM.

124   Her married life . . .: OLC to OLL, Feb. 2, 1879, MTM.

124   "We have spent . . .": OLC to OLL, Feb. 2, 1879, MTM.

125   "France has neither . . .": OLC to OLL, Dec. 22, 1878, MTP.

NOTES

PAGE

125	Livy had observed . . .: OLC to OLL, Dec. 22, 1878, MTP.
125	Clemens grumbled . . .: *MMF* 229.
125	Livy informed him . . .: OLC to CL, Mar. 9, 1879, MTP.
125	She mildly regretted . . .: OLC to CL, Mar. 9, 1879, MTP.
125	"I wish that . . .": OLC to OLL, Mar. 16, 1879, MTP.
125	"It seems to me . . .": OLC to OLL, Mar. 16, 1879, MTP.
126	"I often reproach . . .": OLC to OLL, Mar. 16, 1879, MTP.
126	"I have no dress . . .": OLC to OLL, Mar. 16, 1879, MTP.
126	"Spending money . . .": OLC to OLL, Mar. 16, 1879, MTP.
126	"I do hate . . .": OLC to OLL, Apr. 28, 1879, MTP.
126	She wrote her mother . . .: OLC to OLL, Apr. 28, 1879, MTP.
126	"We live . . .": OLC to OLL, May 13; 16, 1879, MTP.
126	Despite the social . . .: *MMF* 230.
127	When Livy inquired . . .: Paine 2:640.
127	She wrote her mother . . .: OLC to OLL, Apr. 28, 1879, MTP.
127–128	"Susie has little arithmetic . . .": OLC to OLL, July 20, 1879, MTP.
128	"I have had . . .": OLC to OLL, July 20, 1879, MTP.
128	Livy was not unpacked . . .: *MMF* 232.
128	Despite the fact . . .: OLC to OLL, Nov. 1879, MTP.
128	Susie reproached, . . .: OLC to OLL, Nov. 1879, MTP.

CHAPTER 13

PAGE

129	She had almost . . .: Notebooks SDP.
129	No wonder she . . .: OLC to OLL, Nov. 2, 1879, MTP.
129	She hung . . .: OLC to OLL, Nov. 16, 1879, MTP.
129	Clemens described it . . .: SLC to OLL, Feb. 23, 1879, MTP.*
130	"The new things . . .": OLC to OLL, Nov. 16, 1879, MTP.
130	News of this troubled Livy . . .: OLC to OLL, Jan. 1, 1879, MTP.
130	On their return, . . .: OLC to OLL, Jan. 1, 1879, MTP.
130	She feared . . .: OLC to OLL, Jan. 1, 1879, MTP.
130	Those who indulged . . .: K. Leary 19–20; GK to Nina Ansley King, June 19, 1887, GKP.
131	Livy confided to her mother . . .: OLC to OLL, Nov. 30, 1879, SDP.
131	"I told Mr. Clemens . . .": OLC to OLL, Nov. 30, 1879, MTM.
131	Although she boldly declared, . . .: OLC to OLL, Dec. 28, 1879, MTP.
131	For Livy . . .: OLC to OLL, Nov. 30, 1879, SDP.

NOTES

PAGE

132   When her mother . . .: OLC to OLL, Dec. 8, 1879, MTM.

132   He had become . . .: *MTBM* 140.

132   At one point . . .: OLC to OLL, Nov. 2, 1879, SDP.

132   Her daughters lifted . . .: OLC to OLL, Nov. 30, 1879, MTM.

132   He followed the advice . . .: *MTHL* 1:286.

132   He told Howells, . . .: *MTHL* 1:290.

132   Finishing *A Tramp Abroad* . . .: *MTHL* 1:286–87.

133   "I have even fascinated . . .": *MTHL* 1:292.

133   Livy was again pleased . . .: Howells 130.

133   An alarm . . .: *MTHL* 1:306.

133   Clemens reported . . .: *MTHL* 1:318–19.

133   No twins . . .: *MTHL* 1:318–19.

133   Clemens explained . . .: *MTHL* 1:321–23

134   More likely Livy . . .: *MTHL* 1:321–23.

134   Ironically, Jean, . . .: OLC to MC, Dec. 7, 1880, MTP.

134   In contrast, Elinor . . .: *MTHL* 1:321–24.

134   "Susie and Bay . . .": *MTHL* 1:320.

134   Clemens had once written . . .: SLC to OLC, Apr. 26, 1873, MTP.*

134   Mark Twain would remark, . . .: *MTN.*

135   Susie once said, . . .: Paine 2:684.

135   Susie could not contain . . .: Neider, *Auto* 197–98.

135   Livy asked her daughter, . . .: Neider, *Auto* 197–98.

135   She told her mother, . . .: Neider, *Auto* 197–98.

135   In his autobiography . . .: Neider, *Auto* 197–98.

135   Whether out of jealousy . . .: "Record of Small Foolishnesses," Mark Twain Collection.

136   When Livy came through . . .: K. Leary 4; 125.

136   As elaborate . . .: Paine 2:691–92.

136   "We haven't all had . . .": Paine 2:652–57.

137   "And if the child . . .": Paine 2:652–57.

137   Clemens triumphantly reported . . .: Paine 2:652–57.

138   Clemens wrote his sister . . .: Paine 2:696.

138   One, obviously Huck's story, needed . . .: Paine 2:696.

138   Despite the fact that Bliss . . .: Paine 2:697.

138   Clemens's agreement . . .: *MTHL* 1:349.

138   Clemens, with perfect . . .: Paine 2:903–4.

139   When an agent from Bell . . .: *MTE* 163–64.

139   Sue Crane thought . . .: *MTBM* 142.

139   "It is like adding . . .": *MTBM* 137.

139   For the holiday season . . .: K. Leary 71–72; *MFMT* 35–36.

139   The new year of 1881 . . .: Paine 2:699–700.

140   Although Clemens insisted . . .: OLC to EH, Feb. 28, 1881, MTP.

NOTES

PAGE

140	Livy convinced . . .: *MTHL* 1:355.
141–141	It made the Gerhardts . . .: *MTHL* 1:354.
141	In March the Clemenses . . .: OLC to LW and GW, Mar. 1, 1881, SDP.
141	Even Livy . . .: *MTBM* 166.
141	The driveway . . .: *MMF* 245–46.
141	At last Livy . . .: *MTBM* 54.
142	Livy informed . . .: OLC to CW, Aug. 25, 1881, MTP.
142	Clemens worried . . .: *MTL* 1:419.
142	Clemens began to wish . . .: *MTL* 1:419.
142–143	The bill . . .: *MTBM* 150–51.
143	Samuel and Olivia Clemens . . .: Paine 2:729.

CHAPTER 14

PAGE

144	It was dedicated "To those good-mannered . . .": Neider, *Auto* 212–13.
144	"The book is . . .": Neider, *Auto* 212–13.
144	Mrs. Fairbanks . . .: *MMF* 245.
144	Howells stressed . . .: *MTHL* 1:378.
144	"beautiful book,": *MTHL* 1:378.
145	When her daughters were adults, . . .: *MFMT* 63.
145	By the time Clemens . . .: *MTBM* 183.
145	Clemens told Howells . . .: *MTHL* 1:386–87.
145	With Clemens, preparing for war . . .: *MTHL* 1:386–87.
145	He intended to write . . .: *MTHL* 1:386–87.
145	Livy, naturally, . . .: *MTHL* 1:386–87.
145	She urged her husband . . .: *MTBM* 183.
145	Clemens asked his already . . .: *MTBM* 183.
146	Clemens had gotten himself . . .: *MTHL* 1:386–87.
146	"Only three profane . . .": *MFMT* 75.
146	"In her mouth . . .": Neider, *Auto* 212.
146	"There, now you know . . .": Neider, *Auto* 212.
146	Clemens said, . . .: Neider, *Auto* 212.
147	"We often listen . . .": Neider, *Auto* 212.
147	Susie related . . .: *S&MT* 141.
147	Livy requested, . . .: Paine 2:1015.
147	On another occasion . . .: OLC to SLC, Jan. 3, 1885, MTP.
147	The southern writer . . .: GK to May King McDowell, June 22, 1887, GKP.
148	"More than ever . . .": OLC to SLC, May 3, 1882, MTP.
148	Although her husband . . .: Paine 2:730.
148	Livy was relieved . . .: Paine 2:730.

CHAPTER 15

NOTES

PAGE

157	"In Susan Gridley's make . . .": Tuckey 167–68.
158	When Clemens was on his reading tour, . . .: OLC to SLC, Nov. 1, 1884, MTP.
158	Livy approved, . . .: OLC to SLC, Jan. 3, 1885.
158	In Mark Twain's great affinity . . .: Paine 2:784.
158	Livy's "tour" . . .: Neider, *Auto* 31.
159	Ultimately Livy and her husband . . .: K. Leary 87.
159	Livy wrote her husband . . .: OLC to SLC, Apr. 9, 1885; reprinted in *The Twainian*.
159	"You & the children . . .": *LL* 223.
159	"You cannot be gone . . .": OLC to SLC, Nov. 21, 1884, MTP.
159	Livy lovingly declared, . . .: OLC to SLC, Nov. 3, 1884, MTP.
159	Occupied with the house, . . .: OLC to SLC, Jan. 23, 1885; reprinted in *The Twainian*.
159	With Livy's further . . .: OLC to SLC, Jan. 26, 1885; reprinted in *The Twainian*.
160	Susie wrote that even little Jean . . .: *S&MT* 190.
160	"Papa acted his part . . .": *S&MT* 190.
160	Jean was only three . . .: Paine, *Auto* 2:61–62.
160	The play was produced . . .: Paine, *Auto* 2:61–62.
161	In his autobiography . . .: Neider, *Auto* 91.
161	They were told by the editor, . . .: Neider, *Auto* 91.
161	Now it seemed . . .: Blair 365–66.
161	Aunt Sally's words . . .: Blair 365–66.
161	It made Livy "sick.": Blair 365–66.
162	By mid-February, . . .: *LL* 237.
162	Clemens wrote Howells, . . .: *MTHL* 2:520.
162	Livy, a product . . .: OLC to SLC, Feb. 11, 1885; reprinted in *The Twainian*.
162	Clemens returned home . . .: Neider, *Auto* 236–39.
162	"He had declined . . .": Neider, *Auto* 236–39.
162	By chance . . .: *LL* 242.
162	Grant was considering . . .: Paine 2:800–1
163	Mortally ill, Grant struggled . . .: Neider, *Auto* 254.
163	Clemens was euphoric . . .: *MTBM* 305.
163	"In all my life . . .": Paine 2:819–20.
163	Susy called it . . .: Paine 2:819–20.
163–164	Finally, Clemens . . .: Paine 2:819–20.
164	Her husband's glowing . . .: Paine 2:819–20.
164	Susy described it. . . .:Paine 2:819–20.
164	In a visitor's book . . .: OLC Journal, June 7, 1885 through Nov. 27, 1885, MTP. This and subsequent information are from this journal.

PAGE

164   She called her daughters . . .: OLC Journal, MTP.
164   "There is much . . .": OLC Journal, MTP.
164   Livy felt Susy gave . . .: OLC Journal, MTP.
164–165 Livy wrote of Susy's recitation, . . .: OLC Journal, MTP.
165   She passed another hour . . .: OLC Journal, MTP.
165   Livy wrote, "I did not want . . .": OLC Journal, MTP.
165   "She seems a docile . . .": OLC Journal, MTP.
165   Riding the donkey . . .: OLC Journal, MTP.
166   The gesture made Livy . . .: OLC Journal, MTP.
166   Livy recounted . . .: OLC Journal, MTP.
166   For Jean's birthday, . . .: OLC Journal, MTP.
166   "It is terrible!": OLC Journal, MTP.
166   "She was such a lovely . . .": OLC Journal, MTP.
166   Livy sadly closed her account . . .: OLC Journal, MTP.
166   "This afternoon . . .: OLC Journal, MTP.
166   Livy chided . . .": OLC Journal, MTP.
166   It began . . .: OLC Journal, MTP.

CHAPTER 16

PAGE

167   "I am frightened . . .": Paine 2:831.
167   Clemens had already proclaimed . . .: Paine 2:840.
167   Clemens worked on the story . . .: MTBM 355.
168   "Only two or three chapters . . .": MMF 258.
168   Clemens was as enchanted . . .: Paine 2:904–5.
168   In 1881 . . .: Paine 2:904–5.
169   Clemens called it . . .: Paine 2:910.
169   She desired a particular sofa, . . .: MTBM 358.
169   In April, Livy . . .: MTBM 358.
170   By May 1886 . . .: LL 247.
170   She wrote, . . .: MTBM 370.
170   In Clemens's words, . . .: MTBM 363–64.
170   The grandeur of the audience . . .: MTBM 363–64.
171   Clara reacted . . .: Paine 2:845.
171   "Did you ever try . . .": Will Clemens, 183–84.
171   Quarry Farm proved . . .: MTL 2:471.
171   As Livy once remarked, . . .: OLC to OLL, 1887, MTP.
171   Clemens became a reader . . .: OLC to OLL, 1887, MTP.
172   Livy wrote her mother, . . .: OLC to OLL, 1887, MTP.
172   Proudly he told . . .: MMF 258–61.
172   Cherished even more . . .: OLC to OLL, Jan. 13, 1887, MTP.
172   Livy echoed . . .: OLC to OLL, Jan. 13, 1887, MTP.
172   The Clemenses flirted with "mind cure" theory . . .: S&MT
         226–27; Harnsberger 23.

NOTES

PAGE

173   "Yesterday a thunder-stroke . . .": *MTHL* 2:575–76.

173   Susy recorded in her biography . . .: Harnsberger 69–70.

173   As an adult Clara . . .: Harnsberger 69–70.

173   Clemens estimated a "three quarters . . .": *MTBM* 375.

174   The residents of Nook Farm . . .: Andrews 88; K. Leary 35.

174   The kindhearted Livy . . .: Andrews 88; K. Leary 35.

174   If you didn't know . . .: Paine, *Auto* 2:242–43.

174   As a little girl, . . .: Paine, *Auto* 2:242–43.

174   Henry Ward Beecher's death . . .: *MTBM* 394.

175   "There you see the hand . . .": *CY* 55–56.

175   Still a mother . . .: OLC to OLL, July 24, 1887, MTP.

175   Clemens wrote his sister . . .: *MTL* 2:489.

176   "I blame myself . . .": *MTBM* 380–87.

176   To Pamela, . . .: SLC to PM, July 1, 1889, MTP.*

176   Susy once stated, . . .: Paine, *Auto* 2:156–58.

176   "The children got a screen . . .": Paine, *Auto* 2:156–58.

177   Livy hinted . . .: Paine, *Auto* 2:156–58.

177   At only eight, . . .: Harnsberger 117.

177   Clemens apologized . . .: Paine 2:858.

177   "We'll be through . . .": Paine 2:858.

177   Worry from the machine . . .: *S&MT* 251.

178   Clemens could always entertain . . .: GK to Nina Ansley King, June 10, 1887, GKP.

178   Although Livy described . . .: OLC to GK, Mar. 24, 1889, GKP.

178   She called Livy . . .: GK to Nina Ansley King, June 10, 1887, GKP.

178   King visited . . .: OLC to GK, June 17, 1888, GKP.

179   When he didn't complete . . .: Paine 2:908.

179   Despite his illness, . . .: OLC to OLL, Nov. 30, 1888, MTM.

179   Livy struggled . . .: OLC to OLL, Dec. 14, 1888, MTM.

179   She wrote Grace . . .: OLC to GK, Dec. 4, 1888, GKP.

179   Despite all her difficulties, . . .: OLC to GK, Dec. 4, 1888, GKP.

179   Livy felt relieved . . .: Paine 2:908.

179   Sadly, human beings . . .: *MMF* 264.

180   "Jean's grief . . .": *MMF* 264.

180   "If you speak . . .": OLC Journal, 1892–93, Villa Viviani, MTP.

CHAPTER 17

PAGE

181   When she tried to read . . .: SLC to PM, July 1, 1889, MTP.*

181–182   Livy insisted . . .: *MTHL* 2:608–9.

NOTES

PAGE

182   Still, he graciously . . .: *MTHL* 2:610.
182   She wrote her mother, . . .: OLC to OLL, Mar. 24, 1889,
       MTP.
182   Each letter echoed, . . .: OLC to GK, Jan. 14, 1891, GKP.
182   Livy reminded . . .: OLC to GK, Mar. 24, 1889, GKP.
182   "I am unable . . .": OLC to GK, Mar. 24, 1889, GKP.
183   "However, as I meant . . .": *MTHL* 2:623–25.
183   Clemens disgruntedly described . . .: SLC to OLL, Dec. 18,
       1889, MTM.
183   In February . . .: OLC to GK, Feb. 25, 1890, GKP.
183   "Mother, Sweet I have something . . .": OLC to OLL, Mar.
       10, 1890, MTP.
183–184 "She was always . . .": Neider, *Auto* 185.
184   Livy wrote her absent husband . . .: OLC to SLC, May 20,
       1890, MTP.
184   "I dread to have to say . . .": Susy to SC, March 24, 1889,
       MTP.
185   Livy confided . . .: OLC to GK, Sept. 10, 1890, GKP.
185   He wrote . . .: SLC to PM, Oct. 12, 1890, MTP.*
185   Livy wrote . . .: OLC to GK, Jan. 14, 1891, GKP.
185   "At the time, it seemed . . .": *S&MT* 282; *MTHL* 2:636.
185–186 Jean at ten, . . .: *MMF* 266.
186   Clemens wrote his sister . . .: SLC to PM, Oct. 12, 1890,
       MTP.*
186   Livy had written her husband . . .: OLC to SLC, Nov. 27,
       1890, MTP.
186   Clemens had stayed behind . . .: *MTHL* 2:633–34.
186   "I feel so much older . . .": OLC to GK, Jan. 14, 1891, GKP.
187   "Everybody asked after . . .": *LL* 259.
187   Clemens wrote Howells . . .: *MTHL* 2:635.
187   It was not right . . .: *S&MT* 288.
187   The moment Susy met him . . .: *S&MT* 288.
188   "I was sitting with Olivia . . .": *S&MT* 288.
188   "While she cried . . .": *S&MT* 288.
189   Livy searched for ways . . .: OLC to OLL, Oct. 26, 1890,
       SDP.
189   "Such is . . .": OLC to OLL, Oct. 26, 1890, MTM.
189   She had long worried . . .: K. Leary 109.
189   Livy wrote Grace King . . .: OLC to GK, May 28, 1891, GKP.
189   Clemens, ignoring . . .: *MTHL* 2:644–45.
189   To Mrs. Fairbanks . . .: *MMF* 267.

CHAPTER 18

PAGE

198 Susy recalled, . . .: *S&MT* 309.

198 "How aggravating . . .": Susy to LB, Nov. 7, 1892, LBSP.

198 "I am getting . . .": Susy to LB, Nov. 7, 1892, LBSP.

198 Susy confided to Clara . . .: *S&MT* 312.

198 "She has three . . .": OLC to AHD, Feb. 20, 1893, SDP.

198–199 "I feel that it is . . .": OLC to AHD, ca. Feb. 23, 1893, SDP.

199 Susy warned Clara, . . .: *S&MT* 313.

199 When it appeared she would . . .: OLC to CC, Dec. 11, 1892, MTP.

199 "J. L. & Co. are in no . . .": OLC to CC, Dec. 1, 1892, MTP.

199 "It seems so dreadful . . .": OLC to CC, Jan. 15, 1893, MTP.

199 "I want you . . .": OLC to CC, Jan. 15, 1893, MTP.

199 "I am *heartily* tired . . .": Susy to LB, Nov. 13, 1892, LBSP.

199 "Still I feel constrained . . .": *S&MT* 313.

200 "Don't get used . . .": OLC to CC, Dec. 20, 1892, MTP.

200 "The average intelligent . . .": Harnsberger 140–42.

200 "There is not . . .": Harnsberger 140–42.

200 "You mustn't misunderstand . . .": Harnsberger 140–42.

201 Livy scolded, . . .: OLC to CC, Jan. 26, 1893, MTP.

201 Even with the language . . .: Susy to LB, Dec. 31, 1892, LBSP.

201 Livy now had reason . . .: *MFMT* 36.

201–202 "America looks further . . .": Susy to LB, Jan., 1893, LBSP.

202 Livy, in bewilderment, . . .: OLC to CC, Jan. 5, 1893, MTP.

202 "I say to Mr. Clemens . . .": OLC to AHD, ca. Feb. 23, 1893, SDP.

202 As a little girl . . .: K. Leary 293.

202 In the carriages . . .: Harnsberger 104–5.

202 Jean insisted . . .: Harnsberger 104–5.

203 "In that way . . .": Harnsberger 104–5.

203 Once he asked his wife, . . .: Harnsberger 104–5.

203 Livy supported, . . .: Harnsberger 104–5.

203 Even her father . . .: *MMF* 269.

203 Susy, who had once . . .: Susy to LB, Dec. 27, 1892, LBSP.

203 "Florence has been . . .": Susy to LB, Apr. 3, 1893, LBSP.

203 "But I feel perfectly . . .": *S&MT* 323.

203 "He *is* a fascinating . . .": *S&MT* 321.

203 Even though he was . . .: Susy to LB, Apr. 3, 1893, LBSP.

203 When he didn't ask . . .: Susy to LB, Apr. 3, 1893, LBSP.

204 Sadly, she concluded . . .: *S&MT* 324.

204 "I do think . . ." Susy to LB, Dec. 31, 1892, LBSP.

NOTES

CHAPTER 19

PAGE

214 To Clara she admitted, . . .: OLC to CC, Nov. 27, 1893, MTP.

214 "We shall think as little . . .": OLC to CC, Nov. 27, 1893, MTP.

214 With Susy and their . . .: *LL* 284.

214 "I tried the mind-cure . . .": *LL* 284–85.

215 "Don't lose a minute,": *MTHL* 2:659.

215 She also disliked . . .: OLC to AHD, Feb. 4, 1894, SDP.

215 It "offends one's taste": OLC to AHD, Feb. 4, 1894, SDP.

215 For Livy it was far . . .: OLC to AHD, Feb. 4, 1894, SDP.

215 From Helen Wilman's chapter . . .: OLC Journal, 1893–1902, MTP.

215 "Every time you turn away . . .": OLC Journal, 1893–1902, MTP.

215 Clemens told Livy . . .: *LL* 289.

215 She wrote Sue Crane . . .: Paine 2:978.

216 "I will live in literature, . . .": Paine 2:978.

216 The cable read, . . .: Paine 2:978–79.

216 Too agitated . . .: *LL* 293.

216 To his sister . . .: SLC to PM, Feb. 25, 1894, MTP.*

216 Clemens informed Livy, . . .: SLC to OLC, Apr. 16, 1894, MTP.*

217 Rogers understood . . .: Paine 2:984.

217 "If you don't do . . .": Paine 2:984.

217 They were "bent on . . .": Paine 2:984.

217 Remembering it in 1909 . . .: Neider, *Auto* 262.

217 Clemens admitted to Livy, . . .: *LL* 301–2.

217 She wrote Sue Crane, . . .: Paine 2:987.

218 Clemens wrote her words . . .: Neider, *Auto* 258.

218 In an effort to convince herself . . .: OLC to AHD, May 23, 1894, SDP.

218 Rogers agreed with her . . .: Neider, *Auto* 260.

218 "Sue, if you were to see . . .": Paine 2:987.

218–219 "What we want is to have . . .": *LL* 309.

219 "Suppose father . . .": *LL* 306.

219 He promised, . . .: *LL* 306.

219 Susy was right: . . .: Susy to CC, Aug. 10, 1894, MTP.

219 The event prompted . . .: *LL* 304.

220 Deep down, Clemens . . .: Paine 2:991–93.

220 She was reluctant . . .: Paine 2:994.

220 Susy had come . . .: Susy to LB, Aug. 1, 1894, LBSP.

220 Also, "the house has stood . . .": OLC to AHD, Jan. 26, 1895, SDP.

220 "There are so many things . . .": OLC to Franklin Whitmore, June 18, 1895, MTP.

NOTES

PAGE

221   Clemens marveled, . . .: Paine 2:994.
221   Clemens gave Livy . . .: Paine 2:996–97.
221   Susy recorded, . . .: Paine 2:996–97.

CHAPTER 20

PAGE

222   "I think there is no season . . .": OLC to AHD, Jan. 26,
        1895, SDP.
222   Once inside, . . .: LL 314.
222   "Katy had every rug . . .": LL 312.
222   "I was seized . . .": LL 312.
222   For Clemens, "It seemed . . .": LL 312.
222–223 To Mrs. Fairbanks . . .: MMF 277.
223   "Words cannot describe . . .": LL 312.
223   Susy had admitted . . .: Susy to LB, Apr. 3, 1893, LBSP.
223   Charles Langdon . . .: HHR 147.
223   Livy admitted, . . .: Paine 2:1003.
224   This thirteen month . . .: Neider, Auto 261.
225   From Cleveland, . . .: Neider, Auto 263–64.
225   "From my reception . . .": Paine 2:1007.
225   "Lecturing is . . .": San Francisco Examiner, Aug. 24, 1895.
225   "He insisted, . . .": San Francisco Examiner, Aug. 24, 1895.
226   "My wife and daughter . . .": San Francisco Examiner, Aug.
        24, 1895.
226   Susy wondered . . .: Harnsberger 151–52.
226   He had told Rogers, . . .: Paine 2:998.
226   He had his own way, . . .: Paine 2:1005.
226   They had to content . . .: Paine 2:1008.
227   Livy, troubled . . .: OLC to Susy, Aug. 30 & 31, 1895, MTP.
227   She wrote Susy, "People . . .": Harnsberger 155.
227   "And so it goes, . . .": Harnsberger 155.
227–228 "They made me laugh . . .": OLC to Susy, Sept. 20, 1895,
        MTP.
228   Clemens appreciated . . .: Neider, Auto 182–83.
228   "For one audience . . .": Neider, Auto 182–83.
228   Clemens admitted, . . .: Neider, Auto 182–83.
228   The pause Livy . . .: Neider, Auto 182–83.
228   If the audience was sharp, . . .: Neider, Auto 182–83.
228   They sailed . . .: OLC to Kinsey, Nov. 21, 1895, MTP.
228   Livy wrote . . .: OLC to Kinsey, Nov. 21, 1895, MTP.
229   "We comfort . . .": OLC to Kinsey, Nov. 21, 1895, MTP.
229   After seeing the village . . .: Harnsberger 157.
229   Livy could write, . . .: OLC to SC, Sept. 5, 1895, MTP.

PAGE

229   "I am sure if his life . . .": OLC to SC, Sept. 5, 1895, MTP.
229   He turned sixty, . . .: Paine 2:1011.
229–230   "I wonder if we . . .": OLC to SC, Nov. 24, 1895, MTP.
230   She asked that Sue . . .: OLC to SC, Dec. 20 & 26, 1895, MTP.
230   "Everything takes longer . . .": OLC to Susy, Dec. 2, 1895, MTP.
230   In fact, she feared . . .: OLC to Susy, Dec. 2, 1895, MTP.
230   To Susy, Clemens blamed . . .: Harnsberger 158.
230   Livy wrote, "I am . . .": S&MT 375.
230   She thought mind cure . . .: S&MT 371.
230   "I have become . . .": S&MT 371.
230–231   "One doesn't . . .": S&MT 375.
231   While Clemens's health . . .: OLC to JC, Feb. 16, 1896, MTP.
231   She also noted . . .: OLC to JC, Feb. 16, 1896, MTP.
231   Livy went to a museum . . .: OLC to JC, Feb. 16, 1896, MTP.
231   Livy found . . .: OLC to JC, Feb. 16, 1896, MTP.
231   Surprisingly, Clemens wrote . . .: Harnsberger 160.
231   He added, . . .: Harnsberger 160.
231–232   The wind burned . . .: OLC to SC, Mar. 30, 1896, MTP.
232   Her goal . . .: OLC to AHD, Apr. 13, 1896, SDP.
232   "I love that house . . .": OLC to AHD, Apr. 13, 1896, SDP.
232   She wrote her sister . . .: OLC to SC, Mar. 30, 1896, MTP.
232   "He does not believe . . .": OLC to SC, Mar. 30, 1896, MTP.
232   Once on the stage . . .: OLC to SC, Mar. 30, 1896, MTP.
232   By the time . . .: OLC to SC, June 16, 1896, MTP.
233   "We feel now . . .": OLC to SC, Mar. 30, 1896, MTP.
233   She loved and missed . . .: OLC to SLC, May 19, 1896, MTP.
233   "I want them to feel . . .": OLC to SLC, May 19, 1896, MTP.
233   "I should think . . .": OLC to SLC, May 19, 1896, MTP.
233   "So I went, . . .": OLC to JC, Feb. 16, 1896, MTP.

CHAPTER 21

PAGE

234   She had written . . .: S&MT 381.
234   Looking forward . . .: S&MT 381.
234   She found Hartford . . .: S&MT 381.
234–235   Katy Leary remarked, . . .: K. Leary 132–33.
235   Susy, pale and flushed, . . .: K. Leary 134–35.
235   By the afternoon, . . .: K. Leary 134–35.
235   She sensed . . .: K. Leary 134–35.

NOTES

PAGE

235   Susy had continued . . . .: Leary 134–35.

235   "Nothing serious," . . .: Neider, *Auto* 322–23.

236   Katy's reply, . . .: Neider, *Auto* 322–23.

236   Before it left, . . .: Neider, *Auto* 322–23.

236   She criticized . . .: K. Leary 134–35.

236   She wrote, "In strength . . .": Leary 134–35.

236   "I am blind, . . .": OLC to Mrs. Whitmore, Apr. 22, 1897, MTM.

236–237   Susy's last gesture . . .: OLC to Mrs. Whitmore, Apr. 22, 1897, MTM.

237   "How gracious . . .": Neider, *Auto* 322–23.

237   Clemens was in Guildford, . . .: Neider, *Auto* 322–23.

237   'It is one . . .": Neider, *Auto* 322–23.

237   On August 16, . . .: LL 320–23.

237   His greatest pain . . .: LL 320–23.

238   He searched through letters . . .: LL 320–23.

238   Mentally, he whipped . . .: LL 320–23.

238   Without Livy . . .: LL 320–23.

238   "I eat—because . . .": LL 320–23.

238   Alternating between . . . .: MFMT 168.

238   The captain . . .: MFMT 168.

238   Her immediate thought, . . .: MFMT 168.

238   Livy swooned, . . .: MFMT 168.

238   Joseph Twichell, . . .: Paine 2:1024.

238   Katy commented, . . .: K. Leary 138.

238   All Livy . . .: K. Leary 138.

238   In ironies . . .: Neider, *Auto* 323.

239   Clemens, unbearably alone . . .: LL 326.

239   He looked for . . .: LL 326.

239   He wrote Livy, . . .: LL 326.

239   In his despair, . . .: LL 322.

239   Livy, unbearably alone . . .: K. Leary 138.

239   "On the 23rd . . .": Neider, *Auto* 324.

239   "Warm summer sun, . . .": Paine 2:1024.

240   "If she had died . . .": Paine 2:1023.

240   How prophetic . . .: OLC to Mrs. Whitmore, Apr. 9, 1896, MTP.

240   She would eventually . . .: OLC to GK, Mar. 9, 1897, GKP.

240   At twenty-one years . . .: Susy to LB, Apr. 3, 1893, LBSP.

240   Clemens wrote Howells . . .: MTHL 2:664.

240   Livy, he wrote, . . .: MTHL 2:664.

240   "What a mystery . . .": OLC to GK, June 27, 1897, GKP.

240–241   From an unidentified . . .: OLC to Mrs. Whitmore, Apr. 22, 1897, MTP.

241   Katy Leary recognized . . . .: K. Leary 140.

NOTES

PAGE

241   "Now my world . . .": OLC to AHD, Oct. 22, 1896, SDP.

241   "I cannot find . . .": OLC to AHD, Oct. 22, 1896, SDP.

241   "No one knows, . . .": OLC to AHD, Oct. 22, 1896, SDP.

241   "terrific evil influence": OLC to AHD, Oct. 22, 1896, SDP.

241   "natural and wise protectors": OLC to AHD, Oct. 22, 1896, SDP.

241   "badly managed": OLC to GK, Mar. 9, 1897, GKP.

241   "Yet, I cannot . . .": OLC to Mrs. Whitmore, Apr. 22, 1897, MTP.

241   With a loss . . .: OLC to Mrs. Whitmore, Apr. 22, 1897, MTP.

241   Yet this woman . . .: *MTHL* 2:663, Notebook 320.

241   "It is an odious . . .": *LL* 328.

241   In pity, not hate, . . .: Paine 2:1026.

242   The raw spots . . .: Paine 2:1038.

242   "This would enrage . . .": Harnsberger 171.

242   The New York *Herald* . . .: Paine 2:1025–26.

242   "I am sorry . . .": OLC to GK, June 27, 1897, GKP.

242   Clemens made his famous . . .: Paine 2:1039.

242   To Mrs. Fairbanks . . .: *MMF* 278.

243   Christmas morning . . .: Paine 2:1027.

243   "Page 1002. I don't like . . .": Paine 2:1040.

243   Katy recalled, "He'd say . . .": K. Leary 306.

244   Clemens had once remarked . . .: King 172–73.

244   Each was upset . . .: Leary 182–83.

244   When Livy could complete . . .: Paine 2:1083.

244   "Susy" requested . . .: Documents File, 1900, MTP.

244   Livy wanted to believe . . .: *LL* 325.

245   Livy had described the letters . . .: OLC to AHD, Oct. 22, 1896, SDP.

246   In the poem . . .: OLC to Mrs. F. Cheney, Oct. 7, 1898, MTP.

246   "I loved Susy, . . .": *LL* 321–22.

CHAPTER 22

PAGE

247   Clemens noted, . . .: *MTHL* 2:665.

247   They received . . .: K. Leary 162.

247   A Vienna newspaper . . .: Paine 2:1052.

248   "Such funny . . .": Paine 2:1059.

248   After two years in Vienna, . . .: Paine 2:1072.

248   Or if his brother . . .: Paine 2:1053.

248   Livy characterized Orion; . . .: OLC to Samuel Moffett, Jan. 6, 1898, MTP.

PAGE

248   Livy's greatest diversion, . . .: *MTHL* 2:670.

248–249   She read them over . . .: *HHR* 325.

249   Clemens experienced . . . .: Paine 2:1059.

249   "I was hoping and praying . . .": Paine 2:1059–61.

249   "Seems a kind of pity . . .": Paine 2:1059–61.

249–250   She wrote John and Ellen O'Neill . . .: OLC to John and Ellen O'Neill, Feb. 27, 1898, MTP.

250   When the United States . . .: OLC to CL, Apr. 24, 1898, MTP.

250   At first supportive . . .: Paine 2:1064.

250   After Jean and Livy . . .: *HHR* 358.

250   "We don't know who made . . .": *HHR* 356.

250   She wrote Mrs. Cheney, . . .: OLC to Mrs. F. Cheney, Oct. 7, 1898, MTP.

251   "I . . . kept trying to think . . .": *MMF* 278.

251   In January 1899 . . .: *MTHL* 2:684.

251   One German opera singer . . .: Harnsberger 183.

251   Livy once more mused . . .: Paine 2:1084.

251   "absent-mindedness": *HHR* 403.

251   They were ready . . .: *HHR* 403.

252   He admitted to Rogers, . . .: *HHR* 405.

252   "It is vigorous . . .": *HHR* 404.

252   Clemens commented . . .: *HHR* 408.

252   Clemens announced . . .: *HHR* 424.

253   Jean's "ailing" . . .: "Jean's Illness," MTP.*

253   "parental restraint and watchfulness": "Jean's Illness," MTP.*

253   When Livy came down . . .: *HHR* 425.

253   "It was assassination . . .": *HHR* 425.

253   Considering the health record . . .: *LL* 316.

253   Livy preferred entertaining . . .: OLC to Mrs. J. V. W. MacAlister, Nov. 7, 1899, MTP.

253–254   At the birth . . .: OLC to Katherine Clemens, Mar. 10, 1900, MTM.

254   "the Vienna albumen": Paine 2:1102.

255   Livy recognized . . .: Paine 2:1102.

255   She wondered . . .: Paine 2:1102.

255   Then in her indecision . . .: Paine 2:1102.

255   "When I was comparatively young . . .": Paine 2:1102.

255   "I hate the correcting . . .": Paine 2:1102.

255   "I don't think . . .": Paine 2:1102.

255   If she felt she wasn't . . .: Paine 2:1102.

255   Kellgren announced . . .: SLC to PM, Apr. 25, 1900, MTP.*

255   "cross[ing] the ocean": SLC to PM, Apr. 25, 1900, MTP.*

255   The whole situation . . .: SLC to PM, Apr. 25, 1900, MTP.*

256   As Clemens told Howells, . . .: *MTHL* 2:717.

256   "hay and sheep": Paine 2:1109.

NOTES

PAGE

256   "beautiful & peaceful": Paine 2:1109.

256   Clemens described himself . . .: Paine 2:1109.

256   Livy had pondered, . . .: OLC to Mrs. Taft, May 6, 1900, MTP.

CHAPTER 23

PAGE

257   "a fighting cock": *MTHL* 2:723.

257   Clemens attributed . . .: *MTHL* 2:723.

258   Settling first . . .: OLC to Mrs. F. Whitmore, Sept. 23, 1900, MTP.

258   "How fast . . .": OLC to Mrs. Frank Cheney, Feb. 25, 1900, MTP.

258   "I cannot trust . . .": OLC to Mrs. F. Whitmore, Sept. 23, 1900, MTP.

258   Livy believed, . . .: Paine 3:1112.

258   She hired a cook . . .: *HHR* 453.

258   "She had resisted . . .": Neider, *Auto* 326.

258   "I declined 7 banquets . . .": Paine 3:1121.

258   He laughed about . . .: Paine 3:1121.

259   "rushing life": OLC to GK, Feb. 24, 1901, GKP.

259   "festivities": OLC to Katherine Clemens, May 29, 1900, MTP.

259   To Clara, she could . . .: OLC to CC, Sept. 25, 1901, MTP.

259   "We do not oppose . . .": OLC to GK, Feb. 24, 1901, GKP.

259   "Agents seem . . .": OLC to GK, Feb. 24, 1901, GKP.

260   "I bring you the stately nation . . .": Paine 3:1127.

260   Once again he spoke . . .: Paine 3:1128.

260   "three hundred taels . . .": Paine 3:1128.

260   Despite the controversy, . . .: OLC to GK, Feb. 2, 1901, GKP.

261   Now sitting by a lake . . .: OLC to Maria Gay, June 24, 1901, MTP.

261   "The air is . . .": OLC to AHD, Aug. 18, 1901, SDP.

261   "Rowing & bathing . . .": OLC to AHD, Aug. 18, 1901, SDP.

261   "We caught a Chinee missionary . . .": Paine 3:1140.

261   "I do wish something . . .": OLC to Sam Moffett, July 17, 1901, MTP.

261   She shared her dreams . . .: OLC to CC, July 4, 1901, MTP.

261   She based her excitement . . .: OLC to CC, July 4, 1901, MTP.

261   "How I wish . . .": OLC to Sam Moffett, Sept. 17, 1901, MTP.

NOTES

PAGE

262   Livy had remarked . . .: OLC to GK, Feb. 24, 1901, GKP.

262   Livy was still against . . .: SLC to Franklin Whitmore, Dec. 7, 1901, MTP.*

262   "dreaded": OLC to AHD, Oct. 1, 1901, MTP.

262   She wrote Alice . . .: OLC to AHD, Oct. 1, 1901, MTP.

262–263 "We rented 1st of October . . .": OLC Guest Book, MTP.

263   "with us": OLC Guest Book, MTP.

263   A few months previously, . . .: OLC to Mrs. Franklin Whitmore, Nov. 20, 1901, MTP.

263   An undated message from Livy . . .: OLC to SLC, MTP.

263–264 "I am absolutely wretched . . .": LL 333.

264   To Katherine Clemens . . .: OLC to Katherine Clemens, May 4, 1902, MTP.

264   "Sometimes I feel . . .": OLC to Franklin Whitmore, May 9 & 10, 1903, MTP.

265   "To us our house . . .": Paine 3:1023–24.

265   She began to kindly . . .: OLC to Mrs. Franklin Whitmore, June 21, 1902, MTP.

265   She suggested . . .: OLC to Mrs. Franklin Whitmore, June 21, 1902, MTP.

265   She adds in her usual method . . .: OLC to Mrs. Franklin Whitmore, June 21, 1902, MTP.

265   "Don't let him . . .": OLC to Katherine Clemens, May 27, 1902, MTP.

266   She records in her . . .: OLC Guest Book, Apr. 22, 1902, MTP.

266   And in a letter . . .: OLC to Mrs. Franklin Whitmore, May 27, 1902, MTP.

266   "It would have been equivalent . . .": HHR 490.

266   "It comes near to killing . . .": HHR 490

266   "Mrs. Clemens's five years . . .": HHR 496.

267   "alarmed her": Neider, Auto 328.

267   "I am alarmed . . .": HHR 496.

267   In watching the fireworks, . . .: Neider, Auto 329–31.

267   The afternoon . . .: Neider, Auto 329–31.

267   "I am dying.": Neider, Auto 329–31.

267   "But the worst of all . . .": HHR 499.

268   Whatever the cause, . . .: MTHL 2:745.

268   "up & down & down-&-up": MTHL 2:745.

268   He found another osteopath, . . .: HHR 506.

268   With "no light . . .": HHR 509.

268   With that and the encouragement . . .: HHR 509.

268   Clemens admitted . . .: HHR 505.

268   His words to Howells . . .: MTHL 2:747.

269   In his autobiography . . .: Neider, Auto 327.

269   "Twelve years before, . . .": Neider, Auto 327.

PAGE

269   "Physicians of repute . . .": Neider, *Auto* 327.
269   Clemens wrote Twichell . . .: Paine 3:1180–81.
269   She replied to his letters—: Neider, *Auto* 331–32.
269   Katy remembered, . . .: K. Leary 221.
270   Sometimes he waited . . .: Paine 3:1193.
270   "I was sitting . . .": Paine 3:1193.
270   When Clemens saw his wife . . .: Neider, *Auto* 337.
270   "With a word . . .": Neider, *Auto* 339.
270   At the top of a letter . . .: *LL* 339–40.
270   It evoked many memories, . . .: *LL* 339–40.
270   "I was [thoughtful] careful": *LL* 339–40.
270   But the beautiful memory . . .: *LL* 339–40.
270   "Now, there is one invisible guest . . .": Paine 3:1183–84.
270   "And now my wife and I, . . .": Paine 3:1183–84.
271   "a chill": Paine 3:1190–91.
271   "holy lies,": Paine 3:1190–91.
271   "She had never told . . .": Paine 3:1190–91.
271   "Clara furnished . . .": Paine 3:1190–91.
271   When Clara ran out . . .": Paine 3:1190–91.
271   "Clara could tell . . .": Paine 3:1190–91
271   Clara practiced . . .: *MTHL* 2:756.
271   "We guard her . . .": *MTHL* 2:756.

CHAPTER 24

PAGE

273   "It seemeth to me . . .": Harnsberger 202.
274   By April . . .: *HHR* 522.
274   Clemens informed Rogers, . . .: *HHR* 522.
274   Clemens told Rogers, . . .: *HHR* 527.
274   As she was forbidden . . .: OLC to Franklin Whitmore, May 9 & 10, 1903, MTP.
275   "these expensive items": OLC to Franklin Whitmore, May 9 & 10, 1903, MTP.
275   "keep for us.": OLC to Franklin Whitmore, May 9 & 10, 1903, MTP.
275   Clemens described her—: Paine 3:1206.
275   As much as Livy loved Quarry Farm, . . .: OLC to CC, July 5, 1903, MTP.
275   When the memories . . .: *LL* 343.
275   In another letter to Clara . . .: OLC to CC, July 29, 1903, MTP.
275   "I don't expect . . .": OLC to SLC, Aug. 5, 1903, MTP.
276   "heroic lie": *LL* 345–46.

NOTES

PAGE

276   Howells felt that . . .: *LL* 345–46.

276   "I am truly thankful . . .": *LL* 345–46.

276   "How much immortality . . .": *LL* 345–46.

276   On February 4, . . .: OLC to Professor Fiske, Feb. 4, 1904, MTP.

276   By the end of February . . .: Paine 3:1214.

277   She remarked to Clemens, . . .: SLC to SC, Mar. 8, 1904, MTP.

277   Clara made her Florentine . . .: *HHR* 561–62.

277   Livy was so excited . . .: *HHR* 561–62.

277   Two days later . . .: *HHR* 561–62.

277   Clemens remarked to Rogers, . . .: *HHR* 560.

277   Her end came . . .: *MTN* 387.

277   He had feared the loneliness . . .: *LL* 324.

277   Two years before . . .: OLC to Laura Schultz, Feb. 4, 1902, MTP.

277   In language reminiscent . . .: *HHR* 569.

277   He couldn't think . . .: *HHR* 569.

277   "And now Susy . . .": SLC to CL, June 8, 1904, MTM.

278   They were accompanied . . .: SLC to CL, June 13, 1904, MTP.

278   After five weeks . . .: Paine 3:1222.

278   "Where she stood . . .": *MTN* 390.

278   "And so good-by. Good-by . . .": Paine 3:1123.

278   The graveside service . . .: Neider, *Auto* 373.

279   Standing at Eve's grave, . . .: *CSS* 295.

BIBLIOGRAPHY

Aldrich, Lilian Woodman. *Crowding Memories*. Boston: Houghton Mifflin, 1920.

Anderson, Frederick, William M. Gibson, and Henry Nash Smith, eds. *Mark Twain-Howells Letters, 1872–1910*. 2 vols. Cambridge, Massachusetts: The Belknap Press of Harvard University, 1960.

Andrews, Kenneth. *Nook Farm: Mark Twain's Hartford Circle*. Cambridge: Harvard University Press, 1950.

Beard, George Miller. *Sexual Neurasthenia, Its Hygiene, Causes, Symptoms, and Treatment*. Edited by A. D. Rockwell. New York: Treat, 1884.

Blair, Walter. *Mark Twain and Huck Finn*. Berkeley and Los Angeles: University of California Press, 1960.

Branch, Edgar Marquess, Michael B. Frank, Kenneth M. Sanderson, eds. *Mark Twain's Letters, Volume 1, 1853–1866*. Berkeley and Los Angeles: University of California Press, 1988.

Burr, Anna Robeson. *Silas Weir Mitchell*. New York: Duffield and Company, 1929.

Centennial Album. Elmira, New York: Park Congregational Church, 1946.

Center for Mark Twain Studies at Quarry Farm. Elmira, New York.

Chemung County Historical Society. Archives. Elmira, New York.

Clemens, Clara. *My Father, Mark Twain*. New York: Harper & Brothers Publishers, 1931.

Clemens, Will. *Mark Twain: His Life and Work: A Biographical Sketch*. San Francisco: Clemens Publishing Company, 1892.

DeVoto, Bernard. *Mark Twain in Eruption*. New York: Capricorn Books, 1968.

Eastman, Max. "Mark Twain's Elmira." In *Mark Twain in Elmira*. Edited by Robert D. Jerome and Herbert A. Wisbey, Jr., 129–147. Elmira: Mark Twain Society, 1977.

BIBLIOGRAPHY

Elmira College. Archives. Elmira, New York.
Ferguson, DeLancey. *Mark Twain: Man and Legend.* New York: Russell and Russell, 1965.
Gleason, Rachel Brooks. *Talks To My Patients.* New York: Wood & Holbrook Publishers, 1870.
Grace King Papers, Louisiana and Lower Mississippi Valley Collections, LSU Libraries, Louisiana State University, Baton Rouge, LA.
Haller, John S., and Robin M. Hailer. *The Physician and Sexuality in Victorian America.* Urbana: University of Illinois Press, 1974.
Harnsberger, Caroline Thomas. *Mark Twain, Family Man.* New York: The Citadel Press, 1960.
Hill, Hamlin, ed. *Mark Twain's Letters to His Publishers, 1867–1894.* Berkeley and Los Angeles: University of California Press, 1967.
Howells, William Dean. *My Mark Twain.* New York: Harper & Brothers, 1910.
Jerome, Robert D., and Herbert A. Wisbey, Jr., eds. *Mark Twain in Elmira.* Elmira: Mark Twain Society, 1977.
King, Grace. *Memories of a Southern Woman of Letters.* New York: Macmillan, 1932.
Krauth, Leland. "Mark Twain: At Home in the Gilded Age." *Georgia Review* 28 (Spring 1974): 105–15.
Langdon, Ida. "Elmira's Langdon Family." *Chemung County Historical Journal* 1, No. 2 (December 1955): 51–58.
Leary, Katy. *A Lifetime with Mark Twain.* 1952. Reprint. New York: Crowell, 1962.
Leary, Lewis, ed. *Mark Twain's Correspondence with Henry Huttleston Rogers, 1893–1909.* Berkeley: University of California Press, 1969.
Louise Brownell Saunders Papers. Hamilton College, Clinton, New York.
Mark Twain Collection (MSS 6314), Clifton Waller Barrett Library of American Literature, Special Collections Dept., Univ. of VA Library.
Mark Twain Memorial, Hartford, Connecticut.
Mark Twain Papers. University of California, Berkeley, California.
Mitchell, Silas Weir. *Fat and Blood and How to Make Them.* Philadelphia: J. B. Lippincott, 1877.
Paine, Albert Bigelow. *Mark Twain, a Biography.* 3 vols. New York: Harper & Brothers Publishers, 1912.
Paine, Albert Bigelow, ed. *Mark Twain's Letters.* 2 vols. New York: Harper & Brothers Publishers, 1917.
Paine, Albert Bigelow, ed. *Mark Twain's Notebook.* New York: Harper & Brothers Publishers, 1935.
Salsbury, Edith Colgate, ed. *Susy and Mark Twain.* New York: Harper & Row Publishers, 1965.
Smith, Harriet Elinor, Richard Bucci, Lin Salamo, eds. *Mark Twain's Letters, Volume 2, 1867–1868.* Berkeley and Los Angeles: Univ. of CA Press, 1990.
Smith, Henry Justin, and Lloyd Lewis. *Chicago: The History of Its Reputation.* New York: Harcourt Brace and Company, 1929.
Stowe-Day Papers, Harriet Beecher Stowe Center, Hartford, Connecticut.

BIBLIOGRAPHY

Towner, Ausburn. *Our County and Its People, A History of the Valley and County of Chemung.* Syracuse: D. Mason and Company, 1892.

Tuckey, John S., ed. *Mark Twain's Which Was the Dream? and Other Symbolic Writings of the Later Years.* Berkeley and Los Angeles: University of California Press, 1967.

Twain, Mark. *A Connecticut Yankee in King Arthur's Court.* New York: Harper & Row, Publishers, 1917.

Twain, Mark. *Adventures of Huckleberry Finn.* Boston: Houghton Mifflin Company, 1962.

Twain, Mark. *Adventures of Tom Sawyer.* New York: Harper & Brothers Publishers, 1920.

Twain, Mark. *The Autobiography of Mark Twain.* Edited by Charles Neider. New York: Harper & Brothers, 1959.

Twain, Mark. *The Complete Short Stories of Mark Twain.* Edited by Charles Neider. New York: Doubleday & Company, 1967.

Twain, Mark. *Mark Twain's Autobiography.* Edited by Albert Bigelow Paine. 2 vols. New York: Harper and Brothers, 1924.

Twain, Mark. *Mark Twain's Speeches.* New York: Harper and Brothers, 1923.

Twain, Mark, and Charles Dudley Warner. *The Gilded Age.* 2 vols. New York: Harper & Brothers Publishers, 1901.

Varble, Rachel M. *Jane Clemens: The Story of Mark Twain's Mother.* Garden City: Doubleday and Company, 1964.

Wagenknecht, Edward. *Mark Twain: The Man and His Work.* New Haven: Yale University Press, 1935.

Webster, Samuel, ed. *Mark Twain: Business Man.* Boston: Little, Brown and Company, 1946.

Wecter, Dixon, ed. *The Love Letters of Mark Twain.* New York: Harper & Brothers, 1947.

Wecter, Dixon, ed. *Mark Twain to Mrs. Fairbanks.* San Marino: Huntington Library, 1949.

Wisbey, Jr., Herbert A. "Olivia Clemens Studied at Elmira College." In *Mark Twain Society Bulletin* 2, No. 2 (June 1979): 1–3.

INDEX

323